French Military Doctrine 1913

The Decrees of October 28 and December 2

By

Ministère de la Guerre

Legacy Books Press
Military Classics

PRESTON LIBRARY
VIRGINIA MILITARY INSTITUTE
LEXINGTON, VA 24450

Published by Legacy Books Press
RPO Princess, Box 21031
445 Princess Street
Kingston, Ontario, K7L 5P5
Canada

www.legacybookspress.com

The scanning, uploading, and/or distribution of this book via the Internet or any other means without the permission of the publisher is illegal and punishable by law.

This translation and edition first published in 2021 by Legacy Books Press
1

This translation and edition © 2021 Legacy Books Press, all rights reserved.

ISBN: 978-1-927537-55-8

First published as *Service des Armées en Campagne: Conduits des Grandes Unités* by Henri Charles-Lavauzelle, Paris in 1913, and *Décret du 2 Décembre 1913 Portant Règlement sur le Service des Armées en Campagne: Service en Campagne — Droit International* by L. Fournier, Paris in 1914.

Printed and bound in the United States of America and Canada.

This book is typeset in a Times New Roman 11-point font.

Table of Contents

Publisher's Note 5

Service of the Armies in the Field – Conduct of Large Units .. 7
General Provisions 8
Chapter I – Generalities on the Conduct of War 9
Chapter II – Command 12
Chapter III – Freedom of Action. Security. Research of information. Exploration 16
Chapter IV – Command Aids. Instructions. Orders. Reports. Liaisons 21
Chapter V – The Army Group 26
Chapter VI – The Army 30
Chapter VII – The Army Corps 42
Chapter VIII – Cavalry Corps 56
Chapter IX – Cover and Strongholds 59
Chapter X – Observation Corps 62
Chapter XI – Special Provisions 64
Appendix – Report of the Commission to the Minister of War 65

Decree of 2 December 1913: Regulations on the Service of the Armies in the Field – Service in the Field. International Law 81
Part I – Service in the Field 83
   Report to the President of the French Republic 85
   Report of the Commission 87
   Decree on the Regulation of Field Service 105
   Section I – General Organization of the Army 107
      Chapter I – Formation of the Armies 109
      Chapter II – Command 111
      Chapter III – Staffs and Headquarters 114
      Chapter IV – The Services 116
   Section II – Orders. Liaisons 125

Section III – Marches. Stations.................. 133
    Chapter I – Marches 135
    Chapter II – Stationing 147
    Chapter III – Rules Common to Marches and Stationing 159
Section IV – Security......................... 163
    Chapter I – General Considerations 165
    Chapter II – Security on the Move 167
    Chapter III – Security on Station............. 171
Section V – Battle 189
    Chapter I – Generalities on Combat 191
    Chapter II – Properties and Roles of the Various Arms in Combat 193
    Chapter III – The Offensive 197
    Chapter IV – The Defense.................. 206
    Chapter V – Pursuit....................... 210
    Chapter VI – Retreat 212
    Chapter VII – Particulars Relating to Combat in Various Terrain....................... 214
    Chapter VIII – Particulars Relating to Night Combat 216
    Chapter IX – Action of the Command 219
    Chapter X – Duties of the Leaders and Troops 222
Section VI – Cavalry 227
    Chapter I – General Role of the Cavalry....... 229
    Chapter II – Army Cavalry 230
    Chapter III – Corps Cavalry 233
    Chapter IV – Particulars Concerning the Safety of a Cavalry Troop Operating in Isolation on the March and on Station 237
    Chapter V – The Cavalry Division 240
Section VII – Detachments 247
Section VIII – Fieldworks 257
Section IX – Operation of the Aeronautical service and the Telegraphic Service....................... 263
    Chapter I – Aeronautical Service 265
    Chapter II – Telegraphic Service.............. 267

Table of Contents

Section X – Trains, Depots and Convoys 273
Section XI – Supply and Evacuation, Requisitions .. 281
   Chapter I – Generalities. 283
   Chapter II – Supply of Foodstuffs. 285
   Chapter III – Supply of Ammunition 292
   Chapter IV – Evacuations 296
   Chapter V – Requisitions 298
Section XII – Service of the Gendarmerie in the Field
   301
Appendices. 309
   Appendix No. 1 – Right to Command of Foreign Officers. 311
   Appendix No 2 – Executive Agencies of the Services
   313
   Appendix No 3 – Prescriptions Concerning Orders and Reports. 322
   Appendix No. 4 – Supply of Food to the Troops
   325
   Appendix No. 5 – Logs of Marches and Operations of the Staffs and Corps of Troops. 327
   Appendix No. 6 – Campaign Diaries of Quartermasters 339
Part II – International Law 345
   1. International Convention of Geneva. 347
      Chapter I – Of the Wounded and Sick 349
      Chapter II – Medical Units and Establishments
      351
      Chapter III – Personnel 352
      Chapter IV – Equipment 354
      Chapter VI – The Distinctive Sign 357
      Chapter VII – Application and Execution of the Convention 359
      Chapter VIII – On the Repression of Abuses and Infractions. 360
      General Provisions 362
   2. Declaration of Saint-Petersburg. 364

3. Acts of The Hague.......................... 367
   Convention I on the peaceful settlement of international disputes................... 372
      Section I – Of the Maintenance of the General Peace........................... 375
      Section II – Good Offices and Mediation... 376
      Section III – International Commissions of Inquiry 378
      Section IV – International Arbitration 384
      Section V – Final Provisions 396
   Convention II Concerning the Limitation of the Use of Force for the Recovery of Debts.......... 399
   Convention III Relating to the Opening of Hostilities 403
   Convention IV Concerning the Laws and Customs of War on Land........................ 408
   Appendix to the Convention – Regulations concerning the laws and customs of war on land 413
      Section I – Belligerents................. 413
      Section II – Hostilities 418
      Section III – Military authority in the territory of the enemy State 422
   Convention V Concerning the Rights and Duties of Neutral Powers and Persons in Case of War on Land 425
      Chapter I – The Rights and Duties of Neutral Powers 427
      Chapter II – Belligerents Interned and Wounded Treated by Neutrals 429
      Chapter III – Neutral Persons............ 431
      Chapter IV – Railroad Equipment 433
      Chapter V – Final Provisions 434

Publisher's Note

This translation was created with the assistance of DeepL Pro translation software. While all possible efforts have been taken to avoid translation errors, some errors may still be present in the text.

Service of the Armies in the Field – Conduct of Large Units

Decree bearing regulations on the conduct of large units.

Rambouillet, October 28, 1913.

The President of the French Republic,
On the report of the Minister of War,
Having regard to the decree of May 28, 1895 on the service of the armies in the field,

Decrees:

General Provisions

The present decree applies to the *large units*, which are: the *army group*, the *army*, the *army corps* and, to a certain extent, the *cavalry corps*.

As a result of their organic constitution, these units lend themselves to multiple and varied combinations, which escape any narrow regulation. Moreover, because of their importance, they can be given long term missions, with a large part of initiative.

The *division* is the weakest of the organic units comprising troops of all arms.

It acts most often in a framed manner, and then receives short-term missions that keep it in close dependence on the superior authority.

Its limited size leads it to be used on fronts that are small enough for the leader to be able to exercise direct and rapid action on its various elements.

The conduct and mode of action of the division involve rules which are set forth in the Regulations on Field Service.

Chapter I – Generalities on the Conduct of War

1. The government, which assumes responsibility for the vital interests of the country, has sole authority to determine the political purpose of the war.

If the struggle extends to several frontiers, it shall designate the principal adversary against whom the greater part of the national forces must be directed. He allocates accordingly the means of action and the resources of all kinds, and places them at the complete disposal of the generals in charge of the command-in-chief in the various theaters of operations.

2. Military operations are aimed at the annihilation of the enemy's organized forces.[*]

3. In the present form of the war, the size of the masses involved, the difficulties of their resupply, the interruption of the

---

[*] This principle, which is rigorously applied in the main theater of operations, is subject to exceptions in secondary theaters where it may be appropriate not to seek an immediate decision (Chapter X).

social and economic life of the country, all encourage the search for a decision in the shortest possible time, with a view to ending the struggle promptly.

4. The decisive battle, exploited to the full, is the only way to bend the will of the adversary, by the destruction of his armies. It constitutes the essential act of war. The conquest of a portion of territory, the capture of fortresses, cannot lead to the final result.

The purpose of strategic combinations is therefore, above all, to force the enemy to accept battle. They then tend to impose on him the conditions of the encounter, so as to prepare and facilitate not only tactical victory, but also an exploitation of the victory which is fruitful in results.

5. To win, it is necessary to break the opponent's combat system by force.

This rupture requires attacks pushed to the end, without ulterior motives; it can only be obtained at the price of bloody sacrifices. Any other conception must be rejected as contrary to the very nature of war.

However skilfully conceived, a maneuver prepares, but does not ensure victory.

6. The offensive alone leads to positive results.

Success in war has always been won by generals who wanted and sought battle; those who suffered it have always been defeated.

By taking the initiative in operations, one brings about events instead of suffering them. An energetic commander-in-chief, having confidence in himself, in his subordinates, in his troops, will never let his adversary have priority in the action, under the pretext of waiting for more precise information. From the very beginning of the war, he will imprint on the operations such a character of violence and relentlessness that the enemy, struck in his morale and paralyzed in his action, will be reduced, perhaps, to remain on the defensive.

In the presence of an adversary having taken the initiative of the operations, it is still by an energetic and violent counter-offensive that it will be possible to give the fight a favorable turn.

Generalities on the Conduct of War

In all cases, the first fights are of great importance because of the preponderant influence that they can exert on the subsequent events.

7. In order to wage the supreme struggle which decides the fate of the war, and in which the future of the nation is at stake, one cannot have too many forces. All large units operating in the same theater must therefore participate actively in the general battle.

Given the enormity of the masses currently being deployed, the general battle will be the result of battles of armies, more or less distinct from each other, but all related to the same overall concept. The participation of the totality of the forces in the general battle can be considered as acquired, if all the armies are able to concur in the realization of this conception, with all their means, under the conditions of time and space determined by the commander in chief.

8. Battles are above all moral struggles. Defeat is inevitable as soon as the hope of victory ceases. Success is therefore not for the one who has suffered the fewest losses, but for the one whose will is the strongest and whose morale is the most strongly tempered.

By keeping, at the supreme moment when the balance threatens to tip on the side of the enemy, reserves intended to organize withdrawals, to guard the flanks or to cover the retreat, one lets slip the last chances of victory. Reserves are not intended to limit failure, but to act offensively to win the battle.

A leader disregards his duty who, in the decisive battle, gives up the fight before having exhausted all the means at his disposal.

9. After the victory, a pursuit without truce or mercy, exploiting all energies to their last limits, must ensure the complete destruction of the material and moral forces of the enemy.

It is necessary to put, at all costs, the adversary in the impossibility of recovering a sufficient cohesion to face the fight again. By redoubling his determination and daring in the pursuit, the victorious leader and his troops will obtain such decisive results that a single great battle will perhaps suffice to decide the fate of the war.

Chapter II – Command

10. The command of large units is entrusted to generals of division, having the title of commander of corps, army or army group.

The title of *commander-in-chief* is applied to the general who commands all the troops in the same theater of operations.

11. Whatever his rank and title, the commander of a large unit establishes his authority over his subordinates only on the condition that he inspires their full confidence and commands their respect by the firmness of his character, the elevation of his moral qualities and his professional value.

12. The main data serving as a basis for the decisions of the command are:

The *mission* assigned by the superior authority and which must be carried out in spite of the enemy, whatever the circumstances;

The *forces* to be deployed (number and value of the troops, character and aptitudes of the commanders of the subordinate units, and material means available to the commander);

The *situation* in relation to the enemy, and in relation to the nearest large units (relations of time, space and mission);
All other circumstances (nature of the terrain, state of communications, climate, season, etc.).

THE MANEUVER PLAN.

13. In any operation, the commander first establishes the *general objective* to be achieved, and then he decides on a *maneuver* whose purpose is to combine the use of forces in order to achieve this objective, despite the enemy.

The general goal derives directly from the mission received. Like the mission, it is permanent.

For a large unit, the final result can rarely be achieved at the first attempt. It can only be achieved by degrees, through a series of intermediate objectives. It is essential to pursue these objectives only one after the other. Pursuing multiple outcomes at once leads to fragmentation of effort and diminishes the chances of success.

14. The *maneuver plan* provides the overall goal and outline of the maneuver. It establishes the first objective to be attained, the first direction to be taken, or the first locations to be occupied, and regulates accordingly the distribution and initial disposition of forces.

The maneuver plan must not contain details beyond those required by the situation at the time.

Any provision would be premature, resulting from a final judgment arbitrarily made on the intentions of the adversary, as long as he remains free to move.

Before settling the distribution of his forces, the commander of a large unit considers, without any preconceived opinion, the various plausible hypotheses on the projects of his adversary.

Without ever losing sight of the goal he is pursuing, he plans the measures to be taken, if necessary, to thwart these plans and preserve his freedom of action.

15. In the course of operations, the information provided by the information media makes it possible to eliminate certain assumptions that are recognized as inaccurate and to get a glimpse of the enemy's intentions.

It is therefore essential that forces be distributed, from the outset and at all times, according to an arrangement that is flexible enough to lend itself to the transformations that may be required by the increasingly precise knowledge of the situation.

The situation is, moreover, never established in a certain and complete way. The information often arrives too late; it is almost always insufficient, often contradictory.

From then on, the command can only fulfill its mission and impose its will on the enemy by remaining firm in the main lines of its plan.

Success in war depends even more on perseverance and tenacity in execution than on skill in the conception of the maneuver.

THE INTELLIGENCE PLAN.

16. In drawing up his plan of maneuver, the commander takes into account, insofar as he deems it useful, the information gathered up to that point on the situation, the forces, the dispositions, and the presumed intentions of the adversary.

For large subordinate units, this information is generally contained in the instructions of the superior authority.

The general-in-chief, when he finally decides on his plan of maneuver, uses the information received in peacetime on the organization of the enemy armies, their probable strength, the number and efficiency of their transport lines, the locations of landing docks and yards, etc.

17. In the development of operations, each decision must come at its own time. It follows that, when the time comes, the chief must never delay his decision under the pretext of waiting for additional information. The search for more precise information on the enemy is only intended to limit the field of hypotheses.

18. The commander alone is in a position to determine the information and verifications that will be useful to him in eliminating one or another of the possibilities first considered, and to develop his maneuver in spite of the enemy.

His maneuver plan includes, as a result, *an intelligence plan* in which are determined the essential points on which the investigations of the information organs will have to concentrate.

Information is always requested in the form of precise and simple questions.

19. Information is only of value if, by its nature, scope, and time of arrival, it can be used in the development of the maneuver being executed.

At each echelon, the command therefore requires information that corresponds to the scope of its maneuver.

For example, the commander-in-chief does not have to concern himself with the detailed dispositions taken by the enemy; but he has a major interest in being fixed on the displacements of the center of gravity of the enemy masses. This information would still be useful to him, even if it was several days old.

It would be of lesser value to the commander of a framed army corps, who needs above all precise and recent information on the events taking place in his immediate zone of action.

Chapter III – Freedom of Action. Security. Research of information. Exploration

FREEDOM OF ACTION.

20. To be able to carry out his maneuver, the leader must have his *freedom of action*, that is to say, he must have his forces at his disposal and remain master of using them, in spite of the enemy, to carry out his plan.

In a large unit, it is therefore important above all that the elements of this unit are in a position to participate in the battle and that they are not exposed to being attacked and beaten separately. When these conditions are met, the leader has his forces at his disposal: the unit is then said to be *reunited*.

The reunion of forces, thus defined, constitutes an essential condition of the command's freedom of action.

21. When the forces are united, the best way for a commander to ensure his freedom of action is to impose his will on the enemy by a vigorously conducted offensive, following a well-defined guiding idea. This offensive impresses the adversary, forces him to defend himself, and disconcerts his plans of attack.

22. The arrangements for the execution of the maneuver must be aimed at surprising the adversary in order to deprive him of his freedom of action. Surprise results for the enemy from a danger to which he is unable to respond in a complete and timely manner. It requires rapidity of movement and secrecy of operations.

SECURITY.

23. The essential purpose of *security* is to guarantee the command its freedom of action, by giving it the time and space necessary, first to gather its forces, and then to develop its maneuver.

The time and space available to the commander for the assembly of forces and for the development of maneuver depend on the distance to which the intelligence organs have been pushed and have gathered their information.

Intelligence is sought by the means indicated below and according to the intelligence plan established by the command as a consequence of the maneuver plan.

When additional space and time is recognized as essential, it may be gained by means of elements operating at the desired distance from the main body of the forces and charged with delaying the enemy.

24. Security is completed by provisions taken in the army corps in order to protect the troops against surprises and to guarantee the secrecy of operations.

All of these provisions constitute *protection*.

INTELLIGENCE GATHERING.

25. The higher the rank of the command for which they operate, the earlier the information organs are put into action, the further they are pushed and, consequently, the more strongly they must be formed.

It is not enough to search for information. It is also important to prepare the transmission of information with the greatest care.

26. The principal sources of intelligence are:
Special agent reports;
Aerial observation;
Cavalry and staff reconnaissance;
Combat.

27. In addition, useful indications may be obtained from disclosures in the foreign press and from official or private correspondence, from interrogations of prisoners, deserters or inhabitants, etc.

28. Aerial observation is carried out by two distinct services: a long-range service, placed at the disposal of the commander-in-chief or army commanders, and a more limited-range service, dependent on army, corps, or cavalry division commanders.
Aerial observers recognize the big ones. But their information cannot be relied upon in an absolute manner, due to the delicacy of the aircraft and the atmospheric circumstances that may render these aircraft unusable.

29. The cavalry at the disposal of the general-in-chief and the army cavalry participate in the search for information by exploration.
The cavalry of the army corps provides the complementary information indispensable for the safety of these large units.

30. Staff reconnaissance is carried out by aerial observation or in close liaison with the cavalry.
Their purpose is to clarify certain points that only officers with a complete knowledge of the command's plans can clarify.

31. Combat provides immediate information that can be reported with certainty, provided that only duly observed realities are taken into account.
Reconnaissance resulting from the combat of a unit of all arms cannot provide information beyond the necessarily restricted limits

of the front of action of this unit.

EXPLORATION.

32. The command can only be informed in an exact and continuous manner on the movements and dispositions of the enemy in a given region, on the condition that large cavalry units are sent into this region.

The commander-in-chief and the army commanders have at their disposal, for this purpose, large cavalry forces formed into divisions: several divisions may, for a given purpose, be united under one command: they then constitute a cavalry corps.

The service of these cavalry forces is called *exploration*.

The commanding officer orients the commander of the scouting cavalry to the situation, informs him of his intentions and determines the mission to be accomplished. The instructions he gives specify, among other things, the information to be sought, in the form of precise and simple questions; they include an indication of the region in which the main body of cavalry will have to operate and, if necessary, the attitude to be taken towards the opposing cavalry.

33. The commander of the exploration cavalry has the greatest initiative in the execution of the task assigned to him. This task is simplified if he is able to gain the upper hand over the enemy cavalry. He must, therefore, try to put this cavalry out of the way, whenever his mission does not oppose it. After the enemy cavalry has been defeated, reconnaissance is facilitated, information can be easily transmitted to the rear; the troops are no longer exposed to surprises.

34. Since the exploration cavalry must always be in a position to fight, its leader keeps the bulk of his forces *constantly together*.

The task of searching for information requested by the command is entrusted to light elements (detachments or reconnaissance) sent to certain points or in given directions. All these elements together constitute the discovery.

The elements of discovery can be stopped by the surveillance network that the enemy surrounds himself with.

The exploration cavalry then supports the discovery on the points where the reconnaissance could not pass, by seeking to dislocate the surveillance network of the adversary and to obtain the requested information.

Most often, it only succeeds in delimiting the contours of the enemy infantry. In any case, it indicates with certainty that certain regions are not occupied by the enemy.*

35. *The leader of the exploration cavalry must know how to dare and take risks.* The mobility and the power of the armament of a cavalry division allow it to face even difficult situations.

36. In certain circumstances or on certain terrain, the exploration cavalry may be supported by infantry battalions or mixed detachments: these supports give it the means to force weakly occupied defiles or to limit the outlets accessible to the enemy cavalry; they may also ensure possible withdrawals.

In all cases, it is important that the use of infantry support does not diminish the speed and scope of cavalry movements.

---

* Information of this nature, which has sometimes been called "negative intelligence," is of particular importance.

Chapter IV – Command Aids. Instructions. Orders. Reports. Liaisons

THE HEADQUARTERS. THE SERVICES.

37. Every commander of a large unit has a staff which is designated: in an army, as the *army staff* and in the army group, as the *general staff*.

In each staff, the entire service is headed by a chief of staff who, in an army, bears the title of *chief of staff of the army* and in the army group, the title of *major general*. The major general is assisted by *assistant general staffs*.

38. The General Staff prepares the elements of the General's decisions; it translates these decisions into instructions and orders; it completes these instructions and orders with all the necessary detailed measures and ensures their transmission.

39. The care of provoking the search for information, of centralizing, controlling and reconciling the information gathered, constitutes one of the most important attributions of the staffs.

In war, it is rare that an isolated piece of information can be considered absolutely certain; the degree of confidence to be attributed to it depends on the source or the personality from which it emanates and the confirmations that it receives from all the other information.

All sources of information must therefore be exploited thoroughly and with the greatest care.

40. The chief of staff is the immediate assistant to the commander of the large unit.

He is kept constantly informed of his commander's intentions, in order to be able to foresee and prepare the execution of decisions. In presenting the elements of these decisions, he has the duty to submit the opinions or proposals suggested to him by a detailed knowledge of the situation.

Once the decision has been taken, he studies and proposes all the implementation measures.

He sends all necessary instructions to the departments or bodies responsible for coordinating them (Directorate of Stages and Services, Directorate of the Rear).

He personally directs the liaison and intelligence services.

41. The services are bodies responsible for meeting the needs of the armies.

At the head of each of them, is placed a direction which foresees the needs, gathers the means, orders and ensures the technical measures of execution.

In the army corps, the directorates function under the immediate orders of the general commanding the corps.

In the army, the overall supervision and coordination of the services are ensured by the *director of stages and services*, except for the following forward services: artillery, engineering, liaison, intelligence and aeronautics.

In the army group, the rear services are directed, linked and coordinated by a general officer who has the title of *director of the rear*. The railroad service is under his high authority.

The director of stages and services reports to the general commanding the army under the same conditions as the army corps commanders.

The director of the rear reports to the general commanding the

Command Aids. Instructions. Orders. Reports. Liaisons 23

army group under the same conditions as the army commanders.

42. The functioning of the services is entirely subordinated to the development of operations; the aim to be sought is to enable the command to make its decisions independently of any concern for supplies and evacuations.

To this end, it is essential to inform the directors of the services as soon as possible of the main contingencies envisaged in the maneuver plan. This will enable them to make their forecasts without being surprised by events.

In the event of special technical difficulties, it is up to the command to assess the extent to which it will take into account the operational requirements of the services.

It is also the responsibility of the command[*] to stagger resources in such a way as to bring them to the desired points in a timely manner, while avoiding congestion.

INSTRUCTIONS. ORDERS. REPORTS.

43. Command operates by *instructions and orders*. While respecting the initiative of his subordinates, he has a duty to ensure that his instructions are carried out.

44. Instructions and orders must contain all that is necessary for subordinates and nothing more.

The instruction sets the goal to be achieved, foresees contingencies, expresses intentions. Its purpose is to provide subordinate commanders with the necessary indications to act, in all circumstances, in accordance with the plans of the command.

The order contains formal prescriptions applicable in clearly determined conditions of time and space.

45. An instruction is more or less developed, depending on the

---

[*] Either directly in the corps or through the rear director in the army group or the director of stages and services in the army.

circumstances. Often, it is valid for a fairly long period of time and can be followed, if necessary, by new instructions, as the situation becomes clearer.

46. The instructions are supplemented, if necessary, by orders fixing the conditions of execution of the prescribed operation.
This procedure is customary in the *army*.
In the *corps*, an order will generally suffice, at the head of which are summarized the information on the enemy, the intentions of the corps commander, and the goal to be achieved.

47. Instructions or orders received at various levels of the hierarchy are transformed for the use of immediate subordinates, either into new orders or instructions, or into new orders only.
All efforts must be made to reduce the duration of this transformation.

48. Every unit commander must keep his commander informed, by *reports*, of what he knows about the enemy, the situation, and the operations of his unit.
All significant events are *reported* to confirm, supplement and coordinate previous reports.

LIAISON.

49. The purpose of liaison is to coordinate efforts by ensuring continuity of relations between commanders of units participating in the same operation.

50. Liaisons are established:
Between the commander of a unit and his immediate subordinates;
Between commanders of units operating in adjacent areas.
The former enable the command to transmit its instructions and orders, to complete them, if necessary, and to receive, in return, information, reports and accounts which, by gradually clarifying the situation, provide it with the elements for its subsequent

decisions.

The second is an exchange of information which enables two neighbouring units to combine their efforts for common success and to give each other mutual support.

51. Every unit has an absolute duty to assist neighboring troops to the extent consistent with its mission. On the other hand, no unit has the right to rely on the assistance of elements operating in adjacent zones of action, which may be unable to provide the expected assistance because of their mission.

In no case should lateral connections have the consequence of restricting the freedom of movement of a unit and of obliging it to regulate itself too closely with neighbouring units.

52. It is the duty of every unit commander to relate to his subordinates with the greatest care and at the earliest possible moment.

Conversely, every subordinate must establish liaison with his direct superior.

Every unit commander is, moreover, required to communicate to neighboring units all useful information on his situation and that of the enemy.

53. In principle, the commander of a large unit shall make use of the resources at his disposal to establish his liaison, while avoiding taking resources from neighbouring units.

Materially, the links are made by the use of various types of communications. They can be completed by sending staff officers, liaison agents.

A staff officer is seconded to liaise in all circumstances where the commander of a large unit wishes to be informed in an accurate and continuous manner of events. This officer has the right to request or provide, on behalf of the commander he represents, all useful information or explanations.

Chapter V – The Army Group

54. An army group is a group of armies whose operations are linked together by the plan of the general-in-chief.

55. The purpose of the army group maneuver is to force the enemy into a general battle under conditions that are likely to have decisive results for the outcome of the war.

The army group maneuver consists of a main operation, conducted with as many forces as possible, and secondary operations, intended to prepare or facilitate the development of the main operation.

Each of these operations must have as its end the destruction of the enemy's organized forces in a given area, and must therefore lead to a battle.

56. The general battle is the result of the partial battles which, while contributing to the same final goal, may not be simultaneous.

DISPOSITION AND SECURITY OF THE GROUP OF ARMIES.

57. Each of the partial operations, which together constitute the maneuver of the Army Group, is entrusted to one or more armies.

The Army Group's force structure is adjusted accordingly in width and depth.

The disposition must have enough extension in width to allow for the creation of intervals between the armies of maneuver.

In depth, the armies are preferably placed in echelon with respect to each other. Each of them thus has its own rear zone for the operation of its supply and evacuation organs.

58. The army group is reunited when all the armies are able to participate in the general battle with all their means, under the conditions fixed by the general-in-chief.

59. At the beginning of the war, the operation of reuniting the armies on the borders, at the request of the plan of maneuver, is called *concentration*.

The concentration is carried out by using all the resources of the rail network, under the protection of cover and fortified positions[*] and at a sufficient distance from the frontier so that the group of armies cannot be attacked before having completed its reunion.

60. During operations, the security of the army group is obtained by the articulation of the system, which must allow the development of the maneuver plan of the general-in-chief in spite of the enemy.

In order to be in a position to judiciously adjust his system, the commander-in-chief will have the necessary information sought by his information organs.

---

[*] Chap. IX.

GENERAL BATTLE.

61. The purpose of the general battle is the annihilation of the enemy's organized forces.

The general battle plan must be the natural consequence and development of the maneuver plan. It determines the missions, the zones of operations of the armies, and the general conditions of their entry into action.

62. In the case where the meeting zones of the opposing groups of armies are very far from each other, the passage from the initial formation to the formation of the general battle is carried out by a series of transformations corresponding to the successive modifications of the situation.

When the armies are formed near the borders, the initial formation of concentration contains in germ the formation of the general battle. The armies are reunited according to the measures decided upon in peacetime. However, the commander-in-chief may prescribe the execution of variants to the concentration scheme.

After the troops have completed their landings, he can still, to a certain extent, shift the center of gravity of the system and reinforce certain armies, by means of changes in the order of battle.

63. During the general battle, the commander of the army group intervenes above all to coordinate operations. He may thus be led to activate or slow down the movements of certain armies. He considers the repercussions that partial successes or setbacks in secondary zones of operations may have on the maneuver as a whole. Without losing sight of his main idea, he modifies, as far as possible, the distribution of forces to take these repercussions into account.

Because of the fronts occupied by the armies, such modifications will most often be difficult to achieve. Even by rail, the transport of large reserves always requires a considerable amount of time and can only be used within limited limits.

64. As soon as the enemy begins to yield, the pursuit must be started without respite. It is by a relentless and brutal pursuit, pushed to the extreme limit of the forces

It is by a relentless and brutal pursuit, pushed to the limit of the forces, that one manages to crush the last resistances and to finish the enemy by preventing him from reorganizing himself.

It is then up to the superior command to combine direct attacks, pushed in front of the front of the armies, with vast envelopment movements, directed on the lines of communication of the enemy.

The cavalry masses play a preponderant role in the pursuit. Heavily equipped with artillery and ammunition, supported by detachments of light infantry, they tried to rise quickly on the flanks of the retreating enemy armies and even to anticipate them in order to stop them.

With a view to freeing the armies of the front line from secondary missions, all the other organized forces of the nation must be carried forward as soon as possible, to ensure the occupation of the enemy's territory, to besiege his places and to ruin his resources.

65. When the general battle has been decided in favor of the enemy, the commander-in-chief shall determine for the various armies the general directions of retreat and the zones where they may reorganize. It is his duty to provoke all necessary measures to resume operations as soon as possible.

Chapter VI – The Army

MANEUVER FORMATIONS

66. The battle, fought with all the forces available, is the goal towards which the maneuver of the army tends.

It is important, during the course of the maneuver, to keep the army constantly together, that is to say, to arrange its elements in such a way that they are always able to participate in the same overall action.

But an army that is too closely concentrated is hampered in its movements; it is unable to maneuver. Vis-a-vis a skilled adversary, it is exposed to envelopment.

Even in the vicinity of the enemy, it is essential that the army have sufficient articulation so that all its elements can move with ease and develop all their means of action in battle.

When, because of the inadequacy of the road network, obstacles in the terrain or other circumstances, the army is not assembled, the safety provisions prescribed by the command must make it possible to gain the time necessary for this assembly (art. 75).

67. The army, while remaining reunited, can have a position that is all the wider and deeper the further away the adversary is.

A very open position has the advantage of lending itself to a more complete use of the resources of the country, the cantonments and the road network. A wide articulation spares the troops unnecessary fatigue and deprivation and allows them to be brought to the battle in full possession of their physical and moral means.

On the other hand, the greater the distance from the enemy, the more it is advisable to extend the system in order to adapt it, without difficulty, to all the transformations that the changes in the situation may require.

The extension of the formation in the direction of the width facilitates the march and the enveloping maneuvers; it lends itself moreover, by simple tightening of the intervals, to a later narrower meeting, in view of the battle. The wide position maintains the enemy in uncertainty on the direction in which the main effort of the army will occur.

A deep formation is suitable for the execution of sudden and rapid changes in direction. It allows the drawing of an enveloping maneuver, by advancing a wing, or to protect a flank by a refused echelon. It finally assures the command the possibility of reserving a part of the forces, in view of their tactical use in the battle.

68. Always guided by the plan of maneuver whose execution he is pursuing, the army commander determines the form, proportions, orientation and conditions of articulation of his force, taking into account the needs of the situation and the circumstances of time and place.

Each element of the army, while playing a particular role in the whole, must act in perfect harmony with the neighboring elements.

It is up to the commander of the army, with a view to making the convergence of efforts effective, to establish, between the bodies placed under his orders, by the instructions he gives, the most favorable mission relations for the realization of his projects.

In addition, the commander of the army fixes, by orders, the zones of march or the itineraries of the corps, the direction of their movement or action, the locations of their headquarters, the lines to be reached at the end of the march by the leading elements, and, if necessary, by the trailing elements.

69. In principle, at least one marching road is assigned to each army corps. However, the insufficiency of the road network or the necessity of maneuver may lead to two corps marching one behind the other on one or more roads.

70. As one approaches the adversary, there is a major interest in progressively reducing the depth of the deployment zones to avoid imposing, on the eve of the battle, excessive fatigue on the last elements.

SECURITY OF THE ARMY.

71. The security of the army is achieved:
By intelligence;
By the articulation of the forces;
Exceptionally, by the use of detached forces.
It is completed by the protection organized in the army corps.
The information that the commander of the army has his information organs seek enables him to regulate the organization of his forces and, if necessary, to order the necessary detachments in due course.

72. In addition to its special agents and aeronautical formations, the army has at its disposal the cavalry assigned to it for intelligence research.

73. The cavalry of the army is generally formed into divisions.
It is responsible for the reconnaissance service on behalf of the army commander. His instructions indicate to it the results to be achieved and, if necessary, the limit of its action (chap. III – Exploration).
Because of its presence in the region assigned to its exploration, it will contribute in this region to the security of the army by the information that it provides, by making and maintaining contact with the enemy, and, if necessary, by the

delaying action exercised on the opposing columns.

When the battle becomes imminent and there is no more room for the army's cavalry in front of the front, it operates in liaison with the vanguards, or acts on a wing of the army, according to the orders of the army commander. The latter may at his discretion keep it at his disposal, distribute it among the army corps or place it under the direct orders of a corps commander.

In all cases, the army's cavalry must participate in the battle.

74. The information gathered by the information organs makes it possible to assess the distance at which the enemy is located. They thus provide the means to determine the limits of the extension to be given to the formation so that the army remains united.

The articulation is then regulated in order to allow all the large subordinate units to lend each other support, and to participate in the battle, under conditions of space and time foreseen by the command.

The safety of the army is thus guaranteed.

The elements of the formation which enter first in action, in case of meeting, recognize the enemy, attack or contain him, and prepare the entry in action of the main forces.

75. The use of detached forces, intended to ensure the reunion of forces or to cover the maneuver of the main body of the army from afar, may be justified in certain eventualities (for example, to ensure the opening of the army beyond a defile, to stop one of the forces of a divided enemy while the main body of the army operates against the other force, etc.). But, because of the risks involved in the use of these detachments, they must respond to a definite need or to a well-defined idea of maneuver.

Their mission and, in some cases, their mode of action, are determined by the maneuver plan. Above all, they must save time. To this end, they usually occupy solidly organized positions or oppose the enemy with light elements that delay him and force him to move in combat formation. There are also circumstances where their mission will oblige them to take the offensive.

THE BATTLE.

76. The commander of the army must go into battle with the firm resolve to accomplish, by destroying the enemy, the mission that has been assigned to him.

77. It is not necessary to be superior to the enemy at all times and in all parts of the battlefield. It is sufficient to be the strongest at the right point and time.

The battle consists of :

A main action, carried out with large forces, in such a direction that success in that direction will lead to decisive results.

Secondary actions, intended to prepare or facilitate the main action and involving the use of means measured by the task at hand.

78. Whenever his mission authorizes him to do so, the commander of the army takes the initiative in attacks, in order to force the enemy to submit to his will.

In all circumstances where he is momentarily forced to remain on the defensive, he must nonetheless take advantage of all favorable opportunities to act offensively.

Passive defense is doomed to certain defeat; it is to be rejected absolutely.

The partial fights of which the battle is composed take different forms according to their particular goal, the number of men involved, the circumstances of time, place and terrain; but they are all linked to the same overall conception defined by the battle plan of the army commander.

BATTLE PLAN.

79. The *battle plan* is expressed in instructions which indicate the goal to be achieved, the overall conception of the army commander, and which consequently fix the army's disposition for the battle, as well as the role of subordinate units.

Because of the extent of the battle front of an army, it is

difficult to move, during the course of the fight, large masses, to make them act at the desired point and time. The commander of the army therefore determines in advance the direction of the main action and the conditions of time in which it will take place; he regulates the secondary actions, in order to make them contribute to the success of the main action.

80. The main action can be directed either at a wing of the opponent, or at a point on his front.

The direction which leads to a wing is, in general, the most advantageous.

Enveloping attacks facilitate the use of superior means to those of the enemy. They throw his forces back on each other, and make it impossible for them to develop all their means; they naturally cause successive positions to fall, by threatening the lines of retreat and the communications of the adversary.

The main action directed on the enemy's front presents more difficulties. It does not allow for a quick decision and requires heavy sacrifices. The results of a frontal action are necessarily incomplete if the enemy is simply pushed back and retains the possibility of occupying support points in the rear. On the other hand, when it leads to a tactical breakthrough, frontal action can lead to decisive success, if the army commander has sufficient forces to rapidly widen the breach and envelop the dislocated enemy forces.

81. The timing of the main action is determined by taking into account the general situation, the form of the maneuver system prior to the battle, and the information gathered on the enemy.

When the enemy is well recognized, or when the army starts from a wide position in order to go to the battle by converging movements, one can try to obtain the concomitance of the main action and the secondary actions.

If the situation is not very precise or if the army is spread out in depth, one will often have to wait, before launching the main action, until secondary actions have made it possible to recognize the enemy, to fix him, and to prepare the decision.

82. Because of the power of the armament, which makes approaches difficult and the beginning of engagements painful, and also because of the frequent use of the resources of the fortification, which require the renewal of attacks, the battles will be able to be prolonged during several days.

Taking this fact into account, the army commander will determine the number of troops to be assigned to secondary actions sufficiently to allow them to sustain the battle for the necessary time. In certain cases and on certain parts of the front, he will be able to assign a momentary defensive mission to units which will organize their positions with a view to delaying the enemy, until such time as the decision occurs in the main action zone.

On the other hand, in the latter zone, the concentration of considerable forces will provide the means to ensure the continuity of the effort and the immediate exploitation of the success obtained. It is by imbuing the forward movement with increasing vigor through the influx of fresh troops, that the command will be able to obtain a rapid decision.

The firm will of the leader, the skilful orientation of the attack and the energy of the executors are so many factors which will decrease the duration of the battle.

BATTLE FORMATION.

83. The *battle formation* results from the formation of maneuver of which it constitutes the last and final form.

The formation in which the army marches to the battle can be, according to the plan of the commander of the army, more or less broad, more or less deep.

A broad posture facilitates the convergence and simultaneity of efforts; a deep posture makes it possible to reserve important forces for the main action, when it must be preceded by secondary actions intended to prepare it.

84. In all cases, the general front of engagement of the army must make it possible to contain the enemy until the moment of decision, wherever he shows forces, unless by their distance or direction of march, these forces are not in a position to intervene effectively in the battle.

85. The unequal distribution of fronts among the elements placed under his orders gives the commander of the army the possibility of varying the density of the forces at his discretion and of concentrating larger numbers of troops in front of the points where he wants to act with more power.

The combat front to be assigned to a unit depends above all on the mission assigned to that unit. It also depends on the terrain.

In the vast expanse of an army battlefield, there may be areas that are not suitable for action by troops of all arms, and others where it is sufficient to delay the enemy for a time. The army commander will assign large fronts to units operating in these areas.

On the contrary, in areas more favorable to the action of weapons, he may assign narrower fronts to the units and reinforce them if necessary.

Even in areas where the concentration of forces is the narrowest, the frontage must remain sufficient to allow corps and divisions to develop all their means.

For a corps of normal composition, operating on terrain favorable to the action of troops of all arms, this front must not fall below 4 kilometers. If it exceeds 8 kilometers, the offensive combat escapes any overall direction; the attacks can no longer be fed, and the corps risks being quickly reduced to the defensive.

The army commander distributes the heavy artillery at his disposal among the army corps. This distribution is made taking into account the role assigned to each corps and the nature of the terrain. It must be carried out early enough for the heavy artillery to be able to intervene in the battle in good time.

86. The army cavalry takes part in the battle.

Despite the improvements in firearms, it is still called upon to play an important role. It is the weapon of surprise and, towards the end of crisis periods, its intervention can be decisive.

The army cavalry acts preferably on the wings and the rear of the enemy, or in the gaps of its battle system; it contributes powerfully to the exploitation of success.

On the front, it is most often distributed among the army corps and it then participates in their combat.

87. When prior secondary actions have been deemed necessary, the troops destined for the main action are kept available sheltered from the emotions of the battle. Most often they are placed in advance in the direction in which the main action is to occur.

When they are placed in the rear of a wing, they overrun it largely, in order to spare themselves the benefit of the envelopment.

88. In addition, the commander of the army can keep at his disposal reserves, intended to counter incidents which may occur during the battle.

The size of these reserves is as limited as possible.

ACTION OF THE ARMY COMMANDER.

89. Before the battle, the army commander establishes his plan and distributes the tasks in order to ensure unity of action and convergence of efforts.

To this end, he assigns to the units under his command their missions, their zones of action, their directions of attack or their locations.

He indicates the elements whose use he reserves.

He or she orients the director of stages and services on his or her intentions.

He fixes the point where his command post will be installed.

90. The command post is chosen in view of the ease and rapidity of the connections.

The commander of the army shall avoid moving his command post, at least in the course of the same day.

If he finds it necessary to leave it temporarily, his staff must continue to function there in his absence.

91. In the course of the battle, the commander of the army intervenes mainly by committing the available troops.

He determines the direction and, if necessary, the moment when the forces destined for the main action are put in motion.

He places the reserves at the disposal of the army corps of which they are an organic part, or gives them specific missions and areas of action.

The choice of the moment when the last reserves must be engaged is particularly delicate and serious, since the implementation of these forces is the last means available to the command to make its guiding action felt.

The leader will never hesitate to throw his supreme resources into the battle to wrest victory.

EXPLOITATION OF SUCCESS.

92. All success must be affirmed by the definitive possession of the battlefield. But the uncontested occupation of the conquered ground cannot mark the end of a struggle whose goal is the annihilation of the enemy.

Only the pursuit, immediate and relentless, can achieve this result.

The organization and execution of the pursuit imposes on the command, at all levels of the hierarchy, a difficult duty.

After the expenditure of physical and moral forces required by the battle, the troops, in their satisfaction of the success obtained, are too inclined to believe that their task is accomplished.

It is by force of will that the command will succeed in stimulating their energy and in extracting from them the supreme effort which will put the enemy definitively out of the question.

While the most tried and tested units, obviously unable to resume the forward march, were temporarily maintained on the conquered positions to reconstitute themselves, all the others were immediately carried forward by their leaders. They launched themselves on the adversary without giving him a moment's respite, to prevent him from recovering and to transform his retreat into a rout.

At the beginning of the pursuit, the personal action of the commander of the army can generally only be exercised by the implementation of troops of all arms, and in particular of the cavalry divisions which still remain at his disposal.

CONDUCT IN CASE OF FAILURE.

93. When, all forces having been thrown into the struggle, the army has nevertheless failed in its efforts, it seeks to stop the enemy and contain him until nightfall.

As soon as it is dark, the troops that are in immediate contact with the enemy are held in position; the others are reconstituted into tactical groups and form reserves.

The commander of the army makes arrangements to start the fight again the next day.

When all available forces have been committed to the battle and when the morale of the troops no longer allows for the resumption of the fight, it is important above all to put sufficient distance between the army and the enemy. The army commander then indicates to the various corps the general directions in which they should withdraw.

It is up to the corps commanders to designate, each in his zone of action, units, reinforced with cavalry and artillery, which form rear-guards and sacrifice themselves if necessary to allow the main forces to escape the embrace of the enemy.

As soon as the army has gained sufficient ground, the army commander determines the position where it will stop to recover and re-establish its tactical links, with a view to resuming operations.

ISOLATED OR DETACHED ARMY CORPS.

94. The commander of an isolated or detached corps organizes its position, transforms it and moves it at the request of its maneuver plan, by procedures similar to those indicated in the army maneuver.

When an isolated or detached army corps is constituted with two divisions, its commander will often have an interest in forming mixed groups weaker than the division, in order to combine the use of his forces under better conditions.

The security of the isolated or detached army corps is achieved in the same way as the security of the army, by intelligence, by the articulation of the system and possibly by the use of detached forces.

Protection is provided by the subordinate units.

The battle fought by an isolated or detached army corps is prepared, directed and exploited as an army battle.

Chapter VII – The Army Corps

Within the framework of an army, the corps is an organ of tactical execution.

MARCHES AND STATIONING.

95. Within the limits of the instructions and orders of the commander of the army, the measures taken by the commander of the corps have the essential object of placing his troops in a position to fight with all their means and under the most advantageous conditions.

As long as the distance from the enemy allows the corps to move and rest in complete safety, the marching and stationing arrangements are regulated with a view to facilitating movement and sparing the troops unnecessary fatigue and privation.

As soon as an encounter is possible, all considerations give way to the necessity of using all the means of action of the corps to carry out, in spite of the enemy, the intentions of the army commander.

96. *Far from the enemy*, the commander of the army corps endeavors to leave subordinate units as much independence as possible during the march, and to assign them sufficiently large billets.

97. Unless the orders of the army commander or local circumstances compel him to do so, the corps commander avoids having his troops march on a single road.

A formation based on two or three columns, staggered if necessary in relation to each other, as the situation demands, ensures sufficient independence for the subordinate units and nevertheless remains maneuverable enough to lend itself to changes of direction recognized as necessary during the march.

When the corps operates at a very great distance from the enemy, it is sometimes even advantageous to make full use of the road network and to form a large number of small columns, by assigning distinct routes to the different arms.

The use of this last procedure requires that security be absolute and that one be certain of not having to change direction during the march.

98. The staggering of the cantonments in depth along the roads followed allows the corps to be stationed in good positions, without increasing the length of the march by lateral movements. Moreover, all the elements of the column being able to leave and arrive at the lodging almost simultaneously, it is possible to use all the capacity of march of the troop by avoiding the movements of night.

However, as soon as the possibility of an encounter is foreseen, one must also take into account the obligation that will be imposed later on to bring all the combatant elements closer to the heads of the columns.

In strong columns, in order to avoid the excessive fatigue that this tightening would entail for the tail elements if it were carried out all at once, one will be led to progressively reduce the depth of the deployment zones as one approaches the enemy, and to renounce in part the advantages of the staggering of billets in depth.

99. *In the vicinity of the enemy*, that is, when the corps commander considers that an encounter is possible within twenty-four hours, the troops march and station themselves in the order dictated by the urgency of their employment in combat. The commander of the corps will reduce the depth of the columns and tighten the billets. He completes, if necessary, the security measures (art. 104 and following), and rejects to the rear everything that is not indispensable for combat.

100. There is no normal order of march, nor is there a normal order of combat.

In principle, the artillery is close to the heads of the main columns, ready to intervene quickly in the action. However, it is necessary to take into account the double necessity of not delaying the arrival of the infantry too much and to guarantee the safety of the artillery.

101. The reduction of the depth of the columns can be achieved by the use of enlarged formations (infantry and artillery in doubled formation); but the width of the roads does not always allow the use of these formations. Moreover, the use of massive columns is a cause of great fatigue for the troops and leads to a notable reduction of the speed of march.

The most advantageous method to reduce the depth of the marching formation of an army corps, in proximity of the enemy, consists in forming several columns.

But, when the meeting is possible, the formation must remain sufficiently maneuverable so that the commander of the army corps preserves the total disposition of the bulk of his forces. It is therefore necessary to limit the number of columns to two or three.

It is also important not to slow down the movement and, for this purpose, to use preferably good roads.

102. When marching towards the enemy *in view of a certain and immediate combat*, the marching formation must allow the principal elements of the corps to quickly take their combat formation. It is advantageous, when the nature of the terrain and the condition of the ground permit, to have the corps march in an articulated assembly formation.

The articulated assembly is a formation in which the elements are staggered in width and depth, as required by the tactical situation, under conditions that allow them to use the terrain, move in an orderly fashion, and move quickly into combat deployment.

When the corps commander's intentions are clear, the articulated assembly formation may consist of several columns, each directed at its particular objective.

The width of the formation should not exceed the corps' front line of action. Its depth depends on the terrain and circumstances. It is necessary to have carefully recognized the terrain to be covered and to have foreseen the means to improve the routes.

In the immediate contact with the adversary, the army corps is stationed in an articulated assembly, in cantonments-bivouacs or in bivouacs.

103. The provisions relating to marches and deploying are regulated each day by the corps' order of operations. Exceptionally, at a great distance from the enemy, the order may cover a period of two or more days of march.

THE SECURITY OF THE CORPS.

104. The essential purpose of corps security is to guarantee the main body of the corps the space and time necessary to move, in complete freedom and at the appropriate time, from the marching or stationing position to the combat position.

It may happen that the corps has been ordered to evade by refusing combat. The security must then allow the main body of the army to avoid the adversary's embrace.

The security of the corps is completed by protective measures intended to protect the columns and cantonments from surprise and to stop the incursions of opposing cavalry forces.

105. By the use of detachments of all arms, designated according to the place they occupy in relation to the main body of the army: vanguards, rearguards, flank-guards.

106. The information which reaches the corps commander is of two kinds:

1. that which he receives from the army staff;
2. that which he obtains for his own account, in addition to that which is normally supplied to him by his security detachments.

The corps commander ensures with the greatest care his direct liaison with the army cavalry, when it operates in his vicinity. He has his own cavalry search for additional information; in certain cases, he may even have this cavalry supported by infantry and artillery.

107. The advance guard, in addition to the mission common to all security detachments (art. 23), must put the commander of the corps in a position to engage his main force only at the appropriate time and according to his plan. To this end, when the enemy is not sufficiently recognized, they force him to show his forces.

It is particularly important to appreciate exactly when the main body of the forces should take its battle formation. A corps attacked during its deployment is in a state of marked inferiority. But on the other hand, a premature deployment causes considerable loss of time and deprives the commander of all freedom of maneuver.

The role of a vanguard takes all its extent when it must ensure, beyond a defile, the opening and the deployment of the army corps formed in a single column. In this case, it will most often be necessary to constitute it strongly or to reinforce it by the first elements of the main body of the army.

One or more vanguards are formed, depending on the number of columns and the extent of the march front.

The composition of the vanguards varies with the circumstances.

In principle, the vanguards include troops of all arms.

When several columns are formed, the commander of the corps retains the overall direction of his corps, reserving for himself the exclusive use of all or part of the bulk of the columns.

When marching towards the enemy in an articulated formation, the main body of the corps may be preceded by a unit forming a vanguard. This role of vanguard can be fulfilled simply by the leading elements of the unit.

108. In the retreating march, the mission of the rearguards is to allow the main body of the forces to escape the enemy's embrace and avoid combat.

Their strength and mode of action depend mainly on the time during which they must delay the enemy, the nature of the terrain, and the space they have available to maneuver.

In principle, they do not have to rely on any help. Once their mission is accomplished, they break off the fight, if necessary, to join the main body of the army. It is in the interest, to facilitate this always delicate break, to constitute them strongly in artillery and cavalry.

109. The role of the flank-guards is to stop or at least delay the enemy in the directions in which the commander of the corps does not want to fight.

The flanking guards, depending on the circumstances, are ordered to take position on the threatened flank or to march parallel to the main body, ready to interpose themselves in due course, between it and the enemy.

Because of the resulting weakening of the main force, flank guards are only formed in case of duly established necessity.

PROTECTION.

110. The purpose of protection is to enable the troops to march and station themselves in safety (Art. 24).

In the directions in which security detachments are pushed (vanguards, flank-guards, rear-guards), the protection of the main body of the army is assured by the very fact of the presence of these detachments. These detachments were in turn covered, on the march and in station, by weaker detachments (vanguard heads, outposts, etc.) and were illuminated by the forces of cavalry placed at their disposal.

In the directions less immediately threatened, and where it does not seem useful to push security detachments, the protection measures are reduced to the strict minimum: cavalry patrols during the marches, guarding the cantonments in station, sending protection detachments that are less strongly constituted, and generally operating at a lesser distance than the security detachments mentioned above.

THE COMBAT.

111. The aim of combat is to destroy the enemy forces in the zone of action assigned to the corps. It implies close and constant cooperation of the different arms.

In principle, the corps operating within the framework of an army fights by division;[*] the commander of the corps retains full latitude to make the withdrawals he deems necessary from the divisions.

The splitting into groups of all arms below the division level has the serious disadvantage of breaking tactical links. If this splitting is normally justified for the isolated corps, it must be avoided for the corps operating within the framework of an army; it is nevertheless a necessity which is sometimes imposed and which must then be accepted.

112. Most often, the combat presents at its beginning a series of actions having for object:

To force the enemy to show his forces and to take a front of combat;

To develop in front of the enemy a front of deployment marked out by points of support which the first engaged troops hold.

All of these actions constitute the *engagement*.

The available troops are formed in the shelter of the deployment front. It is from there that they leave to execute the attacks intended to break the enemy's position.

In certain cases, especially if there is a surprise, the

---

[*] The expression "division" means both the division reduced by the withdrawals made by the commander of the corps, and the complete division.

engagement can be reduced or even eliminated.

113. Corps combat comprises a main attack and secondary attacks.

The main attack is characterized by the use of large forces in order to ensure success, to exploit it to the full, and thus to achieve the aim of the combat, as it results from the mission received from the superior authority.

The other attacks are intended to prepare or facilitate the main attack by fixing the enemy, and by attracting his reserves.

COMBAT PLAN. ACTION OF THE COMMAND.

114. The resolution to fight and the choice of the general form of combat (offensive or defensive) must be made prior to the engagement.

The purpose of the combat plan of the corps commander is to determine, according to the goal to be attained:

The conditions of the engagement;
The combat system of the main body of the corps;
The role of subordinate units;
The direction, objective and moment of the main attack.

The more or less complete information gathered before the battle makes it possible to decide, prior to the engagement, certain parts of the battle plan. Sometimes this information can be used to determine the entire plan, but more often than not, the information needed to complete the plan will be provided by the engagement or by the development of the battle itself.

115. The corps commander exercises leadership and coordination throughout the combat. He chooses his command post accordingly. He sets the divisions either the objectives to be achieved or the fronts to be occupied. In the case where they are joined together, he also determines their zones of action.

He keeps at his disposal, at least at the beginning, the forces necessary to exercise his directing action on the general course of the battle.

The artillery, cavalry and engineer commanders of the corps will assist him in ensuring this guiding action.

The commander of the artillery of the corps, without interfering in any way in the conduct of the artilleries of the divisions, will keep himself constantly informed of the situation of all the batteries in the whole of the corps. He informs the commander of the corps on this subject and submits to him in due course any useful proposal, with a view to ensuring the coordination of the action of the artillery in combat.

The cavalry and engineer commanders of the corps have a similar role, with regard to the employment of the troops of their arm.

ENGAGEMENT.

116. The engagement is the responsibility of the vanguards (or of the elements that take their place), reinforced, if necessary, by elements of the main body.

When only one vanguard is formed for the entire corps, the engagement is directed by the commander of the corps, who stands by the commander of the vanguard.

When more than one vanguard is formed, it is up to the division generals, oriented on the intentions of the corps commander, to regulate themselves the march of the engagement in their division.

117. In the engagement:

The infantry must be employed with economy, so that the command can save the greatest possible part of it for the attacks. Its strength will be determined by the obligation to occupy or remove the strongpoints necessary for deployment and to conquer, if necessary, artillery positions.

The artillery has an important role to play. It must, in fact, take advantage of the first infantry conflicts to try to gain the upper hand on the enemy batteries in action. The latter will find themselves, as a result, in a state of material and moral inferiority that will make their subsequent re-entries into action less powerful.

The artillery must therefore be able to intervene early, in large groups.

Cavalry can be advantageously used: before the engagement, to push back or stop the enemy cavalry, to recognize and slow down the opposing columns; and during the engagement, to help and protect the action of the infantry and artillery.

118. The engagement is always a critical period and efforts should be made to shorten its duration.

The duration of the engagement depends on the information available, the attitude of the enemy, the time required for the main force to make its combat dispositions, and the results expected from the engagement. It will be significantly increased if it is necessary to conquer support points to ensure deployment.

119. The engagement differs depending on whether the combat is an encounter combat, a combat against a posted enemy, or a defensive combat.

A unit engages in *encounter combat* when it encounters an enemy on an offensive march who is also advancing offensively.

The engagement is characterized, in this case, by the difficulty of the deployment. It is generally violent and tumultuous. The offensive must be very energetic from the beginning, in order to seize the outlets, the important points of the terrain, and to hinder the enemy deployment.

An advance achieved in the constitution of the deployment front provides a considerable advantage for the subsequent development of the fight.

The direction of the engagement is particularly difficult in encounter combat. It can only be carried out successfully if the corps commander has a guiding idea and if the commanders of subordinate units are clearly oriented to his intentions.

Against a posted enemy, the aim of the engagement is to drive back the opponent's advanced detachments (vanguards or outposts), in order to determine the true defense front.

In the presence of an enemy with all its means of action on organized terrain, the general pace of the engagement must be methodical. There is more time available, and it is essential to conduct a thorough reconnaissance of the enemy's front before attacking with the bulk of the forces.

In *defensive combat*, the first object of the engagement is to determine the directions of march followed by the enemy.

For this purpose, vanguards can be brought forward from the front. They force the enemy to show his forces and to deploy. Their mission accomplished, they withdraw by flowing through the wings or intervals of the position.

When the intentions of the enemy are not doubtful, the - bulk of the forces is covered by simple outposts.

THE COMBAT FORMATION.

120. The combat formation comprises:
The troops in charge of the engagement;
The available troops;
The security detachments, if any.

In the combat formation, the formation is taken by attached units or by successive units.

The formation by joined units avoids the mixing of units and ensures better the continuity of the action in depth. The formation by successive units is more suitable for a possible maneuver during the combat. It is indicated for a wing unit and for an isolated unit. Its use is still justified when, the front of action being restricted, it is necessary to foresee the removal of several successive lines of support points and, consequently, the necessity to bring in fresh troops for new attacks.

121. When the situation has become sufficiently clear during the engagement, it may be in the interest of the corps commander to immediately entrust the main attack to one of his divisions; the other division will then receive the mission of facilitating this attack.

Otherwise, the divisions will be responsible for the execution of preparatory attacks; the corps commander will reserve the troops necessary to carry out the main attack at the point and at the time that he himself will later determine.

In order to deal with combat incidents, the corps commander may keep a few battalions in reserve, which will be used under the conditions indicated for army reserves (Article 88).

The commander of the army corps exercises, in particular, his action in combat by means of the corps artillery. To this end, he will keep it, in whole or in part, under his direction, in order to support, according to need, one or other of the divisions, or he will distribute it among the divisional artilleries, according to the goal he is pursuing.

122. In each division, the road columns are transferred to the combat formation by taking an articulated assembly formation. The articulated assembly allows the commander to have his forces in hand and to deploy them methodically. In the encounter battle, where time is of the essence, road columns move directly to the battle formation.

ORGANIZATION OF A DEFENSIVE FRONT.

123. The tactical situation sometimes requires that all or part of the corps' front of action be put in a state of defense.

In the latter case, each division will organize the front corresponding to its zone of action.

The purpose of the defense of a front is to cover the gathering of resources before going on the attack, or to contain the enemy on this front with reduced manpower, in order to devote more forces to the attack.

The organization of a front includes the creation of resistance centers to each of which is assigned an infantry garrison. It also involves the selection of artillery positions from which it is possible to flank the centers of resistance, to beat their approaches, the intervals between them, as well as the probable locations of the enemy artillery.

The preparation of attacks or counter-attacks implies the study of the conditions in which the big guns will use their artillery and develop all their means of action. It requires, moreover, the recognition of the first locations of the big guns or the reserves, the determination and the development of the routes that they will have to follow to move forward.

THE ATTACKS OF THE MAIN BODY.

124. The commander of the army corps regulates the conditions of the main attack; the division commanders order and combine the other attacks in their respective zones of action. But the relative importance of the attacks must never appear in the execution orders.

For the attacker, the attack is always carried out with the resolution to approach the enemy with a knife and destroy him.

125. Intimate cooperation between the different arms is essential for the success of an attack.

The infantry plays the leading role. It conquers the terrain and drives the enemy from his positions. It is by varying the density of infantry forces on the various points that the command can regulate the intensity of the fight and determine the relative importance of the attacks.

The essential mission of artillery is to support the forward movement of the infantry. In particular, in the crisis period preceding the assault, it defeats, at all costs, the objectives of the attack.

The cavalry is assigned to the attacks to illuminate, cover and protect them from combat surprises. It assists the infantry with all the means at its disposal and completes its action.

126. The execution of an attack includes a preparatory period, during which the attacking troops are brought up in front of their objectives, reinforce if necessary the units engaged and develop a powerful line of infantry and artillery fire in front of the front to be taken.

The attack then enters its decisive phase, during which all efforts are made to push the constantly reinforced line of infantry fire to the assault.

127. The exploitation of success involves:

The occupation of the conquered support points;

The pursuit by the infantry fires and those of the artillery forces brought as quickly as possible on the position taken from the enemy;

The tactical pursuit by the available elements, in particular by the cavalry;

The immediate organization of new attacks by means of fresh troops.

128. In case of failure, all the wills unite to restore the fight.

The engaged troops cling to the ground while waiting for the arrival of reinforcements or the forward movement of neighboring units. In this way, they try to keep the enemy at bay and seek to resume the offensive as soon as possible.

Chapter VIII – Cavalry Corps

129. Several cavalry divisions assigned to an army or group of armies may be united under the orders of a single commander; they then form a cavalry corps. A certain number of selected and lightened infantry battalions are usually attached to the cavalry corps.

130. The constitution of the cavalry corps is prescribed by the general commanding the army or the general-in-chief.

It responds to the need to coordinate the action of two or more cavalry divisions, in view of important operations to be carried out in conditions of time and space which could not be fulfilled by units composed for the most part of infantry. It is particularly justified when it is essential to acquire superiority over enemy cavalry in a given region.

Generally speaking, the supply and feeding of the cavalry corps presents serious difficulties. It is therefore essential that the command take, from the beginning of the operations, special measures to ensure the supply of food and ammunition. To this end, one or more sections of automobile convoys and, if necessary, sections of artillery ammunition, are placed at the disposal of the cavalry corps.

When these conditions are not fulfilled, the duration of the operations of the cavalry corps is limited by the difficulties presented by the subsistence of a considerable number of horses in a restricted space.

131. The missions that a cavalry corps can receive are mainly aimed at exploration, delaying action against columns of all arms, enveloping movements on the battlefield, pursuit, and protection of the retreat.

132. When he has received his mission, the commander of a cavalry corps decides on the plan of the operation, taking into account the greater or lesser proximity of the enemy cavalry, the terrain and the supply facilities. He assigns, if necessary, a special objective to each division.

But he must always take into account the necessity to put the enemy cavalry out of action beforehand, in order to have a free hand in the subsequent accomplishment of his mission.

As long as the enemy cavalry has not been defeated, it is in the interest of the cavalry corps commander, because of the rapidity and brevity of cavalry actions, to keep his divisions close enough together so that they can participate in the same combat.

If the divisions were too far apart to support each other effectively, they would be likely to fight separate battles, and the benefit to be expected from the formation of the cavalry corps would be lost.

When the enemy cavalry has been put out of action, the commander of the cavalry corps can adopt a more broadly articulated arrangement, while retaining his freedom of action, i.e., remaining in a position to achieve in due course the cooperation of the divisions in the common purpose set by the command.

It is then in a position either to attack the enemy with all forces united, or to assault him at the same time on different and relatively distant points.

133. The safety of the cavalry corps is ensured by the

intelligence gathered at the desired distance and in due time, as well as by the articulation of the divisions' dispositions. *

134. In combat, the generals commanding the divisions have the greatest initiative, within the framework of the mission they have received. Each of them acts according to the plan set by the shef or according to the particular mission assigned to him.

In cavalry combat, the leader determines the conditions of the main attack, taking into account the terrain, what he knows about the enemy, and the time at his disposal: the other attacks support and sustain the main attack. Success will most often belong to the one of the two adversaries who takes the initiative of the attack and who, by remaining master, through his decided march, of the place and time of the combat, will be able to impose his will on the enemy.

It may happen that the commander of the cavalry corps does not have enough time to give his orders for combat, or that the initiative of the engagement escapes him. In this case, he seizes the closest division and leads it or launches it into the attack.

This attack becomes, by this very fact, the main attack, to which the other divisions contribute spontaneously and without delay.

Chapter IX – Cover and Strongholds

COVERAGE.

135. The purpose of cover is to protect against the actions of the enemy:
1. The mobilization of the border zone;
2. The landing zones and the concentration of armies.

In addition, it ensures the protection of communication routes, engineering structures, telegraph lines and stores in the frontier zone.

136. The mission of the covering troops consists of: initially, stopping the enemy's reconnaissance or detachments that would seek to penetrate the territory; later, delaying the march of more considerable bodies that could disturb the landings and the concentration of the armies.

137. The zone of coverage extends between the border and the general front of concentration of the armies.

The number of sectors is determined according to the terrain and the mission assigned to the cover.

138. The whole of the troops in the zone of coverage is placed under the authority of the general commander-in-chief, who is responsible for coordinating its operations.

139. In each sector, the system includes:
1. *Covering forces* pushing forward a surveillance network;
2. In the rear, a *large covering force* available for maneuver.

140- The mission of the covering groups is to stop the enemy parties, to inform the commander of the sector and to give him time to make his arrangements.

Their composition and strength are determined according to their mission, the nature of the terrain, the number and importance of the directions to be watched.

141. The end of the period of coverage is clearly indicated by an army order. At this point, the cover is merged with the army's security apparatus.

142. In the course of operations, situations may arise which require measures similar to those involved in the period of cover (reorganization of forces after a battle, protection of a siege corps, etc.).

STRONGHOLDS.

143. Strongpoints are valuable only insofar as they can facilitate the operations of armies in the field.

Fortifications in frontier areas should be used to support cover.

Fortified systems organized near the frontiers allow the saving of forces in the territories they cover.

They force the adversary who would have taken the initiative of the operations to divide his means and, consequently, to weaken himself.

By paralyzing, if necessary, the movements of the victorious enemy, by hampering his communications, by immobilizing part of his forces, the places facilitate the eventual retreat of the field armies, which, thanks to them, can reform and then resume their freedom of action.

144. The commander-in-chief has at his disposal, within the limits of the rights conferred upon him by article 151 of the decree of October 7, 1909, the means of action of the places under his command. In order to ensure the unity of command, he will most often be led to regulate in advance the conditions under which the garrisons of the various places may be associated with the operations of specific armies or army corps.

The commander of an army or corps operating in the vicinity of a place of war must have the constant preoccupation of not allowing himself to be confined to it at any cost.

145. In enemy territory, it is up to the commander-in-chief, guided by his plan of maneuver, to decide on the nature of the operations to be directed against each of the places, taking into account the resources that it contains and the communications that it intercepts.

Whether an enemy fortress is to be concealed, invested, blocked or attacked, the initiative and responsibility for the first measures to be taken against it rests with each army commander in his zone of operations.

The arrangements made at the outset will be designed to initiate without delay the defensive organizations which it is important to oppose any enemy force using the place to break through.

These arrangements will be completed later, if necessary, by the large unit which will receive the mission to operate against the fortress and which will relieve all or part of the forces left by the front line troops.

The siege, if ordered, will not be able to succeed the investment until after the time necessary to gather and bring in all the means of attack.

Chapter X – Observation Corps

146. The greater part of the national forces having to be employed against the principal adversary, the numbers left in secondary theaters of operations, where there is no reason to seek immediate decision, are reduced to the strict minimum. They constitute *observation corps*.

147. The mission of an observation corps is to guarantee freedom of operations in the main theater.

They ensure the protection of the national territory in the zones assigned to their action. It differs from them by its longer duration. The observation corps cannot count on any support; on the other hand, they have much more depth for their operations than the cover.

148. Whatever the size of the area assigned to its operations, often considerable, the commander of an observation corps avoids dispersing his forces.

He adopts an in-depth formation generally comprising In the front line, on the principal directions by which the enemy can present himself, detached forces whose number and strength are reduced to a minimum; In the rear, large units, available for maneuver.

The commander of an observation corps studies the use of large units and prepares in advance their implementation in the different hypotheses that may arise. He decides accordingly on their distribution in his theater of operations.

149. An observation corps will only succeed in fulfilling its mission if it fully exploits, in order to delay the enemy, all the advantages that it can draw from the use of the terrain, as well as from permanent or improvised fortifications.

Moreover, the judicious and complete use of the railroad network gives the means to rapidly concentrate reserved forces and thus facilitates maneuver on lines of interior operations.

Chapter XI – Special Provisions

150. The provisions contrary to the present decree, which are contained in the decree of May 28, 1895, bearing regulations on the service of the armies in the field, are repealed.

Executed at Rambouillet, October 28, 1913.

R. POINCARÉ.

For the President of the Republic:
The Minister of War,

Eug. ETIENNE.

Appendix – Report of the Commission to the Minister of War

The studies undertaken in France, over the last twenty years, on the operations of armies and groups of armies, have brought to light a certain number of principles which dominate the use of these large units. These principles had not been, until now, gathered in an official document.

The decree of May 28, 1895 on the service of armies in the field does not consider the operations of units above the corps. This regulation is mainly concerned with defining the role, the properties, the reciprocal relations of the different arms, in the various circumstances of war. Limiting itself to succinct notions on the action of the command and the conduct of operations, it leaves aside the study of high order combinations that characterize not only army maneuver, but also the overall movements of the army corps, considered as a grouping of units that themselves include troops of all arms.

It seemed logical to take advantage of the moment when the revision of the aforementioned decree appeared necessary, to fill these gaps and to establish the bases of our war doctrine.

In accordance with the program that was drawn up for it, the commission in charge of the revision of this decree considered: on the one hand, the conditions of the combined use of the various arms in the division; on the other hand, the operations of the large units (army corps, army, army group).

The new decree on field service will indicate the rules and procedures for the use of the division; it will set forth the tactical principles that must be known by all officers.

The principles relating to the conduct of large units, of interest especially to the high command and the staffs, have been condensed into a separate regulation.

In submitting the regulation on the conduct of large units to M. LE MINISTRE, the commission has the honor of calling his attention hereafter to the fundamental ideas that it has endeavored to bring to light, and to the modifications that it has thought necessary to make to certain prescriptions of the decree of May 28, 1895.

Generalities on the conduct of war.

The conduct of the war is dominated by the necessity to give operations a vigorously offensive character.

Among all nations, France is the one whose military history offers the most striking examples of the great results to which the war of attack leads, as well as of the disasters which the war of waiting entails.

Carried by us almost to perfection, the doctrine of the offensive has brought us the most glorious successes. And, by a cruel counter-proof, on the day when we disregarded it, it provided our adversaries with the very weapons with which they defeated us.

The lessons of the past have borne fruit: the French army, having returned to its traditions, no longer admits any other law in the conduct of operations than the offensive.

But the application of this law requires, as a preliminary, the gathering of forces:

One must first gather and act offensively as soon as the forces are gathered.

Following the South African war, certain theories reappeared that one might have thought had been abandoned forever, on the inviolability of the fronts and on the possibility of bringing about a decision by maneuver, without combat. Shortly afterwards, the Russo-Japanese war came, it is true, to bring a striking denial to these dangerous theories; but one must always fear that a long period of peace will one day bring them back.

In order to prevent such a backslide, the regulations endeavor to highlight this primordial law that battle, the exclusive goal of operations, is the only way to break the enemy's will and that *the first duty of the leader is to want battle.*

The battle, once engaged, must be pushed to the limit, without any ulterior motive, until the extreme limit of the forces.

The decree of 28 May 1895 weakened the scope of this principle by restrictions on the use of reserves. It could lead to dangerous misunderstandings. This commission clearly affirmed that a leader should never hesitate, in order to secure victory, to throw his last battalions into the fire.

An erroneous interpretation of the prescriptions of the field service relating to safety could also lead to an inaccurate conception of the necessities of war and incite to put the concern to guard oneself before the will to act. In maneuvers, one could often observe a weakening of the forces intended for attacks, as a result of excessive withdrawals made for secondary missions. Without ignoring the importance of security, the commission deemed it necessary to react against this tendency; it insisted on this truth, confirmed by the experience of war, that a vigorous offensive forces the enemy to take defensive measures and constitutes the surest means of guaranteeing the command, as well as the troops, against any danger of surprise.

Command.

In war, all command decisions must be inspired by the will to take and keep the initiative in operations. This offensive will must be asserted relentlessly, in spite of the obstacles and the inevitable accidents. But the development of the maneuver of a large unit necessarily requires an appreciable time, during which the situation will undergo more or less profound modifications. During the execution of the maneuver, the command will have to make a series of decisions corresponding to these modifications. It is also important that the successive decisions are logically linked and that they are made without any disruptions or delays. History shows, in fact, that it is by tenaciously pursuing the same guiding idea that the commander of a large unit manages to dominate events and ensure victory. Thus, it is necessary for the commander to specify his intentions in a plan of maneuver that will serve as a guide for the conduct of operations.

The conditions that must be met by the plan of maneuver and the essential data used as a basis for its development are delineated in Chapter II of the regulations.

In particular, the commission has sought to clarify the degree of influence that intelligence should have in determining and executing the scheme of operations.

Each decision involved in the conduct of a large unit must come at the right time, even if the data collected up to that point on the enemy's forces and dispositions are still obscure and incomplete. A leader who yields to the temptation to wait to act until more accurate information arrives, runs the risk of seeing his adversary tear the veil by decisive acts.

But if the leader, when the moment has come for him to take a decision, must know how to be satisfied with the information already collected, he obviously has a major interest in taking advantage of the time, sometimes very long, which elapses between his successive decisions, to seek out all the data likely to shed light on the situation and to help him develop his plan logically. The leader, who is the only one who knows the points that need to be clarified, will therefore ask precise questions of the information bodies at his disposal. The simpler and less numerous the questions asked, the greater the chance of obtaining the information sought.

The commission was thus led to consider the notion of an *intelligence plan* as a consequence of the maneuver plan.

Appendix

Freedom of action. Safety. Research of information. Exploration.

Security, as defined by the 1895 decree, has the following objectives:
1. To inform the command about the enemy's movements in a given zone;
2. to protect the troops against surprises and to give the command time to make its arrangements.

Since 1895, the concept of security has been broadened, while its essential characteristics have been further defined.

It is admitted today that the object of the security is: In first place, to guarantee the freedom of action of the command (security of the chief); In second place, to protect the troops against the surprises (security of the troop or protection).

SAFETY OF THE LEADER. The freedom of action, an idea of somewhat abstract order, which, until now, had not been defined in our regulations, can be considered as realized when the leader has gathered his forces and is able to develop his plan of maneuver, despite the enemy.

The commission, giving the word "reunion" the meaning common in the Napoleonic era, considers that a large unit is reunited when all its elements, forming a more or less widely articulated unit, are able to participate in the same overall action.

If an intervention by the enemy is possible before this essential condition of the leader's freedom of action is achieved, detachments of all arms will have to interpose themselves in the threatened directions to gain the time and space necessary for the reunion of the main body of the troops.

When the gathering of forces is assured, the leader's safety rests above all on the search for the information necessary to develop the plan of maneuver.

This research, carried out according to the indications of the intelligence plan, is the responsibility of the information organs placed at the disposal of the large unit.

The commission listed these bodies and indicated their functions. As far as the cavalry is concerned, it was necessary to modify the provisions of the decree of May 28, 1895, in order to bring them in line with the ideas currently accepted on the role of the weapon, its mode of use and its distribution.

Until now, the cavalry included:

Cavalry divisions, in charge of exploration on behalf of the commander-in-chief (decree of May 28, 1895, article 19);

Corps brigades, at the disposal of the army commanders for the security of the front line (article 21);

And finally divisional squadrons assigned to the infantry divisions and intended to contribute to the immediate protection of the troops (article 20).

However, if everyone is more or less in agreement on the missions to be assigned to the cavalry divisions and divisional squadrons, the same cannot be said for the corps brigades. Charged with informing the command in a given zone, covering the troops in the rear and opposing the incursions of enemy cavalry, these brigades were obliged to hold, through detachments or reconnaissance, all the access routes that the enemy could use. Thus, on the one hand, they must remain together to fight, and that is why they are often grouped in provisional divisions; on the other hand, they must be diluted to the extreme, if they are to fulfill their surveillance role, as specified in the regulations.

The commission believes that the corps cavalry does not have sufficient manpower to fulfill the multiple tasks imposed upon it and that the front-line security service, as conceived by the decree of May 28, 1895, leads to a dispersion of means contrary to all the principles governing the use of the cavalry, as well as that of the other arms.

It does not seem, moreover, that sending small detachments far away on all usable access routes can be of any real use to the command.

The commander of an army, like the general-in-chief, must have the necessary information sought, at the desired distance, both to ensure the development of his plan and to verify if the disposition of his army is well suited to the situation.

The army cavalry will thus receive missions of exploration analogous, except for the scope, to those of the cavalry placed at the disposal of the general-in-chief.

Appendix

Often obliged, in order to fulfill these missions, to meet with the opposing cavalry, it will only be able to defeat them if it is in strength.

It is therefore essential that it be formed into divisions and that it march together.

This new constitution of the army cavalry entails, as a consequence, a reduction in the strength of the corps cavalry; but this reduction does not seem to present any inconvenience.

Far from the enemy, information of interest to the corps will be provided by the army commander. It is especially in the vicinity of the enemy, when the encounter becomes imminent, that the corps commander will have to take special measures to ensure his freedom of action in view of the battle. Large cavalry forces would not be of much use to him for this purpose; they would lack the field to extend their exploration and would not, moreover, have the pretension of piercing the network of the enemy infantry.

The corps commander will have recourse to more effective means. The use of detachments of all arms (security detachments) will allow him to gain the time and space necessary to develop his maneuver. In particular, the engagement of the vanguards will ensure the possibility of forming its combat system in full knowledge of the facts and of avoiding premature deployment, which would have the effect of taking away from the corps part of its ability to move and maneuver.

The corps cavalry will most often be attached to the security detachments in order to enlighten and inform them; it will thus contribute, to a large extent, to the protection of the troops in station, on the march and in combat. In the special circumstances where it would be deemed appropriate to assemble it, almost entirely, to search for important information, it will always be possible, because of the short range of its exploration, to have it supported by infantry and artillery.

In no case should the role of the corps cavalry be assimilated to that of the army cavalry, launched far away in search of the adversary. Limited to the tasks enumerated above, this role will be easily fulfilled by a regiment of 4 to 6 squadrons, unless an additional cavalry force is assigned to isolated army corps or detached for special missions.

The conception of security, as just indicated, leads to a distribution of cavalry units different from that envisaged by the field service.

If the commission's view were adopted, the cavalry would only include:

Cavalry divisions (or corps) in charge of exploration on behalf of the general-in-chief and army commanders;

Corps cavalry regiments destined to contribute to the security of the army corps (security of the chief and protection of the troops).

PROTECTION. The protection of the troops against surprises completes the security. It is the task of the protection service organized in the army corps to set up a surveillance network around the cantonment areas and columns and to guarantee the troops against the incursions of enemy cavalry. This task, formerly devolved upon the security of the front line, will certainly be fulfilled in a more efficient manner by the security detachments of the army corps, which, lighting and covering themselves for their own account, will protect, by the same token, the large troops on the march or stationed behind them.

The command's assistants. Instructions. Orders. R e p o r t s . Liaisons.

The questions which are the object of this chapter will find their natural development in the instruction on the state service.

The commission limited itself to specifying a few important points of particular interest to the command of large units. It was thus led to insist on the role of the chief of staff, whose activity could not be limited to the material task of transmitting the orders of the general.

Informed at all times on the details of the situation, the chief of staff is the auxiliary and the collaborator of the command. It is his duty, when he is invited, to give his opinion in all frankness and freedom, except to then completely disregard his personal opinion, as soon as the general has made his decision.

The army group.

The maneuver of the army group aims at great strategic results. The considerable importance of the number of troops on the line and the vast dimensions of the theater of operations oblige the command to establish its forecasts well in advance, to exercise the direction from very high up and to leave to the commanders of the subordinate units the care of settling all tactical questions.

The commission outlined, in broad strokes, the conditions that must be tried to achieve in the conception of the maneuver of the army group, as well as the nature and scope of the action of the general-in-chief in the development of operations and in the conduct of the general battle.

In particular, it has sought to emphasize the importance of the main operation, conducted with as many forces as possible, in order to obtain not only tactical successes, but also absolutely decisive strategic results.

The army.

The regulation poses in principle that the army must be constantly assembled. The reunion does not imply the close concentration, at all times, of all the army corps; but it requires a formation all the more tightened as the enemy is closer. The art of the leader consists in distributing the forces over a space as vast as the situation of the moment permits, while at the same time allowing for the possibility of transforming, at the appropriate time, the maneuver system into a battle system.

This judicious articulation of the system, combined with the search for information at the desired distance and with the protection organized in each army corps, guarantees, in almost all cases, the safety of the army. Sometimes, it is true, the use of detached army forces (general vanguards or cover), can become indispensable, notably when the army is in the process of being reunited or when certain terrain conditions require the extension of the maneuver system. But the commission refused to establish the use of general vanguards as a principle of doctrine. It considers this procedure as a makeshift solution imposed by certain circumstances, but whose usual application would be most dangerous. Like all detachments, detached army forces run the risk of being crushed in isolation, or at least of finding themselves unable to attend the battle.

They therefore constitute a cause of weakening for the army.

Whatever the measures taken for safety, the purpose of these measures is to allow the leader to freely develop his maneuver. This maneuver is conducted according to the plan of maneuver that he has adopted, until the battle that constitutes its crowning achievement.

While the general battle is directed with a view to obtaining decisive strategic results in the entire theater of operations, the battle of an army operating in a group of armies aims above all, like the battles of the corps, at a tactical success that is as complete and as rapid as possible. But, in an army, the importance of the numbers involved and the considerable extent of the front do not allow the battle plan to be stopped at the last moment, nor to be modified appreciably during the action. It is prior to the engagements that the commander of the army, always having in view the general goal fixed by his plan of maneuver, will have to determine this formation and to fix the direction of the principal action.

With regard to the conception of the battle plan, the commission found itself in the presence of two different theories.

One, which would be the extension to the army of the provisions of title XIV of the decree on the service of the armies in the field, bases the battle on successive actions (preparatory combats sometimes lasting several days, - decisive action launched when the preparation has been considered sufficient).

The other theory is based on the simultaneity of efforts in the battle (secondary actions fixing the enemy on all or part of the front, - main action against a wing).

After examination, the commission considered that there is no need to oppose two systems, each having their value, and whose application is above all a question of circumstances. It wanted to leave to the chief, who is the only one capable of appreciating the data of all kinds that serve as elements for his decision, the absolute right to exercise his choice in complete freedom.

The army corps.

A distinction has been made between the maneuver of the isolated or detached army corps, and that of the army corps operating within the framework of an army.

In the first case, the corps commander plans his maneuver in advance and operates, proportionately, as an army commander.

In the second case, the corps is only a tactical executing body: the combinations are more immediate and more limited in scope.

MARCHES AND STATIONING. The main points that the commission wished to specify were related to the in-depth cantonment and the articulated assembly.

The decree of May 28, 1895, prescribed the use of staggered billets in depth along the routes followed, in periods of marching at a great distance from the enemy. This very practical stationing procedure, commonly used during the wars of the first Empire, had gradually fallen into disuse in the French army. It is with good reason that we wanted to generalize and regulate its use.

But, in maneuvers on the map and in the field, one could notice a tendency to exaggerate the depth of the deployment zones and especially to carry out too late, and consequently too abruptly, the tightening made necessary by the proximity of the enemy.

Article 98 of the regulations analyzes the conditions of deep quartering and shows the usefulness of a progressive reduction of the staggering to spare the tail elements a too strong stage on the eve of the battle.

The commission also deemed it necessary to define more precisely the articulated assembly, the notion of which is found in article 63 of the decree of 28 May 1895.

Massed assemblies, which are still frequently seen on maneuvers, would expose the troops to complete destruction if they were to be caught under fire from rapid-fire artillery. It is advisable to replace these dense formations with the articulated assembly, a flexible and manageable formation, lending itself to a complete use of the ground and allowing a rapid deployment in view of the combat.

SECURITY. The special conditions to be met by the security of the corps have been defined above.

The regulations sought in particular to specify the mode of employment of the vanguards in case of an encounter with the enemy.

Differences of interpretation have arisen in this regard, due to some discrepancies between the current regulations. Some people attribute to the vanguards the unique mission of facilitating and covering the meeting of the bulk and use them with perhaps exaggerated circumspection. Others, convinced of the need to recognize and fix the enemy forces, always give the vanguards clearly offensive missions.

In fact, the role of the vanguard can be considered from two different points of view (protection of the main body, recognition of the enemy), one or the other predominating, depending on the circumstances. Thanks to the existence of new investigation devices and to the improvement of the means of information transmission, the command will be able, more often than before, to be fixed in advance on the forces and the dispositions of the enemy; it will then make pass to the second plan the role of recognition of the vanguards. This role will, on the contrary, take on its full development when one only possesses data on the contours of the adversary's security network.

This is the approach that the committee has tried to bring out in Article 107 of the regulation.

The all-important question of protecting troops against surprise was only sketched out in Rule 110. It will be the subject of a more complete study in the new decree on field service.

COMBAT. The ideas developed in this chapter are, for the most part, those already set forth in Title XIV of the decree of May 28, 1895; but all this part of the aforementioned decree, the most remarkable perhaps, as a substance and as a form, presented the disadvantage of dividing the combat into too many and too marked phases. This division, necessarily artificial, could lead to complications and errors.

Considering the actions of the vanguard as simple preliminaries, the decree of May 28, 1895 admitted that the leader must remain free to accept or refuse combat, as long as only the vanguards were present. Taken literally, such a conception would lead one to believe that the resolution to fight was subordinate to the recognition of the vanguard, as if the commander of an important unit could march to the enemy without a goal or a plan. To avoid any misinterpretation in this regard, the commission clearly stated that *the resolution to fight and even the choice of the general form of combat must be prior to the engagement*.

After defining the preliminaries of combat, Title XIV distinguished, in the combat itself, a preparation phase and a decision phase.

The opposition between the preparatory combat and the decisive action, which the context of Chapter II tended to emphasize in an exaggerated manner, was further accentuated by the somewhat ambiguous prescription of Article 130 (last paragraph), which specified that "the preparatory troops attack thoroughly, like those of the decisive attack, and at the same time as the decisive troops."

Interpreted as an obligation not to give their all on any part of the battlefield before the moment of decisive action, this prescription could obviously have been used as a pretext for half-measures likely to paralyze the attacks on the front, during the sometimes very long duration of the preparation combat.

In the regulation on the conduct of large units, the division of combat into periods had to be maintained, for the convenience of the exposition, but it seemed possible to reduce the number of these periods to two, by distinguishing, on the one hand, *the engagement*, and on the other hand, *the attacks of the main body*.

The engagement starts from the first contact. Its purpose is to force the enemy to unmask his forces, to allow the commander to bring the bulk of his forces to work, in front of the enemy's position, and finally to conquer the support points necessary for the deployment of the various weapons. It therefore most often involves more or less closely localized attacks. It varies in duration, intensity, and physiognomy, depending on the circumstances and the particular form of the combat (encounter combat, combat against an enemy in position, defensive combat).

As for the attacks of the main body, they all have this common character of aiming at the clear and definitive rupture of the enemy's position. The main attack differs only in that it is more extensive, has a longer range and has more decisive consequences on the outcome of the combat.

The regulations specify that *this classification of the various attacks, according to their importance, is carried out only in the mind of the commander and must never appear in the orders*. For the executor, the attack must, in all cases, be carried out with the utmost vigor and the firm resolution to approach the enemy to destroy him.

This same resolution must also animate the command during the battle and guide it in the use of the units it has reserved for itself. It is not conceivable that reserves could usefully fulfill certain roles assigned to them by the decree of May 28, 1895, and which would consist of guarding lines of retreat during attacks or limiting failure in the event of a setback.

During the entire development of the action, the leader must look forward; in case of failure, all his efforts will tend to re-establish the fight and to take the offensive again. Such is the doctrine of combat that the commission has tried to specify and summarize in the last part of chapter VII.

The preceding considerations apply, in a general manner, to the division as well as to the corps. With regard more specifically to the latter, the commission has established the principle that it must fight by division. In doing so, it wanted to react against the systematic use of groups of all arms, to which the term "momentary groups" has sometimes been applied. These groupings can be useful in certain compartmentalized or covered areas, but they lead to the breaking of tactical links and the dispersion of efforts.

The regulations further define the coordinating role of the corps commander and show how he can be powerfully assisted in this essential role by the artillery, cavalry and engineer commanders of the corps.

Cavalry corps.

Ideas concerning the organization and employment of cavalry in large masses have evolved considerably since 1870. In map exercises and staff trips, the reunion of several cavalry divisions and their constitution into a cavalry corps was frequently considered.

The cavalry corps being to some extent assimilated into a large unit, the commission felt it appropriate to summarize the essential principles of its employment: concentration of forces in front of the enemy cavalry; broad interconnection of divisions when the enemy cavalry has been put out of action.

Cover and strongholds.

Until now, the rules concerning the use of cover had never been the object of official prescriptions. The term "cover" was sometimes used to refer to safety measures taken by a troop on station. The commission wished to clarify what was meant by cover: it was the provisions which were intended to protect the mobilization in the frontier zone and the concentration of armies. As soon as the armies are in a position to provide for their own security, there is no longer any need for cover.

Fortified places and systems have value only insofar as they facilitate the operations of field armies. This is the fundamental principle that justifies their existence, especially at the beginning of the war, when they must serve as a support to the cover and help to protect the concentration of armies.

Observation corps.

The commission felt it necessary to mention the observation corps which are used in secondary theaters of operations where there is no need to seek immediate decision.

Their essential role is to guarantee freedom of operations in the main theater. Their mission can be likened, to some extent, to that of cover.

The regulations do not contemplate the conduct of operations in secondary theaters where, as a result of the support of Allied troops, it may be useful to seek decision by the immediate annihilation of the enemy's organized forces.

These operations are, in fact, subject to the same general rules as those which take place in the main theater.

These are the considerations which justify the principles and rules contained in the *Conduct of Large Units* regulations.

This regulation will serve as a guide to the army staffs for the preparation and execution of maneuvers on the map and in the field; it will form the body of doctrine on which the teaching given both at the Ecole Supérieure de Guerre and at the Centre des Hautes Études Militaires must be based. Finally, it will be the starting point for the work of the commission for the preparation of the regulation on the service of the armies in the field.

This last regulation, all the provisions of which are inspired by the general spirit of the regulation on the conduct of large units, will constitute the fundamental document to which the practical instructions and maneuver regulations of the different arms will be linked.

All the prescriptions concerning the tactical use of troops will, from then on, be grouped in a single document. Thus will be established, at all the levels of the hierarchy, a community of principles and tendencies which will ensure in case of war a convergence of the efforts fruitful in great results.

Decree of 2 December 1913: Regulations on the Service of the Armies in the Field – Service in the Field. International Law

Part I – Service in the Field

Report to the President of the French Republic

Paris, December 1, 1913.

Mr. President,

A commission was charged by one of my predecessors to proceed with the revision of the decree of May 28, 1895, bearing regulations on the service of the armies in the field. This commission divided its work into two parts.

The first part, which is devoted to the exposition of the principles relating to the conduct of the army corps and superior units, is of interest above all to the high command and the staffs; it constitutes the regulation on the conduct of large units, which you were kind enough to put into effect by the decree of October 2 last.

The second part, indicating the rules and procedures for the use of the division, is currently presented to you in the form of a draft regulation on field service, the principles of which must be known by all officers.

In its work, the commission has endeavored to respect as much as possible the substance and form of the decree of 1M5, to which the army will remain indebted for the return to the traditional principle of French tactics. It has only made the modifications required by the constant improvement of the armament and the equipment of the army.

It has only made the modifications required by the constant improvements in armaments and war material, as well as by the tactical lessons learned from recent campaigns.

These modifications did not seem to me to be better justified than by the integral reproduction of the report established by the commission.

Report of the Commission

Plan of the new regulations.

The first duty of the commission was to specify the framework of the new regulation.

The 1895 decree does not contemplate the operations of units above the corps. However, Section XIV deals with the general battle as much as with the combat of small units, and it is addressed rather to the commander-in-chief, an upright personality, than to the sub-ordinate commanders, who are the largest number.

However, the studies undertaken in France in recent years have highlighted the need to establish the principles that dominate the use of large units: there was therefore a gap to be filled. On the other hand, these studies have shown that the conditions of execution, if not the very principles, differ profoundly according to whether it is a large or a small unit, so that it is extremely difficult, unless one does not go beyond generalities, to explain in the same text the battle of the army and the combat of the division.

These are the reasons why the commission in charge of the revision of the 1895 decree was led to condense in a separate instruction,* intended above all for the high command and the staffs, the principles relating to *the conduct of large units* (army corps, army, army group). It was thus possible to give the new regulations a limited and precise framework.

This regulation, which the commission proposes to call "field service" and no longer "army field service", applies, in all matters of tactics, to the elementary unit, comprising troops of all arms, that is to say, *to the division as well as to the lower units.* The principles and rules it sets forth must be known to all officers.

The field service consists of twelve sections, namely:

I. General organization of the army.
II. Orders, liaison.
III. Marches, stations.
IV. Security.
V. Combat.
VI. Cavalry.
VII. Detachments.
VIII. Fieldworks.
IX. Operation of the aeronautical and telegraphic services.
X. Trains, depots and convoys.
XI. Supplies, evacuations, requisitions.
XII. Service of the gendarmerie in the field, Annexes.

The prescriptions relating to marches and stationing have been brought together in a single section, because of the correlation that exists between the marching formation of a troop and the mode of stationing that it adopts at the end of the march. In addition, certain police, hygiene and discipline measures are common to both marching and stationing.

The section relating to combat, which was numbered XIV in the 1895 Order in Council because it was developed after the fact, has taken its natural place after marches, stationing and security.

The important modifications recently made to the organization

---

* This instruction was the subject of the decree of October 28, 1913, on the regulation of the conduct of large units.

of the cavalry led the commission to devote a special section to the use of the troops of this arm, in which it transferred the prescriptions relative to exploration, which was the subject of section III of the decree of 1895.

The operations of the detachments, including those related to the attack or the protection of convoys, are dealt with in a single section. The same applies to the supply of food and ammunition, evacuations and requisitions.

New sections have been devoted to field work, aeronautical and telegraph services, trains, depots and convoys. Finally, the commission, considering that reconnaissance is a matter of security or combat, did not believe it necessary to reproduce section XI of the 1895 decree.

Such is, in summary, the context of the new field service. In the following presentation, the commission indicates and explains, for each of the sections, the principal modifications made to the prescriptions which have been regulatory until now.

Section I – General Organization of the Army.

Section I is merely an update of the corresponding section of the 1895 decree. In order to lighten it, the commission limited itself to indicating, in the new text, the main lines of the military organization and the provisions which have a character of relative permanence. The details of the functioning of the services, which are frequently modified according to the improvements brought to the equipment and to the technique, have been transferred to the annexes.

Section II – Orders. Liaisons.

The text of the prescriptions of the decree of 1895 has been completed in a practical sense as regards the definition and classification of orders, reports and accounts.
The principles relating to liaison are new.
The detailed rules concerning the drafting and transmission of orders and reports have been placed in the annexes.

Section III – Marches. Stations.

The arrangements for marching and stationing must always be subordinated to the tactical necessities of the moment: under this essential proviso, the command has the duty of reducing to a minimum the fatigue of the troops and of carefully watching over their hygiene. Such is the fundamental principle, common to both marching and stationing, of which Section III is merely the development.

Marches. Most of the prescriptions of the 1895 decree on marches have been reproduced, but some modifications and additions have been made.

With regard to the constitution of columns and the execution of marches, certain new indications have been added to the provisions concerning halts, column crossings and the ease to be given to troops in marches far from the enemy.

From a tactical point of view, the main changes made to the 1895 decree concern the place to be assigned to artillery in the columns and the marching formations in the immediate vicinity of the enemy. The great range of modern guns obliges to place the artillery in the columns, far enough behind the most advanced elements of infantry, so that it is not exposed to fall, in road formation, under the fire of enemy batteries. It is recommended, in particular, that no artillery be placed in vanguards that do not include at least one infantry regiment. These necessary precautions in no way negate the permanent obligation to assign to the groups of batteries, in the columns, a place such that the division commander can have all his artillery at his disposal from the beginning of the battle.

The text of the article in the 1895 decree entitled "Marching to the enemy in view of immediate combat" has been the subject of fairly significant changes because it no longer refers to anything other than the march of the division into combat. On this point, which no regulation had dealt with until now, it seemed necessary to make some clarifications.

The division's marching pattern naturally evolves from the road column to the combat formation, as the encounter becomes more imminent. This gradual transformation is intended to prepare the elements of the division to enter into action quickly, and especially to give the division commander the possibility of personally taking the lead in the battle from the outset.

In this order of ideas, the commission admitted the necessity, for the division, even if it marches in more than one column, to have *only one tactical vanguard* in the last hours of march which precede the engagement. This is the division's actual vanguard, and the division commander marches with it. Secondary columns, if any, provide their own protection with small vanguards.

The evolution that immediately precedes the taking of combat dispositions consists of leaving the road formations for the *articulated assembly*, a flexible formation, in which the elements of the division are staggered and spaced at the request of the tactical situation, so as to move easily and be able to deploy without delay. In the immediate vicinity of the enemy, the articulated assembly formation can be taken from the stationing.

Stationing. The new text envisages exclusively the stationing of the division. It reproduces most of the prescriptions of the 1895 decree, while insisting only slightly more on the subordination of the mode of stationing to the tactical situation.

A few detailed changes have been made to the provisions concerning the preparation of the cantonment.

With regard to bivouacs, the commission considered that it was sufficient to regulate the bivouac formations of elementary units, company, squadron, battery, in order to give more flexibility to the bivouac formations of higher units and to make better use of the terrain.

In the chapter entitled "Rules common to marches and stationing," the commission introduced new prescriptions relating to the hygiene of the troops, to the measures to be adopted to avoid indiscretions, to the precautions to be taken against aerial observation, and finally to the stationing and subsistence of small detached forces.

Section IV – Security.

The "security service," as understood by the decree of May 28,

1895, implied the exclusive idea of protection against surprises, for the chief and for the troops. It was already a great advance over the 1883 field service to have highlighted the need for the commander to be informed well beyond the zone of protection of the troops. But the conception of security remained purely defensive.

Today, this conception has been broadened, and what the leader must ask of security is no longer only tranquility, *but above all freedom of action*. As long as he keeps it, it is quite obvious that he, and with him, the troop he commands, is protected against surprises.

Thus understood, the purpose of security is:

1. To guarantee the freedom of action of the commander, that is to say, to give him the time and space he needs to make his arrangements (security of the leader);
2. To protect the troops on the march or at the station against surprises (security of the troops or protection).

The leader's freedom of action is guaranteed: Firstly, by the information that he sends out, in the directions that he designates and at the distance that he deems necessary; Secondly, by the security detachments, vanguards, rear guards or flank guards.

The protection of the troops against surprises is assured, in the directions where the security detachments operate, by these detachments themselves; it is completed, if necessary, in the less important directions, by small forces or patrols.

In sum, there is no marked opposition to the principles of the 1895 decree. But the details of execution differ on the following points: The first line security is abolished, because the mission assigned by the decree of 1895 to the first line security cavalry was deemed impossible to fulfill. The same cavalry could not be asked to search for information in certain directions and oppose incursions of enemy cavalry in all directions. The cavalry remains responsible for informing the command; the protection of the columns against cavalry attacks is the responsibility of the security detachments, which have to guarantee the troops against all unexpected attacks, without distinction of arms.

The security is uninterrupted in the sense that at the end of the march and during the stationing the security detachments stop and continue their security mission in the directions indicated by the command. The protection of the troops against surprises is then completed by *outposts* provided and established by the security detachments themselves.

Thus, in a forward march (and, on this point, the new regulations have not changed anything in the 1895 decree), the outposts are always provided by the vanguard, and if the latter is small in number, it is transformed entirely into outposts. *This is the usual case for the division and the lower units.*

The only exception to this rule is at the end of the day's fighting. In this case, so-called "combat" outposts are established; they are provided by the troops in the front line.

It is up to the division commander to specify clearly and personally, in the orders he gives to each security detachment or to any troop called upon to set up outposts, the mission to be carried out and the terrain to be held in case of an attack. This care is no longer left to the brigadier generals, but it remains understood that these general officers may be charged by the division commander to supervise the execution of the service.

Some changes in detail have been made in the prescriptions relating to the mode of reconnaissance of isolates and detachments, and to night service at outposts.

Section V – Combat.

Section V applies to the combat of the division and inferior units. Its scope is thus much narrower than that of the corresponding section of the 1895 decree. But this is not the only difference between the two texts, and there are some discrepancies of principle which it is necessary to explain.

Purpose of the fight. The purpose of combat is the destruction of the enemy. The will to reach the enemy in order to destroy him must therefore animate the leader first, and, with him, all those he leads into the fire. This is the very basis of combat tactics, as conceived by the new regulations.

Form of combat, offensive and defensive. Both regulations

state that only the offensive succeeds in breaking the will of the opponent and that the defensive never gives the victory. Both rules recognize, however, that defense may be necessary for some of the forces involved, under certain circumstances. But they differ in the definition of these circumstances, that is to say, in the justification of the defensive.

The 1895 decree considers the defensive as a means of "attracting the enemy to a terrain where one believes one can fight under good conditions." From there, to accepting that the value of a position could determine the command to prefer defense to attack, it is not far, and no conception is more dangerous. In order to avoid any misunderstanding on such an important point of doctrine, the new regulation admits only one justification for defending in combat, namely the *need to save troops on certain points, in order to devote more forces to attacks.*

Understood in this way, the defensive is now strictly speaking only an auxiliary to the offensive, but it is necessary for the command to be able to demonstrate the full capacity of resistance of the units to which it has ordered to contain the enemy on a given front. This resistance must be, like the attack, pushed to the end, that is to say, to the point of complete sacrifice.

It follows from the preceding considerations that, in a battle, offensive by its whole, certain secondary units, such as the division, can receive from the higher command a purely defensive mission. This is why the new regulations, after having exposed the principles of offensive combat, which is the normal combat, devote a special chapter to the defensive combat of the division.

Phases of combat. Under the terms of article 128 of the 1895 decree, the command must remain free to refuse combat, or to engage in it, as long as the vanguards are alone in presence. The commission could not agree with this way of seeing things, and it deemed it necessary to affirm, on the contrary, *that the resolution to fight must be prior to the engagement.* It seems, in fact, difficult to admit that the leader of a troop should march to the enemy without having a mission to fulfill, and that he should wait, in order to decide to fight, to be determined on the strength and the intentions of his adversary. Moreover, from the moment when the vanguard is at grips with the enemy, it is usually too late to refuse to fight with the bulk of the forces, unless he agrees to the sacrifice of the vanguard.

Apart from the engagement of the vanguard, which it excludes from the combat proper, the decree of 1895 distinguishes in the combat *a phase of preparation and a phase of decision*. But, which is not without danger, it also seems to distinguish two ways of attacking, depending on whether it is a matter of preparatory combat or of the decisive attack. This is at least what is implied by the text of articles 129 and 130, where it is stated that the preparatory troops must wear down the enemy, constantly threaten him, immobilize him, and that they attack thoroughly at the same time as the decisive attack; an ambiguous prescription which can be interpreted as the obligation not to give a full attack on any point before the moment of the decisive attack.

The new regulation also divides the combat into two main phases, for the convenience of the exposition; but these phases are not the same as in the 1895 decree: the first, which it calls the *engagement*, includes the preliminaries of the combat and the action of the vanguard; the second includes the *attacks of the main body*.

The *engagement* is the responsibility of the vanguard, which the artillery supports from the beginning, and which the first elements of the main body can reinforce, if the order is given. Its purpose is to force the enemy to unmask his forces, to allow the commander of the division to make his dispositions, and to conquer the support points necessary for the deployment of the main body.

The *attacks of the main body* all have the common character of aiming to break the enemy's position. They can be successive or simultaneous. The one that the division commander expects to have the most important result, and which is in his mind the main attack, is organized more strongly than the other attacks, intended to prepare or facilitate the main attack. But the relative importance of the different attacks must never appear in the orders. *For the executors, all attacks are pushed to the limit, with the firm resolution to approach the enemy to destroy him. There is now only one way to attack: that is the way to attack.*

The same offensive energy must animate the division commander and guide him in the use of the units he has kept at his disposal. The decree of 1895 prescribes (art. 128) to keep a reserve "sheltered from the emotions of the battle, until the final solution of the affair, to complete the success or limit the failure"; that is to say that the reserve must be employed only after the battle and not in the battle. This conception can no longer be admitted. If it was not necessary to engage all the troops to defeat the enemy, there is nothing better than to launch in pursuit those who have not yet fought. But to give up the fight before having exhausted all one's resources is a military fault without excuse.

Use of different weapons in combat. The changes made by the new regulations to the text of the 1895 decree are mainly aimed at the use of artillery.

It was accepted, until recent years, that the first duty of the artillery in combat was to take the superiority of fire over the enemy artillery, and then its role was to prepare the infantry attacks by riddling with projectiles the objectives assigned to these attacks, before the entry into action of the infantry.

It is now recognized that the *essential role of artillery is to support infantry attacks by destroying everything that opposes the progress of these attacks*. The search for superiority over enemy artillery has no other purpose than to strive for maximum action against infantry attack objectives. It remains obvious that no opportunity to acquire this superiority must be neglected, and it often happens that the first obstacle encountered by the infantry is precisely the fire it is subjected to from the enemy artillery. This is why the divisional artillery must be able to intervene in its entirety from the beginning of the engagement.

As for the preparation of attacks by the artillery, it cannot be independent of the action of the infantry, because the fire of the artillery has only a limited effectiveness against a sheltered adversary, and that to make this adversary discover himself, it is necessary to attack him with infantry. Cooperation between the two arms must therefore be constant. *The artillery no longer prepares the attacks, it supports them.*

But it should not be concluded from this that the artillery responsible for supporting an attack must be subordinate to the commander of the attack. The locations from which this artillery can most effectively support the infantry advance will often be, for reasons of terrain, outside the zone of action of the latter. In addition, it may happen that the same group of batteries cannot support the same attack from start to finish, and that, on the other hand, at a certain moment, its fire can very effectively support another attack.

Thus appears the necessity, for the commander of the division to remain master of modifying, during the combat, the distribution of the batteries, as well as their mission in the interest of the attacks themselves, in the interest especially of the execution of his combat plan: and it is by this that his directing action can usefully be felt from one end of the combat to the other.

Therefore, the new regulation prescribes that, from the beginning of the engagement, all the divisional artillery, including the batteries that may be attached to the vanguard, is at the exclusive disposal of the division commander, who alone has the authority to determine the overall mission of the artillery, and to designate, in a general manner, the successive objectives that it must take under its fire.

The only case where the subordination of the artillery to the commanders of the different attacks is justified is when the division is fighting in a compartmentalized terrain, with limited views, where any overall direction is impossible. It is then a necessity that must be endured.

Command action. The commission has endeavored to specify the responsibility of the division commander in the direction of the combat. *This direction must not escape him at any time.* In particular, it is his responsibility, and his alone, to set the conditions of engagement and to regulate or coordinate the attacks of the bulk. Once his orders have been given in writing, he leaves the choice of means to his subordinates, and makes his directing action felt through the use of the artillery and the units he has kept at his disposal. To defeat the enemy, he must not hesitate, if necessary, to throw all his forces into the fight.

The text of article 138 of the 1895 decree, relating to the "duties of officers and soldiers," has been reproduced almost literally. It was impossible to give a higher or truer idea of military duty in the fire, as well as of the amount of energy and self-sacrifice that each one must expend in combat to wrest victory from the enemy.

Section VI – Cavalry.

As a result of its recent reorganization, the cavalry now comprises, in time of war, only cavalry divisions charged with exploration on behalf of the commander-in-chief or army commanders, and corps regiments, destined to contribute to the security of the army corps.

It seemed necessary to group, in the same section, which is new, the principles relating to the use of cavalry in the army and in the corps. A special chapter is devoted to the cavalry division.

Exploration naturally finds its place in the chapter relating to the army cavalry, and is no longer the object of a separate section. It is not that its importance is diminished, but the commission thought that the clear separation established until now between exploration and security was no longer justified. In an army, the real object of exploration *is to provide the army commander with the information he deems necessary, both to maintain his freedom of action and to develop his plan of maneuver*. This is the role of the army cavalry divisions, outside of battle. One can therefore no longer oppose exploration to security, since exploration guarantees precisely the security of the leader by the information it provides.

In the same vein, but at a lower level, the main mission of the corps cavalry regiment is to provide the commander of the army corps with *the information he deems necessary for his safety (corps cavalry proper) and to participate in the protection of troops against surprises (divisional cavalry)*.

The security mission assigned to the corps cavalry was naturally much smaller in scope than that of the front line security cavalry in the 1895 decree.

There can be no question of protecting the corps with two or three squadrons, against possible incursions of enemy cavalry. It is only a question of searching for the information requested by the commander of the corps, within a restricted radius, and which will never exceed one day's march in front of the main body of the corps. But this search may require the use of more or less strong cavalry, depending on whether the exploration cavalry has unmasked the front of the army corps, or whether it is operating, on the contrary, in front of this front. Hence the necessity of leaving the commander of the corps complete freedom in the distribution of the corps regiment between security and protection; and the immediate consequence of this necessity is that the strength of the divisional cavalry can no longer be uniformly fixed at one squadron, as it was until now. The new regulation merely prescribes that this strength, variable according to the place or mission of the division in the corps, cannot go below one platoon.

The prescriptions relative to the marches, the stationing and the safety of cavalry troops operating in isolation have been brought together in a single chapter of section VI.

The chapter on the cavalry division deals primarily with the division's combat against cavalry and against units of all arms.

No action of war is less easy to confine to fixed rules than cavalry combat. There are however essential principles to which this combat, in spite of the speed of its development and the variety of its forms, could not escape: First, the necessity of an idea of maneuver, and for the cavalry, the best maneuver is surprise, because it gives the initiative of the attack; Then the organization of a powerful attack, or main attack, that other attacks can facilitate, support or complete; Finally, and above all, the obligation to throw all forces into the melee, without looking back, with the obstinate will to destroy the adversary in hand-to-hand combat, and not only to force him to retreat.

These principles constitute the essence of the combat doctrine common to all arms.

As for the form of combat, as for judging in particular whether the main attack should be combined with the other attacks, so as to achieve envelopment, or whether it is better to make a breaking effort on a selected part of the enemy's position, this is a matter for the division commander.

The regulations cannot give the cavalry commander the formula for victory: he can only indicate the principles of the use of forces in combat.

Even above these principles, there is an element of success that the commander will find only in himself, and without which the rest is nothing: *it is the resolution to attack.*

Section VII – Detachments.

The new regulations have combined into a single section the sections X (detachments) and XII (convoys and their escorts), of the 1895 decree. The text was the object of some modifications.

It seemed necessary to recall that the formation of a detachment must respond, in each case, to a well-defined necessity, because any detachment is a weakening for the troop which provides it.

As far as the composition of detachments is concerned, it was agreed that they should always include cavalry, but that artillery should only be assigned to them if their infantry or cavalry strength reaches one regiment.

Apart from the small operations studied in article 108 of the 1895 decree, the new regulations set forth the principles of conduct for detachments charged with stopping or delaying enemy columns, and for detachments employed as support for the cavalry.

Section VIII – Fieldworks.

In this section, which is new, the regulation assigns to fieldworks the following object: First, to facilitate the progression of troops towards the enemy; Second, to allow a troop marching to the attack and momentarily obliged to stop under fire, to use or improve natural shelters, or to create some if necessary; Lastly, to increase the force of resistance of a troop placed on the defensive, in order that its strength may be reduced as much as possible to the benefit of the attacking troops.

Thus understood, the final goal of fieldwork is to facilitate the offensive.

Report of the Commission 101

Section IX – Operation of the Aviation and Telegraphic Services.

The aviation and telegraph services are army services. However, it seemed necessary to indicate briefly the conditions of their functioning because of the assistance that troops of all arms may be called upon to lend them momentarily. This assistance consists in particular in protecting the landing grounds, in helping the airship personnel in the descent operations, in guarding the radiotelegraphic posts, etc.

The commission also found it useful to set forth the conditions under which small units and reconnaissances must link up with corps telegraph stations and may use telegraphic communications.

Section X – Trains, depots and convoys.

The commission has deemed it essential to bring together in a single section the rules concerning the organization and use of combat trains, regimental trains, depots and convoys.

It also tried to facilitate the transmission of orders from the command to these various supply organs.

It has also tried to facilitate the transmission of orders from the command to these various supply organs, as well as the maintenance of order in the elements that compose them, by grouping these elements under the same authority whenever circumstances permit.

It has sometimes been admitted that the elements of the same supply organization or service could be grouped together for marching and stationing: thus, one would have had the depot group, the convoy group, the regimental train group, etc. This is an attractive concept because of its simplicity, but it is difficult to implement in practice, because as soon as the depots, convoys, and trains begin to provide supplies, they dissociate and remain dissociated as long as they are in operation. On the contrary, it happens that elements belonging to different organs or services.

On the contrary, it happens that elements belonging to different organs or services, depot echelons, administrative convoy sections, medical formations, etc., are momentarily brought, by the very game of supplies, to follow the same route and to be stationed in the same area. It is thus quite natural to form temporary groupings of depot elements, convoys or medical units, whose momentary existence it seemed necessary to regulate in some way, with the aim of order and discipline.

Section XI – Supplies. Evacuations. Requisitions.

Section XI of the new regulations is the combination of sections VII, VIII and IX of the 1895 decree.

The prescriptions relating to the feeding of troops in the field have been modified, particularly with regard to the consumption of reserve foodstuffs.

Under the terms of the 1895 decree, these supplies "must be consumed only on the orders of the command and when any other method of feeding is impossible.

Experience has shown that this requirement is applied too narrowly, in that the commander of the corps alone is given the right to consume the reserve food. The consequence of this interpretation is that it has become the habit to have reserve food consumed only by all the troops of a corps at once, and by entire rations.

However, it is rare that, in a large unit, all the troops are in the same situation with regard to supplies. If there are exceptional circumstances where no force can be supplied, it will frequently happen that the majority of the corps will receive their distributions before nightfall, while certain corps or certain more advanced detachments will receive them too late.

It seemed necessary, consequently, to specify: That any corps or detachment commander is qualified to prescribe the consumption of reserve foodstuffs whenever regular distributions could not be made in due time; That this consumption must be limited to strictly necessary foodstuffs.

The provisions relating to the supply of fresh meat have been brought up to the level of the provisions recently adopted for the transportation of slaughtered meat in special motor vehicles. - Finally, it has been found necessary to substitute for the appellation "stockyard" of an army or corps the appellation "herd of cattle" of an army or corps, in order to avoid any confusion and to reserve the appellation "stockyard" for the artillery and engineer stockyards.

Section XII – Gendarmerie.

The text of the decree of 1895 has been brought into line with that of the instruction on the service of the gendarmerie in the field.

These, Mr. President, are the principal modifications established by the new regulations.

If you are willing to approve them, I have the honor of requesting that you sign the following draft decree on field service regulations.

Please accept, Mr. President, the homage of my profound respect.

The Minister of War,
Eug. ETIENNE.

Decree on the Regulation of Field Service

Paris, December 2, 1913.

The President of the French Republic,
On the report of the Minister of War,
Having regard to the decree of May 28, 1895, bearing regulations on the service of the armies in the field, completed and modified by the decrees of March 29 and May 2, 1900, January 4 and June 20, 1901, and August 7, 1905,

Decrees:

Section I – General Organization of the Army

Chapter I – Formation of the Armies

Art. 1. The forces acting in the same theater of operations are united under a single command.

The Minister of War shall determine the initial order of battle regulating the general distribution of these forces: according to their importance, they shall be constituted into army groups, armies and army corps.

An army group includes armies, cavalry divisions, an aeronautical service and a telegraph service.

A rear command is attached to the army group.

An army includes army corps, one or more cavalry divisions, heavy artillery, a bridge crew, an aeronautical service, a telegraph service. To each army is attached a direction of the stages and services.

In principle, an army corps includes two or three infantry divisions, a corps cavalry, a corps artillery, corps engineering companies, a bridge crew, a searchlight section, a telegraph detachment, medical formations, depots and convoys.

In principle, an infantry division comprises two or three infantry brigades, a cavalry force taken from the corps cavalry, a divisional artillery, one or more engineer companies, a medical detachment.

In principle, a cavalry division includes three cavalry brigades, an artillery group, an infantry cycling group, an engineer cycling section, a telegraph service, an ambulance.

Several cavalry divisions may be grouped under one command to form a cavalry corps.

Division of the territory and of the theater of operations.

Art. 2 At the beginning of the war, the Minister fixes the limits separating the territory placed under the authority of the commander-in-chief, which is called the "army zone," from the territory remaining under his authority, which is called the "interior zone."

These limits may be modified, according to the course of events, at the request of the commander-in-chief.

The part of the "zone of the armies" where the troops of operations (army corps, cavalry divisions, etc., with their constituent elements) move is called the "forward zone".

The rest of the army zone is called the "rear zone".

Each army has at its disposal, for its movements, a part of the front zone, and, for the play of the supply and evacuation organs that belong to it, a part of the rear zone, called "zone of the stages" of the army.

The services are directed in each army by a "director of stages and services" placed under the immediate authority of the army commander.

The services are linked and coordinated throughout the rear area by the director of rear, under the immediate authority of the commander-in-chief.

For each army, the commander-in-chief establishes the lateral boundaries of the forward area; the rear director establishes the lateral and rear boundaries of the staging area; the army commander establishes the boundary between the forward area and the staging area.

Chapter II – Command

Art. 3. The commander of all the forces assigned to the same theater of operations is a marshal of France or a divisional general, who has the title of commander in chief. He receives a letter of command.

The commander of each army is a marshal of France or a major general who has the title of army commander.

He receives a letter of command.

Any commander-in-chief may, during the course of the campaign, change the order of battle. He may also make, among the generals, officers and civil servants under his command, the transfers that losses or the good of the service make necessary.

This power may be delegated.

Right to command.

Art. 4. In the absence of a letter of service designating a possible successor, any holder of a command, who fails for any reason, is temporarily replaced by the most senior officer in the highest rank of the command.

Under the same conditions, if an army commander is missing, he is provisionally replaced by the one of the army corps commanders who is the most senior in the duties of an army corps commander.

The appointment of a detachment commander is made by the authority ordering the formation of the detachment. In all cases, the designated commander must be of a rank at least equal to that of the highest-ranking members of the detachment.

Any officer assigned to a special mission shall exercise command over all other officers employed on the same mission at equal rank.

Military personnel with the rank of officer, belonging to a corps or personnel with its own hierarchy, with or without correspondence with the ranks provided for by the law of April 14, 1832, have, in matters of command, no rights other than those resulting from the special regulations for their services.

With regard to reserve and territorial army officers, retired or resigned officers, officers serving in a foreign capacity and indigenous officers, command rights are regulated in accordance with the provisions of the regulations on the internal service of the troops and the instructions governing the special status of these officers.

Administration in the armies.

Art. 5. In the field, the Minister delegates his administrative powers, within the necessary limits, to each army commander, who then represents the Minister in relation to the army corps commanders.

The army commander is assisted in the administration of his army by a major general, who is directly responsible to him under the same conditions as the corps commanders. This general officer has the title of director of stages and services of the army.

The general commanding a corps is responsible to the commander of the army for the administration of his corps. The same is true of any unit commander to his immediate commander.

General officers have the duty to foresee the needs of the troops and to prescribe or provoke the necessary measures to satisfy them. They give orders to provide and distribute and see that each receives the allowances due to him.

Chapter III – Staffs and Headquarters

Art. 6. A staff is placed under the Commander-in-Chief, under each army, corps and division commander, under the director of the rear and under each director of the stages and services.

In each staff, the entire service is directed by the chief of staff.

The staff of an army group is designated as the general staff. The Chief of Staff is a general officer with the title of Major General and is assisted by general officers with the title of Assistant General Staff.

Role of the General Staff.

Art. 7. The general staff acts in the name of the command, of which it is the auxiliary. Its role is:

1. To prepare for the general the elements of his decisions;

2. To translate these decisions into instructions and orders;

3. To complete the instructions and orders by any necessary detailed measure, which the general would not have decided himself;

4. To ensure the transmission of the instructions and orders and, if necessary, to control their execution.

The chief of staff regulates the action of the staff, directs that of the services and exercises his authority over the entire headquarters.

He personally directs the intelligence service and the liaison service.

The headquarters.

Art. 8. The combination of the staff and the various personnel attached to the same command forms the headquarters.

A specially designated officer, who bears the title of commander of the headquarters, ensures, according to the instructions of the chief of staff, the installation, the service and the guard of the headquarters.

Chapter IV – The Services

Art. 9. The purpose of the services is to satisfy the needs of the armed forces. Their functioning is entirely subordinated to the development of operations.

The services of an army are generally divided into two echelons: one, the "forward echelon," which marches with the combatant elements; the other, the "stage echelon," which functions in the stage zone.

In principle, at the head of each service is placed a head of service[*] who, informed in due time of the intentions of the command, foresees the needs and the means to satisfy them, and then ensures the technical measures of implementation.

The department heads are under the authority of the command, which gives them their orders. In addition, they may receive technical instructions from the senior service manager.

In each army, the director of the stages and services has the overall supervision and direction of all the services of the army,

---

[*] The term "head of service" is used here in its most general sense and applies in each service to the person in charge of the service, regardless of its specific name.

both at the front and at the stages, with the exception, however, of the following front services: artillery, engineering, telegraphy, aeronautics and gendarmerie.

Artillery and engineering services.

Art. 10. The artillery service* is in charge of supplying the troops with ammunition, as well as the replacement of weapons, artillery equipment and military crews.

The engineer service is in charge of supplying the troops with tools, engineer equipment and explosives, of all works concerning the establishment, maintenance or destruction of communications of any kind, permanent or improvised, and possibly the installation of troops.

In an army, the artillery and engineering services of the front are directly under the command of the army.

In each corps, they are directed, under the authority of the corps commander, by the corps artillery or engineer commander.

In the stages, the artillery and engineering services are directed, under the authority of the director of the stages and services, by the directors of the artillery or engineering services of the stages.

Aeronautical service.

Art. 11. The aeronautical service is in charge of the use and maintenance of reconnaissance or aerial observation machines.

It is directed: In an army group, under the authority of the major general, by a general or senior officer designated as director of the aeronautical service;

In an army, under the authority of the army chief of staff, by a senior officer designated as director of the army aeronautical

---

* The attributions of the artillery and engineering services which relate to the attack and defense of places are defined by the regulations on siege warfare.

service.

Telegraphic Service.

Art. 12. The purpose of the telegraph service is to organize and operate the electrical, radio-telegraphic and optical communications necessary for the armies.

In the army group, the telegraph service operates under the authority of the major general and forms two distinct branches:

Telegraphy, directed by the director of the rear, who is assisted, for this purpose, by a senior military official of the post and telegraph administration;

Radiotelegraphy, directed by a senior engineer officer, part of the general staff.

In an army, the telegraph service is directed:

At the front, under the authority of the chief of staff of the army, by a senior engineer officer, chief of service, part of the army staff;

At the stages, by a senior militarized officer of the post and telegraph administration, reporting to the chief of staff of the director of stages and services.

The army radiotelegraphy is attached to the forward telegraph service.

In an army corps, the telegraph service is directed by the officer in command of the telegraph detachment, under the authority of the corps chief of staff.

In a cavalry division, the service is directed by the captain of the engineer, under the authority of the chief of staff of the division.

Intendance Service.

Art. 13. The intendance service is in charge of:

1. The organization, the direction and the technical execution of the services of subsistence, clothing, the camp, the harnessing of the cavalry, as well as the authorization of the expenses of these

services;

2. The authorization of pay;

3. The verification and the closing of accounts of the distributions and consumptions concerning the funds and materials which are under the responsibility of the intendance service;

4. The verification of the accounts of the troops and the administration of the personnel without troops;

5. The control of the service of the treasury and of the posts, within the limits fixed by the regulations. The stewardship services are directed under the authority of the command:

In an army, by an intendant general or a military intendant, head of the stewardship service of the army. This senior official is at the same time director of the stewardship of the stages and reports to the director of the stages and services of the army; In an army corps, by a military intendant or a subintendent. director of the stewardship service of the army corps; In a division, by a military subintendent.

The quartermaster of an army receives from the Minister of War the delegation of all the credits intended to ensure all the services of the army; he subdelegates them as and when necessary to the directors of the services concerned, on the order of the director of the stages and services of the army, who receives for this purpose the instructions of the general commanding the army

Health Service.

Art. 14. The health service has in its attributions the forecast, the preparation and the technical execution of all the measures relative to:

1. Hygiene and prophylaxis;

2. Treatment and evacuation of the sick;

3. Recovery, transport, treatment or evacuation of the wounded, whatever their nationality;

4. Replacement of personnel and replenishment of equipment of the troops and medical units.

The health service is directed, under the authority of the command: In an army, by a medical inspector general or inspector, chief of the army health service, who is at the same time director of the health service of the stages, and who reports to the director of the stages and services of the army; In an army corps, by a medical inspector. or principal, director of the health service of the army corps; In a division, by a principal physician, divisional physician.

Service of the gendarmerie.

Art. 15. The service of the gendarmerie in the armies is responsible for:
1. the research and the ascertainment of crimes, misdemeanors and contraventions, the pursuit and the arrest of the guilty, the transfer of prisoners;
2. the police and the maintenance of order in the army zone:
3. The surveillance of non-military individuals who follow the armies, as well as vagrants and individuals suspected of espionage;
4. The service of the prisons established in the headquarters;
5. The surveillance and policing of the safeguards.

In addition, the gendarmerie may be entrusted, by order of the commanding officer, with:
1. The grouping, command and surveillance of regimental trains;
2. The surveillance of prisoners of war.

The gendarmerie service is organized by army.

It is directed, under the authority of the command and through the intermediary of the chief of staff: In an army, by a colonel or lieutenant-colonel, "provost marshal of the army"; In an army corps and at the stages, by a squadron leader called "provost marshal of the army corps" or "provost marshal of the stages"; In a division and, when necessary, in a weaker unit, by a junior officer, who also takes the title of "provost marshal."

Veterinary service.

Art. 16. The veterinary service has in its attributions the

forecast, the preparation and the technical execution of all the measures relative to:
1. The veterinary hygiene and prophylaxis;
2. The treatment of the sick horses;
3. The hygienic direction of the herds of livestock and the inspection of the animals on the ground and the meat of slaughter.

The veterinary service is directed, under the authority of command: In an army, by a senior veterinarian, who is both chief of the army veterinary service and chief of the stage veterinary service, and who reports to the director of stages and services; In an army corps, by a senior veterinarian 2nd class, who reports to the chief of staff of the corps.

Service of the treasury. Post office service.

Art. 17. The treasury service is in charge of all the receipts coming from the public treasury or made on behalf of the State, and of discharging all the expenses, regularly paid for the COI'P& of troops or serves.

The postal service is responsible, in the area of the artillery, for transporting funds and correspondence to and from the troops in operation.

These services are directed, under the authority of the command and through the Chief of Staff:

In an army, by a paymaster general, head of the treasury and postal service, who is at the same time head of the treasury and postal service of the stages, and who reports to the director of the stages and services of the army;

In an army corps, by a principal paymaster; In a division, by a particular paymaster.

Service of the rear.

Art. 18. The purpose of the rear service is to ensure the continuity of relations and exchanges between the field armies and the national territory.

It forms two large divisions: the service of the roads and the service of the stages,

It includes, moreover, the automobile service and that of water transport.

Railroad service. At the beginning of the war, the Minister drew the line between the "interior network," which remained under his direct orders, and the "army network," which included the railway lines placed under the authority of the commander-in-chief.

The service of the railroads to the armies is in charge of the organization, the maintenance, the exploitation and the destruction of the railroads constituting the network of the armies. This service is directed by a general or senior officer, who takes the title of "director of railroads" and reports to the director of the rear.

Service of the stages. The service of the stages embraces the whole of the services of the rear which do not return in the service even of the railways. Its main purpose is to ensure the supplies and evacuations of the armies and to maintain order and security in the rear area.

This service is directed, in the zone of the stages of each army, by the director of the stages and services of the army, and, in the part of the rear zone not included in the special stage zone of each army, by the director of the army.

By delegation of the general commanding the army, the director of stages and services exercises, in national territory, all or part of the attributions of the territorial command, to the extent determined by the commander-in-chief and according to the instructions of the Minister. In enemy territory, he is responsible for the provisional direction of the civil administration of the occupied territories.

In addition to the railroads, automobile convoys and water transport may be used for supplies and evacuations.

Automobile service. The purpose of the automobile service is to provide the command with safe road transport units designed to extend or replace the railroad for the execution of supplies of any kind and possibly for evacuations.

The entire automobile service operates under the direction of the director of the rear, who, according to the needs of the moment, keeps at his disposal, or distributes among the directions of the stages and services, all or part of the automobile formations.[*]

Water transport service. The service of water transport on the navigable network of the armies is centralized, under the direction of the director of the rear, by a permanent commission called the "field navigation commission."

---

[*] However, the large units include organically, apart from the motor vehicles assigned to the headquarters, special motor sections for their supply of fresh meat and their health service.

Section II – Orders. Liaisons

Orders.

Art. 19. The decisions of the command are notified to the subordinates in the form of orders.

The orders must contain all that is necessary for the subordinate and nothing more. The leader who gives them must not leave to his subordinates the burden of prescribing the measures for which he is normally responsible. On the other hand, he must avoid hindering their initiative by specifying the details of execution.

Every operations order must inform the subordinate about the situation and the role of the unit in the overall operation.

It must contain:

Information on the enemy;[*]

The intentions of the leader who gives the order and the goal he is pursuing; The objectives to be reached and the movements to

---

[*] These indications must be reduced to what directly interests the addressee.

be carried out by the unit to which the order is addressed; The place where the leader will be; The movements of neighboring units.*

Orders are, in principle, given in writing. The observance of this rule specifies the respective responsibilities of the leader and subordinates, while at the same time providing a guarantee against inaccurate interpretation.

Only orders of pure execution, concerning small units, can be verbal.

The executor, unexpectedly placed in the presence of unforeseen circumstances, is no longer obliged to comply strictly with prescriptions which have ceased to be applicable to the new situation. He has the duty to take, on his own initiative, the necessary steps to realize, in spite of all obstacles, the intentions of the command. He reports as soon as possible.

Orders are called instructions when the ordering authority merely makes known his intentions and sets the goal to be achieved, without formally prescribing the conditions of execution.

The greatest precautions must be taken to prevent the disclosure of orders and instructions.

Classification of orders.

Art. 20. Orders are *general* or *individual*, depending on whether they are addressed to all or only a fraction of the troops placed under the command of the authority from which they emanate.

The simultaneous sending of individual orders to several subordinate units should be avoided as much as possible. In the event that this procedure is used, the general order must nevertheless be established, because it eliminates the chances of omission and makes all inferiors aware of the changes in the situation.

When circumstances make it possible to fear that the general

---

* These indications must be reduced to what directly interests the addressee.

or individual order will not be received in a timely manner, a *preparatory order* should be used, the purpose of which is to briefly define the initial conditions for the movement of subordinate units. The preparatory order is always confirmed and supplemented by a general or special order, which must reach those concerned as soon as possible.

All orders and instructions given by generals, corps or service chiefs, must be recorded.

Summary Reports.

Art. 21. The *summary report* is a summary account of a fact or situation, drawn up at the very moment when the events occurred or came to the knowledge of the person giving the report.

The commander of a unit must keep his superior constantly informed of what he knows about the enemy, the situation and the operations of his unit. Any event of interest to the superior will be reported immediately.

In addition, the command may require periodic reports.

Every unit commander is required to inform neighboring units without delay of important events occurring in his area of action.

In principle, the reports are written. Exceptionally, they can be verbal, when they are made from leader to leader, without intermediary.

Debriefs.

Art. 22. The debrief is a detailed report written as soon as possible after the events that are the subject of it.

Every important event gives rise to a debrief intended to confirm the previous reports, completing and coordinating them.

The report is always in writing.

Liaisons.

Art. 23. The purpose of *liaisons* is to coordinate efforts by ensuring continuity of relations between troops participating in the same action; each one must know what his leader wants and what his neighbors are doing.
To this end, liaisons are established :
Between the commander of a unit and his direct superior;
Between the commander of a unit and his immediate subordinates;
Between leaders of units operating in neighboring areas.
Some of them allow the command to transmit its orders or to receive information, reports and statements which, by shedding light on the situation, provide it with the elements necessary to make its subsequent decisions.
The other is an exchange of information that allows neighboring units to combine their efforts for common success.
Every unit has an absolute duty to assist neighboring troops to the extent consistent with its mission. In particular, an uncommitted force is obliged to march with cannon, whenever its mission permits.
On the other hand, no unit has the right to rely on the assistance of elements operating in the immediate areas of action, as these may be unable, because of their mission, to provide the expected assistance.
Between neighbouring units, reciprocal support results above all from the convergence of missions assigned by the higher command.
In no case should lateral liaison result in a weakening of the will to act on the part of the executors, or in delaying the effective moment of action. Subordinate units do not have to adjust themselves closely to each other in order to obey a concern for alignment and elbow to elbow. Moreover, by employing itself without reserve to the accomplishment of its mission, a troop comes by this very fact to the aid of the neighboring forces.

Establishment of liaisons.

Art. 24. The liaison of a unit with the immediate superior authority, the subordinate units and the neighboring units, must be assured in a permanent way, but the procedures to be used to carry out this liaison vary with the circumstances.

During marches away from the enemy, brigades (or regiments) second to the division (or brigade) commander a mounted officer as liaison officer.

During marches close to the enemy and in combat, every unit detaches to its immediate commander one or more liaison officers (mounted officers, cavalrymen, cyclists, or planters).

The unit commanders detach in liaison, to any sub-unit momentarily separated from the main unit, and, if they deem it useful, to neighboring units, an officer or a rank, in charge of sending reports and accompanied by the desired number of horsemen, cyclists or plantons.

Telephone and signal communications are established whenever the troops stop for a sufficient period of time (in combat, during prolonged halts, at outposts).

In the cantonment, the existing telegraphic and telephone network may also be used, to the extent authorized by the command.

Transmission of orders and reports.

Art. 25. The transmission of orders must follow the hierarchical way, without omitting any intermediary, except in case of emergency. In the latter case, the chief who gives the order shall inform the intermediate authority and the one who receives the order shall report without delay to his immediate superior.

Important orders are carried by officers who are aware of the situation and familiar with the contents of the dispatches. In some cases, they are drawn up in several dispatches and sent through different channels.

Any officer charged with carrying an order into a country occupied by enemy posts must be accompanied by one or two well-mounted horsemen.

Any bearer of orders or reports must be prepared to have his dispatches removed. If he is wounded or ill, he shall address himself to the commander of the nearest troops and transmit to him the order or report for which he is responsible. The latter will acknowledge the order or report and make arrangements for it to reach its destination without delay.

The commander of a cavalry troop is obliged to provide a good horse to any officer bearing an order, who requests it, if the condition of the mount of this officer does not allow him to accomplish his mission in due time. In the absence of cavalry, this obligation extends to any commander of a troop provided with horses.[*]

All troops, in particular those belonging to the vanguards, flank-guards and outposts, have the duty to facilitate, by all means in their power, the transmission of information.

The bearer of a dispatch must receive an acknowledgement of receipt from the recipient.

The exchange of orders, minutes and reports, which are not of an urgent nature, takes place at the daily report.

Telephone messages shall be written on departure and on arrival and collated.

Telegrams and messages are always confirmed.

---

[*] The horse must be returned as soon as possible to the corps that provided it.

Section III – Marches. Stations.

Chapter I – Marches

Purpose of the regulations on marches.

Art. 26. The purpose of the regulations concerning marches is essentially to put the troops in a position to fight under the most advantageous conditions, by facilitating movements and avoiding useless fatigue. Marches are executed according to rules that vary with the military situation, and in particular with the distance from the enemy.

The measures to be taken for the marches depend, moreover, on the nature of the country, the number and condition of the communication routes, the arrangement of the troops before and after the march, the condition of the troops, the length of the stage and the atmospheric circumstances.

Constituent elements of the columns.

Art 27. The troops, the combat trains and the regimental trains constitute the elements of the columns. Fleets and convoys always form separate columns.

The *combat trains* follow the troops in all circumstances; they transport the ammunition and material immediately necessary on the battlefield (tools, explosives, medical material).

The *regimental trains* carry the food, baggage and equipment necessary for the daily needs of the troops. They are generally divided into several echelons, the most advanced of which follows the battle trains as closely as possible, when the situation permits.

The *depots* carry additional ammunition and equipment needed for combat.

The *convoys* carry additional food supplies.

Order of march of the elements.

Art. 28. There is no normal order of march, nor is there a normal order of combat: the elements of a column march in the order determined by the command, according to the situation.

During the march, security is ensured by the cavalry, the vanguard, the flank and the rear guard, in accordance with the rules set out in the section "Security".

In principle, in a forward march, the commander of the column is in the vanguard. The officer immediately following him in the hierarchical order marches at the head of the main body, of which he takes command.

Every troop corps is accompanied by its battle train.

In a division, the combat train marches at the tail of the troops, but before the rear guard, if the division provides one.

The various constituted fractions of the column are separated, at the start, by sufficient distances so that the march can be executed with regularity and without jerks. These distances can increase or disappear during the march. They are taken up again at each halt.

Preparation of the march.

Art. 29. The division marches in one or more columns. It can also be part of a larger column.

The superior command regulates the whole movement. He fixes for the division: a marching zone or an itinerary; the time of departure or of passage at a given point or on a given line, of the vanguard or of the head of the main body; the general prescriptions relative to the trains; possibly the general conditions of the main halt and the parking zone at the end of the march.

The division commander determines: the leader, the composition and the route of each column; the order of march of the main column; the particular provisions concerning safety; the conditions of departure; the position will occupy during the march; the prescriptions relating to the trains; possibly, the general conditions of the main halt and the stationing at the end of the march.

If necessary, the column commanders will determine: the order of march of their column, the particular provisions concerning security, the conditions of departure.

The division general, as far as the division's marching area is concerned, and each column commander for his route, have the duty to study in advance, with all the information they can obtain, the conditions of execution of the prescribed march.

Whenever they foresee difficulties in following the itineraries, either because of the poor layout of the roads (particularly through the woods), or because of the insufficiency of maps, they obtain guides and have reconnaissance carried out, in due time.

They order and execute as soon as possible the necessary works for the repair and development of the roads of the imarche.

They study the transverse communications allowing to connect with the neighboring columns.

Preparations for departure.

Art. 30. In principle, the soldiers eat before departure and take a cold meal with them. The cans are filled. As much as possible, the horses are made to drink and eat.

The fires are extinguished, the bivouacs and billets put in order. All inscriptions are erased and all papers destroyed.

At all levels of the hierarchy, the command has the duty to set the conditions of the march, so as to avoid the troops the fatigue of a useless wait, before they enter the column.

The departure is never delayed. If the leader of a unit is not at the head of his troop when the troop must leave, the most senior officer starts it.

Starting of the columns.

Art. 31. The marching is preceded by a general assembly only for a column of small strength.

The measures to be taken in order to form a column depend on the extent and the shape of the stationing area.

If the troops occupy: extended cantonments in the direction of the front, the column 'is formed by' the successive arrival of the various elements at the same point, the so-called 'initial point'.

The command fixes the times of passage at this point of the leading element of the main units and, if necessary, the routes to be followed to get there. It designates, if necessary, a particular starting point for certain troops. The leaders of the subordinate units have the route to be followed to reach the initial point recognized, evaluate the time necessary for their head of column to arrive there, and fix, consequently, the time of departure of their troop. They can, if necessary, designate for their unit an intermediate initial point.

Any initial point must be of easy access, and have clear approaches, so as to allow units arriving before the fixed time to stop without obstructing the route of march. It must never be chosen at the exit of a parade, village, wood, etc.

If the cantonments of the column are staggered in depth along the route to be followed, or if they are very close together, the column is formed by the timely setting in motion of its different forces. The command fixes the time at which the main elements will leave their respective billets; the subordinate commanders act in the same way for the forces under their orders.

March formation.

Art. 32. The march is executed, in principle, on the right side of the road, in order to leave the left side free for traffic.

In general, the infantry and cavalry march in groups of four; the artillery and train carriages in one line, the hand horses and the high-footed animals in two.

Speed of march.

Art. 33. The speed of march of a column of all arms is that of the infantry.

This speed varies with the nature of the terrain and roads, the atmospheric circumstances, the length of the stage and the state of the troops; it must be maintained as uniform as possible during the entire duration of the march.

Execution of the march.

Art. 34. The good execution of the march depends on the regularity of pace of each of the elements of the column. The head of each battalion, squadron or battery, must advance at a uniform speed, without sudden slowing down, and without sudden acceleration.

In any column or significant fraction of a column, a foot officer is responsible for regulating the pace.

Each element of the column is required to link up permanently, by sight, or by a chain of markers, with the troops in front of it, to avoid losing the route. This requirement applies in particular to the element that marches at the head of the main column, which must link up with the tail of the vanguard. Any element that breaks away from the column must inform the unit that is marching behind it, in order to avoid being followed by this unit.

At the beginning of the march, the column commander ensures that the troops advance in the prescribed order.

Hourly halts.

Art. 35. Whenever the situation permits, after each period of fifty minutes of march, a halt of ten minutes is made, called an hourly halt. In principle, unless otherwise ordered, the hourly halt takes place ten minutes before the full hour.

Each battalion, squadron and battery commander stops and restarts the unit he commands at the precise time.

At the moment of the stop, the troops and the cars close on the head of the unit. Troops on foot form bundles and drop bags; troops on horseback dismount.

The hourly halt is not mandatory. In particular, a unit on the verge of engagement no longer halts at a fixed time.

Its leader chooses, according to the situation, the most favorable times or points to rest his troop.

Grand halt.

Art. 36. A grand halt is made if the distance to be covered, the weather or any other circumstance makes it necessary.

This great halt, whose duration is fixed by the command, takes place for all or part of the column. The desired number of resting places is designated for the various elements of the column.

Every location of the grand halt is chosen close to the water and, as far as possible, two thirds or three quarters of the way along the route to be covered by the troops who stop there.

In strong columns, the grand halt must be carefully prepared. The locations of the different elements must be recognized in advance by a staff officer and by mounted representatives of the troops.

Discipline of march.

Art. 37. The officers and commanders shall see that each soldier marches in his place. By maintaining the strictest order in the ranks at all times, one avoids wavering and changes of pace which are a cause of fatigue for the troops.

As a rule, no one leaves the ranks outside the halts. When, exceptionally, a man is authorized to leave the ranks momentarily, he hands his rifle to his neighbor; he is required to rejoin as soon as possible.

No shouting of marching or halting is permitted.

Gunners march behind their troop and not to the side.

Officers who may be on the flank of their troop, to watch the march, must not in any way impede the movement.

A troop or cars stopped must never intercept the road to be followed. The crossing points of roads are to be kept completely clear. Whenever cars stop on a road, they must pull to the right.

During the high hours, the men remain on the same side as the beams or cars, unless that side of the road is bordered by walls or hedges. In this last case, they can go to the opposite side of the road, on the condition that they completely clear the road.

A detachment of police, marching after each corps, is in charge of catching the stragglers. The police detachment that marches last in the column is reinforced by gendarmes; it visits the localities it passes through, and arrests the marauders and stragglers. On arrival, it hands over to the gendarmerie the marauders caught red handed and directs the other men to their units.

Crossing of columns.

Art. 38. In principle, movements are regulated in such a way as to avoid crossing columns.

When, exceptionally, the situation leads to the crossing of two columns, the command gives the necessary orders so that they can cross each other without any disturbance and with the least possible delay.

When, unexpectedly, a column on the march finds the path it must follow intercepted, its leader immediately agrees with the leader of the unit (brigade or regiment) marching in front of him, to ensure the crossing. The highest ranking or most senior officer present will arrange the details of the crossing.

If the approaches of the point of crossing are free, each column successively masses its elements by constituted forces and carries them, beyond the transverse road, in the intervals, households, in the same way, in the other, column; it then resumes the formation of road.

In the case where it is not possible to leave the roads, the crossing is carried out by forces which take a formation of doubled march a little. before arriving at the point of crossing, pass briskly in the intervals of the similar groupings of the other column; and then take again the formation of march and the normal pace.

As much as possible, an officer representing the higher command attends: the crossing of the columns to settle immediately all the difficulties which can be raised.

Marches far from the enemy.

Art. 39. When the march is carried out at such a distance from the enemy that *an encounter can be considered as completely improbable*, the main concern is to facilitate the movement of the troops and to reduce their fatigue.

The distances between the elements are increased in order to ensure more independence to the march of the units.

If security is absolute, and if one has the certainty of not having to modulate the direction during the march, it can be advantageous to use the road network to the full and to form small columns, by assigning distinct routes to the different arms.

The regimental trains are interspersed in the column, in whole or in part, following the units to which they belong, so as to ensure the distribution of foodstuffs and baggage as soon as they arrive at their lodgings.

Cars for the wounded are placed at the disposal of the troops to ensure the transport of the sick during the march.

At the end of the march, the billets are *staggered in depth* on the road followed and at a short distance on both sides of this road, so as to avoid lateral movements and to allow for the next day the almost simultaneous setting out of all the elements of the column.

Marches close to the enemy.

Art. 40. As soon as an encounter becomes possible because of *the proximity of the enemy*, an effort is made to put the troops in a position to fight under good conditions, while facilitating their movement.

The depth of the columns and billets is reduced.

The troops march in the order dictated by the urgency of their arrival on the battlefield.

In principle, the artillery must be close to the head of the column in order to hasten the moment of its entry into action. However, it must be far enough from the most advanced elements so as not to be exposed to fall, in road formation, under the fire of the enemy artillery and to have the certainty of crossing positions without being forced to turn back.

Only in exceptional cases are batteries marched with vanguards that include less than one infantry battalion.

In the interior of the column, the artillery is placed as much as possible so as not to break the tactical links with the infantry. But it is necessary to ensure during the march the protection of the artillery against the attacks of enemy cavalry and cyclists. For this purpose, a force of infantry is always inserted between two successive artillery groups.

If the width of the road allows it, and if the atmospheric circumstances are very favorable, a column can take for the march doubled formations. But this measure is a cause of fatigue for the troops and leads to a notable reduction in the speed of march.

The regimental trains march grouped behind the combat columns.

Marches to the enemy in view of an immediate combat.

Art. 41. When marching to the enemy *in view of a very near battle*, it is important above all that the division commander be able to personally direct the battle from the beginning and that he have at his disposal all his means of action for this purpose.

The marching pattern changes accordingly as the encounter

becomes more imminent.

When the division forms more than one column, the *main* column is preceded by a vanguard with which the division commander marches and which is called the *divisional vanguard*. The other columns ensure their own protection by small vanguards.

The divisional vanguard begins its deployment by detaching infantry forces on either side of the marching route, which, at the time of the encounter, are likely to constitute a solid combat front or to break down the first resistance by turning them.

Before their entry into action, the troops generally leave the road formation and take an articulated assembly formation.

In close proximity to the enemy, the articulated assembly formation may also be taken by the entire division from the parking area.

The *articulated assembly* is a formation in which the elements are staggered in width and depth, as required by the tactical situation, in conditions that allow them to use the terrain, move with order, and rapidly move to deployment for combat.

It includes, in principle, a large force, formed, according to its importance, in one or more groups, and security detachments.

These different elements are carefully removed from view and fire.

If the nature of the terrain and the state of the ground allow it, the troops march in combat in this formation. As far as possible, the artillery and cars use the roads; the infantry marches across fields or follows, in small columns, practicable tracks. It is necessary, in this case, to have recognized the terrain to be covered and to have foreseen the means to improve the routes.

It is made the largest use of the troops of the engineers to remove the obstacles to the movement.

It may be advisable to have part of the artillery march by leaps and bounds from position to position, so as to always have batteries ready to support the action of the first forces of infantry.

In small columns, this procedure is necessary so that the artillery does not fall, in road column, under the fire of the enemy batteries.

It may also be necessary to make the troops march through the woods. It is important, in this case, to take all necessary measures to preserve direction, maintain order and keep the units well grouped.

When, in a column, the vanguard, having come into contact with the enemy, is obliged to slow down its march, the main body avoids closing in on it or stopping in column on the road. The leading forces are arranged in an articulated assembly. If the march is resumed and an immediate engagement is to be expected, the forces already assembled advance across the fields. The rest of the column continues on the road.

As soon as combat becomes certain, at short notice, the regimental trains are maintained or sent back.

Forced marches.

Art. 42. When it is necessary, because of the situation, to hasten the arrival of the columns, the troops execute forced marches, during which the movement continues night and day.

The duration of these marches cannot, in general, be extended beyond thirty-six hours. If possible, periods of movement are alternated with hourly and longer rests, during which the troops can eat and sleep.

Night marches.

Art. 43. It is often necessary to have recourse to night marches, either for the execution of forced marches, or because of other circumstances, notably the obligation to conceal one's movements from the enemy. But night marches impose great fatigue on the troops. It is therefore necessary to prepare them with the greatest care.

At night, all measures must be taken to ensure the regular march of the column in the prescribed direction. For this purpose, guides are attached to the main elements; the distances between the elements are reduced; the route to be followed is marked out; the forks are blocked, etc.

During night marches, the cavalry and artillery cannot be

usefully employed. As far as possible, the cavalry is assigned special routes where it is well protected by the presence of other columns. If it has to follow the same route as other troops, it is made to leave later than the latter, so that it can march at its own pace. The artillery is rejected towards the tail of the columns.

Orders are given in advance so that at dawn the elements would take up their positions in preparation for the daytime march.

Marches in heat and cold or in difficult terrain.

Art. 44. When the marches are carried out in the heat, one must, if the situation allows it, increase the distances between the elements, decrease the speed, suspend the movement during the hottest hours of the day. It may be advantageous to have the infantry march on both sides of the road, leaving the middle free for traffic. One of the most important precautions is to have the men drink while marching.

In cold weather the ration must be increased and the men prevented from standing still during halts.

In all the circumstances which impose particular fatigues on the leading forces (ground covered with snow, ice, brushwood, high crops, etc.), one frequently raises the forces forming the head of the column.

Whenever the weather or the terrain make the march difficult, one can make more frequent stops, shortening their duration if necessary.

Chapter II – Stationing

General rules.

Art. 45. *Stationing is regulated according to the situation, taking into account the day's march.*

One endeavors above all to shelter the men. But, in order to avoid the rapid wear of mounted weapons, no resource is neglected to protect, in addition, the horses against the bad weather. For this purpose, all existing premises are used.

The division receives a *deployment area.* The divisional commander distributes his troops in this area as best he can according to the situation and the resources of the inhabited places.

Far from the enemy, it is in the interest of the troops to give the division a deployment area with a sufficient number of localities, Near the enemy, the need to keep the troops ready to fight takes precedence over any other consideration; it leads to tightening the stationing.

Most often, it is advantageous to deploy in depth along the routes followed, especially for marches where a sustained and prolonged effort is required of the troops.

In the immediate contact of the adversary, the troops deploy in articulated assembly.

Various types of stationing.

Art. 46. The troops occupying inhabited places are in *cantonment*.

Those who are installed in the open air or under improvised shelters are in *bivouac*.

When, due to the insufficiency of resources in premises, a troop has only a part of its elements in cantonment, the rest bivouacking in the vicinity, it is in *cantonment-bivouac*.

When the stay outside inhabited places must be prolonged, the troops are installed in *camps*, provided with shelters, tents or barracks.

Orders for stationing.

Art. 47. In addition to the provisions prescribed in Section II (Art. 19), the orders for the stationing of the division or of the lower units make known :

The cantonments or bivouac sites assigned to the subordinate units; the place of their headquarters; the mission of the security detachments and the conduct to be maintained in the event of an attack by the enemy; the measures foreseen for the main body in the event of an attack; the location of the headquarters or the headquarters of the authority giving the order; the conditions of supply by the regimental trains; possibly, the times at which the various corps must be under arms the following day.

In principle, the artillery is not stationed alone.

Encampment.

Art. 48. All the personnel responsible for recognizing and preparing the camp are designated as the *campers*.

The encampment includes in principle: one mounted officer

per corps; one adjutant per battalion, half-regiment of cavalry or artillery group; one forage officer, one corporal or brigadier and two men per company, squadron or balloon.

When possible, the camps are reinforced by the units destined to constitute the police guards.

A doctor, belonging to one of the corps to be installed in the cantonment or bivouac is, in principle, designated to study in advance the measures concerning the hygiene of the troops at the camp.

Layout of the cantonment.

Art. 40. A distinct sector is assigned to each headquarters, each troop corps or section of a corps. Within the corps, serials are also assigned to each company, squadron or balloon.

As far as possible, both sides of a street are assigned to the same unit.

Officers of all ranks are billeted in the sector of their troop.

Staff officers are billeted in the premises where their offices are located or in the immediate vicinity thereof.

Each corps has its own *police guard*. The head of the corps is stationed near the police guard.

When several corps are gathered in the same cantonment, a *central post* is established to ensure the transmission of the command's orders to the corps in the cantonment. The central post is placed in the center of the cantonment, usually at the town hall. It may be adjacent to the office of a headquarters or it may merge with the police station of one of the corps.

Preparation of the cantonment.

Art. 50. The allocation of the cantonment is made either by an officer specially designated by the command, or by the officer who represents the authority called upon to exercise the functions of commander of the cantonment.

The preparation of the cantonment must be carried out rapidly, so that the troops do not have to wait for their arrival.

When time is short, this preparation is done summarily and can be reduced to a simple distribution of the locality, done according to the map. The camp leaders precede the encampments to study in advance the conditions of installation of their corps.

The officer in charge of the distribution of the cantonment makes a quick reconnaissance of the locality. He gets information from the municipality and, if he has time, consults the plans deposited at the town hall.

He indicates to each camp leader the sector assigned to his troop. He recognizes or has recognized the drinking troughs, the places where the men will take water and those where they will have to wash their clothes, and has them indicated by signs. If necessary, he places sentries at the watering places.

He then determines, if necessary:

The location of the central post;

The location of the artillery depot, in principle outside the cantonment, on the least exposed side, as much as possible on dry ground, with easy circulation and offering openings;

The location of the infantry corps depots, if there is no suitable location in the corps sectors. These depots should be located as close to the troops as possible, but should never interfere with traffic.

The corps camp leaders, after a summary reconnaissance of their sector, will in turn determine those of the companies, squadrons or batteries. They recognize the location of the depot and fix that of the police station.

They reserve one or, if necessary, several houses to receive the sick and wounded of the corps. They decide, according to the proposals of the doctor attached to the camp, the hygiene measures to be taken in the cantonment.

As soon as they arrive, the camps are directed to the sector of their unit. The police guards set up and place sentries at the exits of the cantonment, to intercept any communication of the inhabitants with the outside.

The guards recognize the houses in the parts of the cantonment assigned to them, evaluate their size and indicate their assignment by means of mobile signs without making any inscriptions.

When the preparation of the cantonment is completed, each camp chief draws up a table of the information that it is useful to communicate to the troops. He then sends the adjutants or quartermasters to the most favorable points to bring each unit directly to its sector, goes to meet his corps or detachment commander in person and reports to him.

Installation in the cantonment.

Art. 51. The troop can enter the cantonment as soon as the reconnaissance of the cantonment is completed. All measures must be taken in order to accelerate the entry into the barracks.

Each corps commander or detachment commander gives the signal for his troop to move in.

The warrant officers and the quartermasters respectively report to the commanders and captains and lead the units into the part of the cantonment reserved for them.

The flag is carried to the colonel's quarters.

If there are prisoners to guard, the police guards lock them up in the house they occupy or in neighboring houses.

The locations of headquarters, ambulances, etc., are indicated by the distinctive flags, and, at night, by the corresponding lanterns.

Alert cantonment.

Art. 52. When a troop is stationed near the enemy or when it may be called upon to leave the cantonment quickly, it shall be placed in an *alert cantonment*.

For this purpose, the ground floors are preferably used and the troops are assembled, by constituted forces, in large premises lit at night.

The doors of the occupied houses are kept open; if necessary, additional exits are made. The streets are lit during the night if possible.

The men lie fully clothed, ready to take up arms, the riders beside their horses, the officers with their troops.

If the situation requires it, the horses can remain saddled and bridled and be assembled in yards, squares, etc.

Cantonment-bivouac.

Art. 53. In the cantonment-bivouac, each corps or unit of a corps is assigned a sector, however small, to enable it to shelter its sick, its workers, to set up its kitchens, to make its distributions, etc.

Each unit uses as fully as possible the premises placed at its disposal. In addition, all the resources offered by the locality are used to improvise shelters, canopies, etc. But the roads and paths must be left completely free.

Bivouacs.

Art. 54. The location of bivouacs depends on the tactical situation and the terrain.

Bivouacs are established in the shelter of the enemy's view, and, as far as possible, on dry land, offering easy access, within reach of water and wood resources. Freshly plowed land and, for mounted weapons, artificial meadows, should not be used as bivouac sites.

When the woods meet favorable conditions and communications are easy, they can be used as bivouac sites, provided that the fires are watched; this has the advantage of concealing the presence of all or part of the troops occupying them.

The command determines the bivouac positions to be occupied and the distribution between the corps. The exact locations of the bivouacs are recognized by the camps.

The preparation of a bivouac and the installation of the troops are carried out under the same conditions as for a cantonment, except for the following points:

The officer in charge of the distribution of the bivouac specifies to the different corps of troops the ground which is assigned to them, avoiding mixing them and squeezing them.

Each camp leader has the boundaries of the bivouac assigned to him staked out.

Whenever possible, headquarters and ambulances are established in nearby housing.

The units for which regulation bivouac formations are provided are:

In the infantry, the *company*;
In the cavalry, the *squadron*;
In the artillery, the *battery*.

For the bivouac of superior units, companies, squadrons or batteries are arranged in relation to each other, either in column or in line or in any other formation respecting tactical links, at distances and intervals which vary according to the terrain and are determined with a view to ensuring the grouping of superior units.

The trains are established on the most favorable locations.

The officers bivouac with their troops.

Service in the cantonments and bivouacs.

Art. 55. The provisions of the regulations on the service in the field and on the internal service of the troops are applicable in the cantonments, bivouacs and camps, in all that is not contrary to the present regulations.

No officer or soldier may be absent from the cantonment or bivouac, except for service or on such authorization as the commanding officer may exceptionally give.

Command of cantonment or bivouac.

Art. 56. In all places where troops are stationed, the highest ranking officer will take the title of *commander of the camp or bivouac*.

In general, his powers are those indicated for the commander of arms in the regulations on the service of the place.

This officer shall regulate the general service from the point of view of protection, discipline and hygiene, without interfering in the internal service of corps which are not normally under his authority.

Any general officer, commanding a cantonment or bivouac in which several corps or units of corps are assembled, shall designate a senior officer to assist him, who shall take the title of *major of the cantonment or bivouac*.

The commander and, if necessary, the major of the cantonment or bivouac, shall be quartered or bivouacked in the vicinity of the central post. The troops detach permanently to this post plantons for the transmission of orders.

Daily duties.

Art. 57. In the field, duties are done by day.

Guards, detachments and workers are always provided by constituted units.

There shall be commanded every day, in each infantry regiment, a company; in each cavalry regiment, a half-squadron, and in each artillery regiment, a battery, to provide the police guard, the other interior guards and the picket. These forces are called *day forces*.

The commander of the day force is in charge of distributions; he is assisted in this service by the day officers of the other companies, squadrons or batteries.

In a battalion or in a group of batteries forming a corps or detachment, the day service is provided by a unit commanded by an officer, taken in turn from the companies or batteries; the officer in command is in charge of the distributions.

The senior officer of the day has the general direction of the day service.

Police guard.

Art. 58. The police guards ensure order in the places where the soldiers are stationed, enforce the police rules, supervise the depots, guard the men who are being punished. They shall provide the necessary sentries and patrols for this purpose. Their strength is determined accordingly. A bugler or trumpeter is part of each police guard.

The police guard of each corps is taken from the day force. In case it is not commanded by an officer, it is under the direct authority of the officer of the day of this fraction.

The number of orderlies necessary to ensure the transmission of orders to the battalions, companies, squadrons or batteries is detached to the police guard.

Picket.

Art. 59. The available part of the day force is called the *picket*. It is intended to provide the detachments and guards that can be ordered extraordinarily. For this purpose, it is under the orders of the senior officer of the day.

The officers, non-commissioned officers and soldiers of the picket are always dressed and equipped, the bags made, the horses ready to be saddled.

The picket provides the soldiers needed to receive and transport food for the guard forces.

Punishments.

Art. 60. Arrests are kept within the limits of the cantonment or bivouac of the company, squadron or battery.

In each corps, the men punished by police room or prison are gathered together and placed under the supervision of the police guard in a room which replaces the disciplinary rooms of the corps.

The soldiers likely to be judged by a council of war are handed over to the gendarmerie to be taken to the prison of the general quarter.

Measures of order in the stationing.

Art. 61. In the cantonments and bivouacs, the command, at all levels, ensures order, discipline and hygiene.

The strictest measures are taken against fires.

The officers and non-commissioned officers supervise the maintenance of the effects, equipment, weapons and fittings, the cleanliness of the body, the care to be given to the horses and harness, the conservation of the ammunition and reserve food; they frequently pass through the cantonments, visit the stables, make sure that the men are provided with everything that the locals must supply them with, severely repress any illegitimate demand, endeavor to maintain good relations between the soldiers and their hosts, take note of the complaints that seem to be well-founded, grant them or report on them. which appear to be well-founded, and to grant them or to give an account of them.

All drums or bells are forbidden in the cantonments or bivouacs, except in the case of an alarm, the signal for which is given by the commander of the cantonment who, if necessary, causes the alarm to be sounded.

In the cantonment as in the bivouac, the troops must be in a constant state of readiness to take up arms. The pack is made up every evening, ready to be completed and loaded quickly; the saddles and harnesses are arranged in such a way as to be placed promptly on the horses.

Upon arrival, each unit commander had the directions of the roads leaving the cantonment recognized.

He indicates a *rallying point* in the cantonment of his unit that all the men must know in order to be able to go there alone at the first signal, even at night.

It is on this point that the meetings for the departures, the calls, the inspections, etc. are made.

It is also designated one or more assembly points for the meeting, in case of alarm, of all the troops occupying the cantonment. The routes to reach the assembly points are recognized. The location of the assembly points is made known to all.

Every sentry must be able to indicate the way to the central post of the cantonment.

It is essential not to disturb the rest of the troop during the night, by transmitting orders. Unless otherwise ordered, every morning, at the time fixed by the command, the companies, squadrons or batteries are formed at their rallying point, ready to leave. It is only at this moment that the orders that could not be given the day before at the evening soup, for the departure, are communicated to the troops by the commanders. An exception to this rule is made only for corps or fractions of corps that must move before the set time. In this case, the awakening is assured at the desired hour by the plantons of the units.

Safeguards.

Art. 62. The purpose of the safeguards is to ensure the inviolability of certain public or private establishments, whose entry must be forbidden to the troops in the interest of the army.

The safeguards include a written order, issued by a general officer and bearing the stamp of his staff. This order is given to the personnel of the establishment concerned.

The safeguards, presented to the troops, must be respected as a sentry.

The service of the safeguards is placed under the supervision of the gendarmerie in the armies.

Security of the cantonments and bivouacs.

Art. 63. Independently of the protective measures adopted for the entire base, each commander of a cantonment or bivouac shall take the necessary measures to ensure, in any eventuality, the security of the troops under his command.

The immediate exits or approaches shall be guarded by forces whose importance varies with the situation. Sometimes one is satisfied to place sentries, sometimes one establishes posts which barricade the access roads and organize the useful points to be held.

Every barricade must be set up in such a way as to allow, if necessary, the passage of liaison officers, couriers, cyclists and automobiles.

In principle, each infantry or cavalry corps guards the exits in its sector. Sometimes a force, taken from one or more corps, but distinct from the pickets, is designated to form a reserve within the cantonment. This force settles in the alert cantonment or in the bivouac.

The communication routes are cleared; if necessary, additional outlets are prepared below or outside the cantonments.

The commander of the cantonment notifies the commanders of the corps of the measures to be taken in the event of an attack for the defense of the cantonment or the bivouac.

In enemy country, he may, if he deems it useful, take hostages, forbid the inhabitants to go beyond the posts he has placed at the exits, and require them to remain at home from a given hour. In general, he takes the appropriate measures to prevent any communication between the inhabitants and the enemy's emissaries.

Chapter III – Rules Common to Marches and Stationing

Honors and external marks of respect.

Art. 64. Troops shall not pay honors during the march, nor during halts. At the halt, the police guards shall render honors under the conditions established by the regulations on square service, but without ringing the bell.

External marks of respect are due under all circumstances.

Alternation of units.

Art. 65. In order to avoid that certain elements are subjected to excessive fatigue, the command makes the units alternate among themselves, as far as the situation allows, for the execution of the different services.

On the march, the constituted forces which compose the combat column take in turn, when nothing opposes it, the head of the unit (regiment, brigade or even division), to which they belong.

In the same way, in each corps, the units alternate between them to ensure the service of the outposts and that of the day.

Rules Common to Marches and Stationing

Reports concerning the state of the troops.

Art. 66. The command must constantly have precise knowledge of the efforts that its troops are capable of making. Therefore, at all times, each unit commander shall report, without delay, to his immediate superior, incidents or particular circumstances, which may have a serious influence on the physical or moral state of his men.

Hygiene of troops.

Art. 67. Because of the depth of the zones occupied by the armies and their services, it often happens that the same localities or the same bivouac sites are occupied successively and several days in a row by different troops. Under these conditions, the development of epidemics, whose repercussion could be seriously felt on the general state of the troops, can only be avoided if extremely severe rules of hygiene are observed at all times. The most important of these rules are the following: It is forbidden to use for drinking water other than that which is marked as potable by the command.

The troop will not, under any circumstances, billet in houses where there are contagious diseases.

At the station, and in any prolonged halt, there will be set up barracks, the use of which is obligatory, to the exclusion of any other location. The sheets are always carefully filled before the departure and indicated in a very apparent way.

The offal of slaughtered animals and the remains of dead animals are buried deep. Debris and garbage of all kinds are burned.

Any case of contagious or epidemic disease is immediately reported to the higher authority, which immediately orders the necessary measures.

Rules Common to Marches and Stationing

Measures to be taken to avoid indiscretions and to teach the command.

Art. 68. It is forbidden to leave any paper, letter, etc. at the encampment or during the march, without destroying it.

It is forbidden for soldiers of all ranks to answer questions asked by persons outside the army.

In private correspondence, one must refrain from any communication relating to the location of troops, their strength and their movements. Private letters must not mention the locality where they were written.

All information and documents giving information on the enemy must be transmitted immediately through the chain of command. Clothing and other effects left behind by the enemy are examined. The report of their number and the inscriptions they bear is sent to the command. Any soldier who recognizes the existence of carrier pigeons in a cantonment reports to his leaders.

Prisoners or deserters must be searched and questioned as soon as possible. The interrogation is done, if possible, by the chief or one of the officers of the detachment having made the capture. The answers are summarized in a summary report immediately transmitted to the superior authority.

Any corps or detachment commander who is the first to enter a locality abandoned by the enemy will immediately seize the letters deposited at the post office or in the boxes, the papers of the town hall, the station, the post office, etc. He will search for all the documents left behind by the enemy. He will search for all documents left by the enemy and any clues that could identify the elements that occupied the locality.

Precautions to be observed against aerial investigation.

Art. 69. In all circumstances, during marches, during assemblies and when stationed, every effort will be made to hide the troops from the sight of aerial observers.

On the march, as soon as an aerial device is signaled, the white parts of the road are cleared; the grassy or tree-lined sides are supported as much as possible, preferably on the side opposite the sun. If necessary, the infantry and cavalry march in the ditches.

Outside the roads, it is the large masses and the moving troops that attract the attention of the aerial observers.

The woods, orchards and hedges are used as much as possible; in open terrain, the formations are open and very diluted.

If necessary, one stops, preferably in a kneeling position. The parts of the ground where one is best hidden from view are the areas separating two different colors (e.g., the boundary between two fields of different colors, the edges of roads, the borders of villages and woods, etc.).

In the cantonment, it is usually the camps and fires that indicate the presence of troops. It is therefore advisable to avoid groups of cars forming regular lines. The cars are placed under sheds, trees, in the courtyards or in a line along the houses and hedges, provided that they do not hinder the circulation.

Kitchens are installed as much as possible in the dwellings.

Special requirements for small units.

Art. 70. The small units, such as the divisional cavalry, the detachments of the engineers, of the train, of the administrative and health services, etc., as well as the small detachments, temporarily separated from their corps, are in principle attached, for the cantonment, the supply of food and ammunition, the medical and veterinary care and the evacuations, to a corps of troops designated by the command. When this designation could not be made in advance, it is up to the commander of the cantonment to attach these units and detachments to corps.

Routine.

Art. 71. In the field, when the troops are not provided with mobile kitchens, they cook either by section (or platoon), or by squad (or piece).

In principle, the non-commissioned officers live the same way.

Section IV – Security

Chapter I – General Considerations

Art. 72. The purpose of security is:
1. To guarantee the freedom of action of the commander, that is to say, to give him the time and space he needs to make his dispositions (security of the commander);
2. To protect the troops on the march or at the post against surprises (security of the troops or protection).

The freedom of action of the commander is guaranteed: By the information provided to him by the superior authority and by that which he has sought in the directions and at the distance deemed necessary; By the use of security detachments (vanguard, rear guard, flank guards, etc.) charged with gaining, by their resistance, the time the commander needs to make his arrangements.

In immediate contact with the enemy, the judicious distribution of forces in view of combat is the best guarantee of safety.

The protection of the troops against surprises is achieved, in the directions where the security detachments operate, by the very presence of these detachments.

These detachments cover themselves on their own account, on the march and when stationed, by weaker detachments (vanguard plates, advance posts) and are illuminated by the forces of cavalry put at their disposal.

In the less important directions, the protection measures include the sending of small detachments, detachments pushed less far than the security detachments; sometimes, they are limited to the surveillance of these directions by cavalry patrols and the immediate guarding of the cantonments.

The procedures of the security forces could not be the object of precise rules. To each situation must correspond special measures taken by the chief in order to inform him on what he has an interest in having and to cover him in the directions where he wants to be covered. It is thus up to the chief to determine, according to the needs, the number of security detachments strictly necessary and to specify the respective missions of these detachments.

Chapter II – Security on the Move

General provisions.

Art. 73. The security of a column is guaranteed by detachments called: vanguard, rearguard, flank-guard, according to whether they are placed in front, behind or on the flanks of the column.

Vanguard.

Art. 74. Far from the enemy, the role of the vanguard is simply to clear the obstacles that might be in the way of the column and to allow the latter to march freely. It is made up of forces of infantry and cavalry whose size is proportionate to that of the column to be covered.

In the vicinity of the enemy, the vanguard must be in a position to fulfill all the missions that may fall to it in the engagement according to the orders of the division commander (see Art. 102), that is to say: to attack the enemy in order to force him to show his forces; to occupy the points of support necessary for the deployment of the main body and to conquer these points of support if necessary.

The vanguard is therefore strongly constituted of infantry and cavalry, the latter being in charge of lighting up the desired distance. Units of artillery march to the vanguard whenever the number of infantry is sufficient to cover the artillery. Otherwise, the artillery of the main body must be able to support the infantry of the vanguard very quickly.

The vanguard includes in principle:

All or part of the cavalry assigned to the column;

A proportion of infantry varying from 1/6 to 1/3 of the total strength of the infantry of the column;

Possibly, a part of the artillery, as well as a detachment of engineers, whose composition is subordinated to the nature and the importance of the works to be foreseen during the march.

All these elements are, *for the march*, under the orders of the same leader who is the commander of the vanguard.

The vanguard is generally divided into a certain number of echelons called *the point, the head and the bulk of the vanguard*.

The point is formed by all or part of the cavalry attached to the vanguard, supported by forces of light infantry. It is always commanded by an officer.

The head includes one third to one quarter of the infantry of the vanguard and the engineer detachment.

The bulk of the vanguard is made up of the majority of the infantry and possibly the artillery.

The distance between the vanguard and the main body of the column varies with the proximity of the enemy, the terrain, the strength and the mission of the vanguard.

This distance must be large enough to protect the main body of the column from surprise by enemy artillery fire. On the other hand, it is limited by the need to support the vanguard in time and not to let it fight in isolation.

The distances between the different echelons of the vanguard are determined according to similar considerations.

Rearguard.

Art. 75. In a forward march, the rearguard has a simple role of protection: to observe what is happening in the rear of the column and to cover it, if necessary, against the action of the enemy cavalry.

Its strength usually does not exceed two companies for a divisional column. Whenever possible, a few cavalrymen are added to it.

In retreating marches, the rear guard's mission is to allow the main body of the column to escape the enemy's encirclement and avoid combat.

Generally speaking, it is composed like a vanguard in the forward march. However, it should not rely on the support of the main body, and it is generally advisable to build it up strongly, especially in artillery and cavalry.

The cavalry marches in the rear, keeping contact with the enemy, and is particularly concerned with illuminating the flanks.

Flank guards.

Art. 76. The flank-guards are intended to protect the flanks or the open flank of a column.

Their mission is either to guarantee the column against the action of light detachments, or to contain the enemy, if an attack is possible.

In the first case, the flank-guard can be constituted by simple forces of cavalry.

In the second case, it includes troops of all arms, taken either from the vanguard, or from the main body of the column.

Its strength is related to the size of the column to be covered and the size of the possible attacks.

According to the instructions which they have received, the flank guards march parallel to the column, either at the level of the main body, or at the level of the vanguard, or else they occupy on the exposed flank the points from which the enemy could threaten the movement; they station themselves there until they are certain that their presence is no longer necessary.

Chapter III – Security on Station

Art. 77. When stationed, security is guaranteed, as when on the march, by the very arrangement of the security detachments: vanguards, rearguards, flank-guards, which are stationed in the directions leading towards the enemy.

The protection of the stationed troops is, in principle, the responsibility of the elements provided by the vanguards, rearguards and flank-guards, and called outposts.

Outside the zone occupied by the security detachments, the main body detaches, if necessary, elements that are placed in outposts for its protection.

In immediate contact with the enemy, the front line elements of the unit provide the outposts.

Role of the outposts.

Art. 78. Outposts have a mission of resistance and surveillance; they do not have to seek combat. In the event of an attack, they do not hesitate to sacrifice themselves in order to give the troops they are covering the time they need to make their arrangements. They do not cease resistance until they are ordered to do so.

The mission of the outposts involves, as much as possible, the close cooperation of infantry and cavalry.

Because of its strength of resistance, the infantry is the main element of the outposts. The bulk of this infantry holds the points of the terrain which it is important to deny the enemy access.

During the day, the cavalry attached to the outposts takes over the entire surveillance mission in order to relieve the infantry.

During the night, the infantry alone assumes the dual role of resistance and surveillance; the cavalry is stationed in the rear.

Surveillance must be assured, regardless of the distance from the enemy. Resistance is only envisaged if the enemy is in a position to intervene, and it is prepared in a manner that is all the more complete the closer one gets to the enemy.

The addition of artillery forces to the outposts is only justified if there is a need to beat particularly important points, such as defiles, at great distance.

The overall arrangement of the outposts depends on the situation, the command's plans, the location of the main body of the division and the terrain.

The outposts are, as far as possible, established in such a way that the most advanced cantonments and the assembly points of the main body of the division are completely sheltered from the fire of the enemy artillery. Their position is chosen primarily because of the facilities it offers for resistance. It is also advantageous to have, from this position, extensive views allowing for good surveillance of the terrain.

The service of the outposts imposes great fatigue on the troops. It is therefore necessary to employ only the number of troops strictly necessary in each particular case.

Outposts at the end of the march.

Art. 79. After a forward march, the mission of providing the outposts on the direction of the march falls to the advance guard.

These outposts are composed of the entire vanguard if it is weak; this is the usual rule for the division and the lower units.

A large vanguard can, on the contrary, depending on the situation, put only part of its forces in the outposts. There is then a large vanguard covered by outposts.

In all cases, the commander of the vanguard is the commander of the outposts provided by his vanguard.

If the area to be guarded lacks depth, if it has cuts or cover making communications difficult, it is advantageous to divide it into sectors each with a particular commander subordinate to the commander of the vanguard.

In the case of a retreating march, the rearguard provides the outposts under the conditions just indicated for the vanguard. It is also possible to have the outposts taken by units belonging to the main body of the column. These units settle down before the arrival of the rear guard, which crosses them to go and camp beyond under their protection.

Security detachments other than vanguards and rearguards also provide outposts on the directions they have to guard; the commanders of these detachments are commanders of the outposts provided by their detachment.

The same unit may remain in charge of security on the march and on station for several consecutive days. An effort is then made to alternate the sub-units for outpost duty.

The outposts are formed more or less strongly, depending on the proximity of the enemy.

Outposts far from the enemy. Far from the enemy, when one has to fear only incursions of cavalry parties or cyclists, the outposts are reduced to a minimum, so as to spare the forces of the troops. The protection is obtained in part by the very device of the cantonments, which are staggered in depth. Each cantonment keeps its exits; some posts are pushed on the main directions to be watched.

Outposts at a short distance from the enemy. When the enemy is close enough for an attack to be possible, the question of resistance of the outposts comes to the fore.

On the important directions, the formation is articulated with a view to combat and generally comprises:

A first echelon, constituted by the grand guards, who hold the points of the terrain that lend themselves to resistance;

A second echelon, formed by a reserve of outposts, intended to support or collect the grand guards.

The grand guards have, in front of them, surveillance elements, small posts, sentries and patrols.

In the directions where an attack is unlikely, simple surveillance posts are used.

Combat outposts.

Art. 80. At the end of a day's fighting, when remaining in contact with the enemy, the troops engaged cover themselves, *without waiting for orders*, with combat outposts.

These outposts are provided by the front line units which, maintained in the immediate vicinity of the combat position or on this very position, cover themselves each for their account by constituted fractions, sections or companies. The elements necessary for surveillance are pushed forward.

The combat position is put in a state of defense.

Command action.

Art. 81. The essential role of the outposts is to gain the time needed by the commander of the division to make his dispositions.

It is therefore up to the division commander to clearly specify, for each detachment called upon to provide outposts, the mission he assigns to the detachment, and the terrain to be held in case of an enemy attack.

According to his mission, the goal he proposes and the possibilities of attack by the enemy, each detachment commander will determine the number of outposts he is called upon to provide, their general line, the overall plan for their resistance, as well as their distribution on the ground according to the importance of the directions to be watched. In his orders, he determines: the directions to be guarded or the points to be held, the locations of the various elements of resistance (grand guards and reserves), their strength, as well as their respective roles in case of an attack, and also gives all useful information on the situation of the division and the neighboring units, that of the enemy, etc.

The commanders of the grand guards and the advance guard have the duty to decide in advance, according to the same principles, the distribution of their troops and the manner in which they will employ them in the event of an attack by the enemy.

GENERAL RULES OF SERVICE AT THE OUTPOSTS.
Installation and raising of outposts.

Art. 82. At the end of the march, the service of the outposts is organized as soon as the advance guard reaches the locations assigned to it by the order of stationing. The installation of the outposts is carried out under the protection of the cavalry or the advanced elements of the vanguard.

The commander of the outposts gives, *according to the map*, his orders for the taking of the outposts.

The indications contained in these orders are the following:

Mission of the outposts and conduct in case of attack; Mission of the cavalry;

Approximate location and sector of surveillance of each grand guard;

Location of the reserve(s) of the outposts;

Information of any kind of interest to the outposts, on the enemy, neighboring units, directions or points to be watched in a particular way, etc.;

Word of order and rallying.

Each major guard and reserve commander of outposts directs his unit as soon as possible to the location indicated by the order, taking the necessary protective measures, and precedes it to reconnoiter the terrain. After this reconnaissance, he determines the final locations to be occupied.

The reserves of the outposts and the grand guards remain under arms until the small posts are in place.

The commander of the outposts visits the reserves, the grand guards and the important posts without delay, prescribes the modifications he deems necessary and establishes himself in his person at the main body of the vanguard.

When the march is to be resumed the next day, the outposts normally remain in position until the first infantry elements of the vanguard have passed the small posts. They then join the vanguard, if the latter has not been relieved, or take, in the column, the place assigned to them.

In the case of a retrograde march, the outposts assemble when the main body of the column has taken the distance prescribed by the command.

The installation and raising of the outposts provided by the other security detachments is carried out according to the same principles.

During the periods of stationing, the service of the outposts is usually of twenty-four hours. The command fixes the conditions under which the outposts are relieved. This operation must be carried out in daylight; the time at which it is carried out must change each day.

Communication to the outposts.

Art. 83. The recognition between the different elements at the outposts is carried out by means of the word and signals.

The word, which includes the word of order and the rallying word, is, in principle, given by the commander of the corps and notified each day by the commander of the division.

If this notification arrives too late to the commander of the outposts, the latter will set the word himself, make it known to the neighboring outposts and report back to the division commander.

He proceeds in the same way if there is reason to fear that the word has been surprised by the enemy.

The commander of the outposts prescribes the reconnaissance signals to be used, if any, by the sentries, patrols and rounds, and makes them known, as aforesaid, to the division commander and to the neighboring outposts.

Reserve of outposts.

Art. 84. The reserve of outposts is generally established at a certain distance behind the grand guards, sometimes on the line of the grand guards themselves. In the event of an attack, according to the mission that has been assigned to it, it reinforces the latter, collects them, or resolutely takes the offensive against any enemy column that has forced its line. It avoids merging into partial reinforcements and acts, preferably, in groups.

The reserve comprises, as far as possible, half the number of troops assigned to the outposts. If the terrain is divided into sectors, each sector has a partial reserve.

The reserve may provide the patrols or rounds prescribed by the commander of the outposts or the sector, as well as the special posts required in certain cases.

It is set up, as much as possible, in alert cantonment, otherwise it bivouacs. It has a police guard.

Distributions are made to the reserve for all the troops in the outposts.

The outpost reserve must be connected by telephone and by liaison officers with the grand guards and with the authority immediately above.

Grand guards.

Art. 85. The general line of the grand guards is determined by the commander of the outposts; it is called the *line of resistance of the outposts*.

The usual strength of a grand guard is one company; it can be decreased; it can also be increased, when it is a question of holding a particularly important point.

To each grand guard, is assigned a sector determined according to the terrain.

The grand guard generally detaches small posts and patrols, to watch the terrain in front of it, and thus give it time to make its combat dispositions.

The total number of personnel employed for small posts and patrols should be as small as possible, so as not to diminish the resistance capability of the grand guard.

The grand guard has a defensive mission. Most often, it must resist on the ground; it uses the natural support points of the position assigned to it; it organizes them if necessary and stations itself in the immediate vicinity of its combat position.

Sometimes, an offensive attitude will be necessary; in this case, the grand guard will be established at a central point, from which it will be able to move quickly to meet the enemy forces that have penetrated its sector. A grand guard must not abandon its mission or its sector to go to the aid of a neighboring grand guard under attack. If possible, it should assist with fire, but it should be extra vigilant on its front line of surveillance.

The grand guard is established out of the enemy's sight, in bivouac, sheltered as much as possible, or in alert cantonment. The men kept their equipment on day and night.

About a quarter of the grand guard is on picket duty, ready to march at the first signal. The picket provides a sentry in front of the weapons, and, if necessary, the men necessary to observe the signals of the small posts.

The grand guard must be in liaison with its small posts, the reserve of outposts and the neighboring grand guards. Cyclists, signalmen, telephonists, mounted scouts and, possibly, horsemen, may be added to it for this purpose.

Small posts and sentries.

Art. 86. Every small post must be commanded by an officer or by a proven non-commissioned officer.

The small posts do not constitute a first line of resistance in front of the grand guard. They are only intended to ensure the surveillance of the sector assigned to them and to warn of the approach of the enemy. In case of surprise, they fire and avoid falling back directly on the main guard, in order to unmask the latter's field of fire.

The strength of each small post is limited to the number of men necessary to provide the sentries and patrols required to monitor its sector.

During the operations of investment of a place, the need to provide a chain of sentries sufficiently close and distributed on all the front assigned to the grand guard, leads to give to the small posts a strong enough manpower which can reach a section and to assign them a narrower sector of surveillance.

The small post provides one or more double sentries, as well as a single sentry in front of the post whenever it provides more than one double sentry. The locations selected for the sentries should provide for strict surveillance.

The general line of sentries is usually referred to as the *outpost guard line*.

The sentries seek to conceal themselves, while remaining able to observe well. They are constantly attentive, and never allow themselves to be distracted from their surveillance, even by the appearance of a superior; they do not pay honors. They may be allowed to leave their packs at the small post. They always have their weapons ready to fire, but do not fire unless they clearly see the enemy or are attacked. They also fire at anyone who tries to force their lockout.

At night, they should not sit or lie down.

The location of the small post is chosen according to those of the sentries; it must allow for easy communication with them on the one hand, and with the general guard on the other. Most often, the small posts will be advantageously established on the roads or in the immediate vicinity. Their location must be hidden as much as possible from the enemy's view.

At the small post, the men remain constantly equipped and keep the weapon within their reach. At night, a part of the force, at least half, remains constantly awake and vigilant; the rest may be allowed to sleep for a few hours; the officers alternate between them to rest; it is generally forbidden to light fires and to smoke.

Food is prepared at the grand guard and taken to the small post.

Manner of arrest and recognition at the outposts.

Art. 87. Independently of their mission of protection, the outposts must see to the observance of the following instruction in the most rigorous manner:

No one is authorized to cross the line of the sentries without having been recognized by the commander of the small post or the large guard, under the conditions fixed below.

Consequently, the sentries stop any isolated person or group passing in their vicinity.

The commanders of the small posts accompany detachments, isolated persons on mission or persons with a pass to the sentries' line. They let in, day and night, after having recognized them, the isolated soldiers, the patrols and the rounds. During the day, they also let in detachments that are part of the troops at the outposts and those for which they have received special instructions.

The commander of the grand guard himself came to recognize the detachments that presented themselves during the night. He would only let them enter if they belonged to the troops covered by the outposts, if their leader carried a written order, or if there was not the slightest doubt as to their identity.

To stop, the sentries shout, day and night: "Halt!" If they do not stop, they shout, as a second warning: "Halt there or I'll fire!" If, in spite of this second injunction, one continues to advance, they fire.

If one stops, they warn the chief of the small post, but they don't let one approach them.

The chief of the small post recognizes by the cry: "Who is there?" When it has been answered, "France, soldier or detachment of such and such a corps, patrol or round," or when the agreed signals have been made, he shouts, "Advance to order."

If the arrested persons are part of small isolated groups, the chief of the small post lets them approach only in succession.

If it is a detachment, a round or a patrol, the commander of the detachment, the round or the patrol must advance alone; his troop is kept at a distance until, its leader having been recognized, it is allowed to enter.

At night, when a detachment presents itself, the commander of the small post notifies the commander of the grand guard.

Even when the order has been given, the chief of the small post must take all precautions to ensure the identity of the persons he is authorized to recognize. In case of doubt, or if the word of order could not be given by them, he has them taken to the commander of the grand guard, who questions them, has them searched if necessary and sends them under escort to the commander of the outposts.

The commanders of the grand guards proceeded in the same way when they came to recognize them.

Whatever his rank, the leader of a troop arrested by outposts is obliged to answer all questions put to him for the purpose of verifying his identity.

Parliamentarians.

Art. 88. When a parliamentarian presents himself, the sentries stop him outside the lines and make him turn to the side opposite the outposts. The chief of the small post comes to recognize him, takes his dispatches and sends them to the commander of the grand guard. The latter received them and sent them without delay to the division commander through the intermediary of the commander of the outposts.

In order to avoid any indiscretion, the chief of the small post remains with the member of parliament; when the receipt of the dispatches arrives, the latter is immediately dismissed.

If the parliamentarian asks to be received by the commander of the troops, the chief of the small post blindfolds him and his trumpeter and leads them to the small post, where they await the order of introduction. This order can only be given by the commander of the troops himself.

While the trumpeter remains at the small post, the parliamentarian is sent, blindfolded, to the grand guard, from where an officer led him to the reserve of the outposts, and then to the commander of the troops. He is brought back with the same precautions to the post where he had presented himself. In certain cases, the member of parliament must be held temporarily, for example, when he has been able to gather information on surprise movements that must be kept hidden from the enemy.

Any conversation with a member of parliament is strictly forbidden.

Deserters.

Art. 89. The sentries to whom enemy deserters present themselves shall order them verbally or by sign to lay down their arms and, if they are on horseback, to dismount and unhitch their horses. They fire on them if they do not obey.

The chief of the small post comes to recognize the deserters, and only lets them approach in succession.

The commander of the grand guard, to whom they are brought, questions them about everything that might interest the safety of the army, and has them taken under escort to the commander of the outposts. The latter questions them again and directs them to the headquarters of the division commander.

Patrols.

Art. 90. Patrols are detachments of varying strength that the small posts, the grand guards and, if necessary, the reserve, send in front of the line of sentries to watch over the parts of the terrain that escape the sight of the latter, or to observe the movements of the enemy, when in contact with him.

Patrols are in principle the mobile element of surveillance. They may, however, according to the instructions received, sometimes stop for a more or less long time, either to better observe by stopping on points from which they have extensive views, or to set up ambushes.

The instructions given to each patrol leader before his departure, indicate:

The specific purpose of his mission;

The general route to be followed or the area to be covered;

The points he is not to pass or the approximate duration of his mission;

The command and rallying word and signals.

The patrols are always composed of at least three men commanded by a corporal, a non-commissioned officer, if necessary by an officer. Intelligent, skilful men who are able to orientate themselves are preferably chosen for this service.

The commanders of the grand guards or the reserve regulate the number, time and route of the patrols, according to the strength of their troops, the nature of the terrain and the possibilities of attack.

When he deems it necessary, the commander of a small post may also send out patrols.

Patrols march carefully and quietly, stopping often to listen and orient themselves; they carefully observe the terrain they are covering.

At night or in cut-off terrain, small infantry patrols generally do not advance more than one kilometer from the line of sentries. If circumstances require that they be pushed further, their strength is increased.

Towards daybreak, patrols should be more frequent and reconnoiter the ground farther out; they do not return until daylight.

The patrols avoid engaging in combat and even more so avoid being cut off; for this reason, they take a different route on the way back. If they encounter an enemy of inferior strength, they try to take prisoners by luring him into an ambush. If the enemy is in strength, they warn the small posts in the rear and withdraw while continuing to observe.

Every patrol leader communicates to his men the order and the signals so that they can return in isolation, if the patrol is forced to disperse.

Upon returning, he reports what he has observed to the leader who sent him. Any important information is transmitted to the commander of the outposts.

When the outposts must stay several days on the same ground, the time of exit and the route of the patrols are changed each day.

Rounds.

Art. 91. The rounds are made by an officer or a noncommissioned officer, accompanied by two or three armed men. They ensure the vigilance of the sentries; they link the small posts and the grand guards and they contribute to the surveillance by observing during their march.

The rounds generally circulate within the surveillance line.

By day and by night, the rounds, patrols and troops in arms are recognized in the following way: The leader who first sees the patrol or the troop shouts: "Halt!" and then: "Who is there?" To the answer: "Round, patrol, detachment of such and such a regiment or France," he shouts: "Advance to the order," receives the word of order from the commander of the round, patrol or troop and gives in exchange the word of rallying.

Examination post.

Sec. 92. In certain cases, it may be advantageous to establish, on the same line of small posts, a special post called an *examination post*, charged with receiving, examining and interrogating parliamentarians, deserters, prisoners and, in general, all persons foreign to the army who request to enter the lines.

The commander of the outposts determines the composition of this examination post and its location, which is generally chosen on the most important access route. This location is indicated to the small post commanders, who direct isolated and non-army personnel to the examination post.

In the vicinity of the enemy, the higher command may absolutely prohibit the entry and exit of the lines.

General prescriptions concerning outposts.

Art. 93. Independently of the special instructions relating to the conduct to be maintained in each particular case, the outposts shall conform, in all circumstances, to the following general instructions:

1. When the outposts are in contact with the enemy, they have the duty to maintain this contact by patrols, led if necessary by officers.

In the event that they notice that the enemy has evaded them, the patrols will warn the commanders of the general guard, who will immediately report to the commander of the outposts.

2. During the night, the small posts, the picket force of the grand guards and the police guard of the reserve of the outposts take up arms for the patrols, the rounds and any troops coming towards them; the sentries in front of the weapons receive the necessary instructions to this effect.

One hour before daybreak, all the elements of the outposts, small posts, grand guards and reserve take up arms and are ready to fight.

3. The troops at the outposts do not pay honors.

Batteries and bells are forbidden.

4. Any indication concerning the enemy must be reported immediately to the higher echelon.

As soon as he has occupied the location assigned to him, the commander of each element of the outpost network must send his immediate superior a report on the installation, summarizing the arrangements made by him. Each morning, he makes a summary report on the events of the night.

Cavalry at the outposts.

Art. 94. At the end of the march, the cavalry of the vanguard covers the establishment of the outposts. To this end, it places patrol detachments and patrols beyond the line of surveillance assigned to the outposts, according to the indications of the commander of the advance guard.

When the infantry outposts have occupied their positions, the main body of the cavalry withdraws to the stationing area, leaving only the force designated by the commander of the advance guard at the outposts. This force was placed under the orders of the commander of the outposts.

During the day, it is generally divided between the reserve and the grand guards and provides:

1. Patrol detachments to relieve the infantry, by assisting in the surveillance on the front indicated by the commander of the outposts;
2. Patrols to search the terrain beyond the line of surveillance;
3. Eventually, special posts to occupy important points in front of the line of surveillance.

At night, the cavalry of the outposts is grouped in the reserve of the outposts or quartered in the rear so as to assure them the rest they need. Exceptionally, in certain special cases, the special posts established during the day may be maintained at night.

In the outposts, it is necessary to avoid using horsemen for liaison and the transmission of orders. This service must be, in principle, ensured by cyclists, when the optical or electric means of communication are missing.

Particulars relating to the night outposts.

Art. 95. At night, the protection of the troops at the station is assured by the infantry.

Darkness facilitates surprises, and significantly reduces the effectiveness of fire. The locations occupied by the outposts are concealed with the greatest care from the enemy's investigations. The various elements of the network of outposts remain, as much as possible, grouped and act preferably by counter-attack.

Mobile surveillance by patrols must be very active, especially around daybreak.

In the vicinity of the enemy, and when the outposts have been established during the day, it may be useful to assign them new locations for the night. It is often advisable to push them further forward.

These locations are especially chosen in such a way as to firmly hold the network of communication routes leading to the enemy. The grand guards and the reserve of outposts are established on the roads and, as much as possible, in localities crossed by these roads. These localities are put in a state of defense.

The assembly places in case of an alert must have easy access for counter-attacks.

In order to give the grand guard the time it needs to make its dispositions, the small posts can be pushed to a greater distance than during the day, and brought to the immediate proximity of the sentries; ambushes can be set up in front.

The chosen sites are occupied at nightfall; they must have been reconnoitred in advance during the day.

Late arrival at the parking area will often require the placement of outposts at night.

The overall arrangements can only be made according to the map. They generally consist in occupying, on the important directions, well marked and easily recognizable points of the terrain, localities, bridges, crossroads, etc.

All measures must be taken to ensure that the locations of the various elements of the outpost network are accurately identified, and that the connections are well assured.

The outpost reserve and the grand guards move together to the point where the reserve is to be established. From there, each grand guard went to his location: a reserve officer accompanied him to reconnoiter this location and the route that led to it.

The installation of the small posts provided by the grand guards is carried out according to the same principles.

As soon as daybreak arrives, the commanders of the guards and reserves make a rapid reconnaissance of the terrain and modify accordingly, if necessary, the positions taken at night.

Section V – Battle

Chapter I – Generalities on Combat

Art. 90. When the division marches in combat, the division commander receives from the higher authority instructions which determine his mission, the general direction to be followed, the objectives to be attained, or, if necessary, a zone of action.

The combat aims at the destruction of the enemy forces. It implies the close and constant cooperation of the different arms.

Only the offensive manages to break the opponent's will. It imposes itself for the major part of the forces.

The need to save troops in order to give more power to attacks may lead to keeping the defensive in certain areas. But, by itself, the defensive can only contain the enemy for a limited time; it never brings success.

To leave no chance untaken, the leader must bring all his forces into the fight, minimizing any detachments he may be forced to make.

Once begun, the combat is pushed to the limit; success depends even more on vigor and tenacity in execution than on skill in combinations. All the units are therefore employed with the utmost energeticness. The task of the executants consists:

In the offensive: to attack right on the indicated objective;
In the defensive: to stop the enemy by sacrificing if necessary to the last man.

Chapter II – Properties and Roles of the Various Arms in Combat

Infantry.

Art. 97. The infantry is the main weapon. It conquers and holds the ground. It definitively drives the enemy out of his strong points.

It alone is capable of fighting at all times, by day and by night, and on all terrains.

The infantry acts by movement and fire.

Only forward movement, pushed to the point of hand-to-hand combat, is decisive and irresistible, but it is generally necessary for effective, intense fire to open the way.

On a very covered ground, or at night, the fire has only a minimal efficiency, and the fight can be reduced to an approach followed by an immediate attack with the bayonet.

Everywhere else, the combination of movement and fire is the mode of action of the infantry. Forward movement is continued as long as possible. Fire is opened only at distances where it can be effective, and only when it becomes impossible for the infantry to advance without firing. The advance is made by rapid leaps, supported by artillery fire and by the fire of neighboring units, until the enemy is approached closely enough to be tackled by a final leap with the bayonet.

The power of the current armament makes impossible any attack in dense formation, carried out, by day, in open ground. The offensive impetus can only be maintained on the condition that flexible formations are employed, and as little vulnerable as possible. The infantry therefore fought in skirmishers.

Skirmishers continue the fight until the assault. They need constant reinforcement. To achieve this reinforcement, the command must arrange the infantry in depth, especially on those parts of the front where it wants to produce a more powerful and sustained action.

The task that falls to the infantry is particularly hard and laborious. It can only be accomplished at the cost of prolonged and often renewed efforts, of an enormous expenditure of physical and moral energy and of bloody sacrifices.

The mission of the infantry, on the battlefield, is therefore the most glorious of all.

Artillery.

Art. 98. The artillery acts only by its fire.

Even after having opened fire, it remains, to a certain extent, available for new missions if it is deflected from the enemy's view. It thus constitutes in the hands of the command a powerful means of action by means of which the commander can make his intervention felt throughout the course of the battle.

Artillery fire alone cannot drive the enemy from his positions. It has only a minimal effectiveness against a sheltered adversary. To bring this adversary to uncover himself, it is necessary to attack him with infantry. The artillery supports the infantry by destroying everything that prevents it from advancing. The close, constant cooperation of the infantry and the artillery is therefore essential in combat in the most absolute way.

The artillery strives to obtain destructive effects. Any firing is justified, if the expenditure of ammunition that it entails corresponds to the importance that the command attaches to the desired result.

The task of the artillery will be considerably facilitated if it succeeds in dominating the opposing batteries; but the artillery battle must have no other object than to allow this weapon to have, thereafter, more forces against the objectives of the infantry attack. It is the responsibility of the division commander to determine, according to the situation at the different moments of the battle, the general objectives which the artillery must take under its fire (see Art. 109), with a view to lending the infantry the most effective assistance.

During the attack, the artillery covers with projectiles the objectives against which the infantry is marching. It seeks to combine as much as possible front and rear fire, both to make the fire more effective, and so that it can be continued until the last moment.

If the assault succeeds, units of artillery will crown the conquered positions as soon as possible, in order to assert possession and to begin, without delay, the exploitation of the success. In case of failure, it is under the protection of the artillery fire that the infantry is reformed to resume the attack.

The artillery in movement is reduced to impotence; even in position, it needs to be protected.

Cavalry.

Art. 99. Cavalry is, par excellence, the weapon of surprise; its speed allows it to intervene unexpectedly and thus produce the greatest results.

In combat, it acts according to the instructions given to it by the commanding officer; it seeks by all means to bring constant and effective assistance to the other troops, with whom it has the duty to remain in liaison.

In the area of action of the unit to which it is assigned, the cavalry informs the command, covers the deployment of the other arms and protects them from combat surprises. It constantly seeks opportunities to intervene usefully in the action, and cooperates with infantry attacks.

It exploits success by a pursuit to excess; in retreat, it sacrifices itself, totally if necessary, to give the other troops time to withdraw from the combat.

The attack on horseback and with the cold steel, which alone gives quick and decisive results, is the main mode of action of the cavalry. Combat on foot is used when the situation or the nature of the terrain momentarily prevents the cavalry from achieving the goal assigned to it by combat on horseback.

Engineers.

Art. 100. The essential mission of the engineers is to establish or improve communications.

In the offensive, it accompanies the other arms; it organizes the points of passage which are necessary for them; it removes or destroys the obstacles which they meet.

In the defense, it participates in the organization of support points, under the conditions set by the command. He establishes the necessary communications for the troops of the defense, and creates obstacles to stop the march of the enemy infantry.

Chapter III – The Offensive

General considerations.

Art. 101. The division commander always seeks to take and maintain the initiative of the attack.

To win, it is not necessary to be superior to the enemy everywhere and at all times; it is sufficient to be the strongest at the desired point and time. Offensive combat therefore includes, against a determined part of the enemy's front, an attack to which the divisional commander allocates as much strength as possible, and which is, in his mind, the main attack.

The other attacks, intended to prepare or facilitate the main attack, by fixing the enemy and attracting his reserves, are conducted with lesser means of action.

The relative importance of the various attacks should never appear in orders. Every troop must go to the fire with the conviction that it will contribute more than all the others to the victory. *For the attackers, the attacks are always pushed to the limit, with the resolution to approach the enemy with a bayonet.*

Before attacking, it is important to determine the objectives of the attack, so as not to run the risk of striking in the void.

To this end, it is most often necessary to force the enemy to unmask his forces, to conquer the support points necessary for the deployment of the main body, or to gain time to bring the main body of the division to work, in front of the chosen objectives.

The battle thus begins, in general, with a series of actions designed to allow the division commander to make his dispositions in complete freedom and in due time.

These actions often take the form of more or less closely localized attacks. They are the responsibility of the vanguard, which the artillery supports from the beginning, and which the first elements of the main body reinforce if necessary; all of these actions constitute the *engagement*.

In certain cases, notably if the information gathered allows the division commander to decide *a priori* on its dispositions, the division advances in an articulated assembly formation; the advanced elements of the formation then fulfill the role assigned to the vanguard in the engagement.

When the vanguard is engaged with the enemy, the division commander can generally refuse combat with the bulk of his forces only by sacrificing the vanguard.

For the commander, the resolution to fight must therefore exist prior to the engagement.

In the offensive, a troop is sometimes stopped by superior forces. It then clings to the ground to ensure the conservation of the ground already conquered; but the only thought of all must be to resume the forward movement.

The engagement.

Art. 102. As soon as the advanced elements signal the presence of the enemy, the commander of the division, who marches with the advance guard accompanied by the commander of the divisional artillery, specifies the mission of the vanguard, indicating in particular the support points of the terrain which he deems necessary to occupy in view of the subsequent development of the combat.

The vanguard quickly occupies these points, or attacks them, in order to dislodge the enemy, if the latter already holds them.

Contact is thus established with the enemy at the various points that will constitute the combat front.

Engagement in the encounter combat.

Art. 103. The engagement takes on its full importance in the encounter combat, that is to say when the division approaches, during an offensive march, an enemy who is advancing offensively.

It is advantageous that the battle array be formed before the enemy has taken his. The need to act quickly generally takes precedence over any other consideration; it can lead the division commander to make a decision without waiting to be better informed about the situation.

The vanguard takes an energetic offensive in order to seize the outlets, the important points of the terrain and to hinder the enemy deployment. It runs to the support points that are assigned to it as objectives; if necessary, it puts all its units in line; it holds on to the ground when it is stopped by superior forces.

The engagement often has a violent character which may require the rapid entry into line of the leading elements of the bulk of the division.

Engagement against an enemy in position.

Art. 104. In combat against an enemy known to be in position, the engagement aims at driving back the opponent's advanced detachments in order to determine his real defense front.

After clearing the initial resistance, the vanguard will often find itself in the presence of very superior forces established on terrain that they know and that they have sometimes organized. The vanguard must therefore act more methodically than in encounter combat, and must identify its objectives and approach routes more thoroughly, in order to engage in a more comprehensive way.

Making contact is made difficult by the absence of smoke and the precautions adopted by the enemy to conceal his troops; the reconnaissance that must be carried out for this purpose is entrusted to officers of all arms, equipped with excellent binoculars.

Role of arms in the engagement.

Art. 105. Whatever the form of the engagement, the infantry plays the principal role in it, as it does throughout the combat. But, from the moment it is under fire, a troop of infantry ceases to be available. The command must therefore avoid taking from the main body of the division any withdrawals that are not absolutely essential to support the action of the vanguard. On the other hand, it is necessary that the number of troops committed be sufficient to conquer and hold the ground necessary for the deployment of the main body, in particular the first artillery positions.

The artillery supports the infantry of the vanguard in conquering or taking possession of the terrain. It results for it the obligation to enter into action as soon as possible.

As soon as the battle is engaged, the artillery takes advantage of every opportunity to try to put the opposing batteries out of action or at least to take on them, from the beginning, an ascendancy that places them in a state of material and moral inferiority for the rest of the action. The artillery of the division must, therefore, be able to intervene entirely, under the sole protection of the troops engaged.

In the engagement, the artillery is, in principle, at the exclusive disposal of the division commander; when batteries have been attached to the vanguard for the march, they remain under the direct orders of the division artillery commander. It is up to the division commander to determine the support that the divisional artillery must lend to the vanguard, the missions that are incumbent upon it in the engagement and, as a whole, the positions that it will have to occupy.

The cavalry endeavors to determine the outline of the enemy. It participates in all the actions of the engagement by extending the action of the vanguard and by covering the positions that the artillery could possibly occupy; it ensures, if necessary, the connections with the neighboring units.

The division's combat system.

Art. 106. The main body of the division is formed in an articulated assembly during the engagement at the latest. It is covered by the troops engaged.

The main body of the division is deployed in close units or in successive units.

The unit formation avoids the mixing of units and better ensures a continuity of the action in depth.

The formation by successive units is particularly suitable for a possible maneuver during the combat. It is indicated for a wing unit or an isolated unit. Its use is still justified when, the front of action being restricted, it is necessary to foresee the removal of several successive lines of support points and, consequently, the need to bring in fresh troops for new attacks.

The battlefront depends, first of all, on the mission assigned to the division; it also depends on the terrain. Even in areas of the battlefield where the density of forces is greatest, the front must always remain sufficient to allow the division to develop all its means of action.

For a division of normal composition, operating on terrain favorable to the combined action of troops of all arms, this front should not, in the offensive, exceed 4 kilometers. Above this limit, the overall direction of the battle becomes difficult, the insufficiently fueled attacks lack vigor, and the division risks being quickly reduced to impotence.

The attacks of the bulk.

Art. 107. The information provided by the engagement is often insufficient or incomplete. If the division commander were to try to be too precise, he would risk losing the benefit of the initiative of the attacks: he must, therefore, make his decision and launch the attacks as soon as the bulk of his forces is in a position to act.

The division commander pursues only one goal at a time. He indicates this clearly, so that all efforts are directed towards the success of the main attack.

When the situation has become sufficiently clear during the engagement, the main attack and the secondary attacks are launched simultaneously.

Otherwise, the division commander may make such secondary attacks as he deems necessary, and retains at his disposal, until the time is right, the forces he has designated for the main attack.

The objectives of the attack are determined by the mission, the situation resulting from the engagement, and the facilities presented by the terrain for the combined use of the various weapons. These objectives are sometimes different from those aimed at in the engagement, but wholesale attacks may also be the normal development of the engagement, giving it greater scope and power.

All attacks are executed according to the same principles; the main attack differs only in its greater development and the consequences expected from it in terms of the outcome of the battle.

The divisional commander determines the relative importance of the attacks by varying the density of forces and more particularly that of the infantry he employs. He concentrates the greater part of his resources in the area of the main attack and arranges the troops there, so as to act with maximum power, to ensure continuity of effort and immediate exploitation of success.

Execution of an attack.

Art. 108. *Approach.* The attack is preceded by an approach, the purpose of which is to bring the units responsible for the attack as close as possible to their objectives and to position them in front of these objectives.

Under fire, an infantry troop can only deploy straight ahead; the direction is no longer subject to change. It is therefore necessary to place the infantry in front of its objectives before the attack. The troops in charge of executing an enveloping attack must take the necessary field in time to deploy straight ahead.

The approach is made by carefully chosen and recognized routes. The directions are identified. Every opportunity is taken to regain control of the units and re-establish tactical links.

The artillery is in a position to intervene to support the infantry as soon as the latter begins its approach.

The line of skirmishers must be formed at the moment when the approach gives way to the actual attack.

Progress of the attack.

Art. 109. The attack requires continuity of effort and extreme energy. Everyone must have only one thought: to go forward, regardless, straight to the indicated objective, to reach the enemy as soon as possible.

Any attack implies the close cooperation of the infantry and artillery. The division commander ensures the liaison between these two arms by the missions he assigns them.

The artillery assists the progression of the infantry with all its means. According to the instructions of the commanding officer, it fires against the support points attacked by its infantry or against the troops whose action stops or hinders the infantry. It destroys, in due course, the material obstacles that the infantry may encounter.

The infantry gains, without firing, as much ground as possible; it opens fire only when it is forced to do so in order to continue to advance. At this moment, the chain of skirmishers must be dense enough to give the fire the maximum power. Each of the forces that constitute it moves forward, by rapid jumps and as long as possible; to gain ground, each force takes advantage of all the moments when the fire of the enemy infantry is rendered less effective by the fire of the neighboring units, or by that of the friendly artillery.

The chain of skirmishers is reinforced as gaps occur in it. The arrival of fresh troops gives the line of fire all its power, redoubles the moral energy and thus facilitates the resumption of the forward movement.

The reinforcements gradually approached the chain by using cover and taking up positions that were not very vulnerable. In open terrain, they move forward by leaps and bounds like the chain, stopping only to catch their breath.

As the attack progressed, the division commander brought the remaining troops closer together in order to be able to exploit the success immediately. Part of the artillery is designated to move as soon as possible on the conquered position.

Assault.

Art. 110. The progression of the attack has only one goal: to bring the chain to assault distance. It is with the bayonet that the infantry breaks the last resistance of the enemy. The assault, that is to say the attack with cold steel, is the only way to solve the conflict.

During the period preceding the assault, the commander of the division makes his action felt especially by the intervention of the artillery. By redoubling the intensity of its fire and by beating the objectives of the attack at all costs, the artillery facilitates the infantry's execution of the last leaps that will bring it to the enemy position; it gives confidence to the skirmishers who feel supported and thus determines the general assault.

Often also, the signal for the assault will come from certain parts of the line, vigorously commanded, which, during the attack, find the opportunity to throw themselves on the enemy position. Their movement must lead to that of the neighboring units and can also determine the assault.

During the assault, the artillery beats the interior of the attacked position by firing in depth, so as to prevent the enemy reserves from entering the line.

As soon as a strong point is taken, the units still available, supported by the batteries which come to crown the position, lunge against the points from which the enemy would attempt counter-attacks, or on which he would still resist, or they support the neighboring attacks by taking in flank the objectives of these attacks. They thus begin the exploitation of success.

In case of failure, all energies are united to re-establish the fight. The skirmishers hold on to the ground, quickly organizing it while waiting for reinforcements to arrive or for neighboring units to advance. In this way, they sought to contain the enemy and resume the offensive as soon as possible.

The cavalry protects the attack against surprises, especially on the flanks, by patrolling the surrounding terrain. It accompanies the attack, charges the counter-attacks and seizes all opportunities to surprise the opponent.

On the wings, it participated in the assault by taking the enemy from behind. As soon as the position was occupied, it threw itself on the enemy to exploit and complete the success.

Continuation of the offensive.

Art. 111. The success of a first attack is not always sufficient to bring about the definitive retreat of the enemy. Often, the enemy will be found installed in the rear on a new position and, to dislodge him, it will be necessary to continue the attack.

The infantry that has just taken a seriously defended strongpoint needs, after the effort it has made, to regain its strength and reconstitute the units that the battle will have more or less mixed up. Most often, the offensive can only be pursued with vigor and without respite by means of elements that have not yet fought.

These fresh troops, brought in at the right time, overtake the conquered position. They take on the new attacks prescribed by the division commander, and carry them out as mentioned above.

The infantry units that have taken the first position support these attacks with their fire. They organize the conquered ground, reconstitute themselves there and supply themselves with ammunition or follow in second line behind the new attack; they then conform their movements to the march of this attack and reinforce it if necessary.

Chapter IV – The Defense

DEFENSE OF A FRONT.
General considerations.

Art. 112. The object of the defensive action is to contain, on a given front, a superior enemy with limited manpower, in order to devote more forces to the offensive action desired and prepared elsewhere.

When, in the context of an offensive action, the higher command assigns a defensive role to a division, it makes use of the division's entire capacity for resistance, in order to determine the front it is given to defend.

Thus placed on the defensive by order of the command, the division must hold on until the end, even if it means a complete sacrifice. It will therefore be careful not to make untimely or unjustified attacks, which could reduce its capacity for resistance and even expose it to failure, the consequences of which could be serious. The cases in which it will have to take the offensive are mentioned in Article 115.

The division commander shall organize the front to be held in such a way as to reduce to a minimum the number of men required to occupy it; this organization must be established according to an overall plan and carried out as far as time and the means available permit. It includes the creation of resistance centers,* to each of which is assigned an infantry garrison, and the choice of artillery positions. These must allow the flanking of the resistance centers, the bombardment of the intervals between them, their surroundings up to the edge of the last cover usable by the attacker, as well as the possible locations of the enemy artillery.

The available troops are kept behind the centers of resistance.

In some cases, especially when a division is operating in isolation, the division commander may have to assign a part of his troops, for example a regiment, a defensive mission.

The following principles apply to this part of the division.

Preparation of the defense.

Art. 113. Most often, the general line constituted by the centers of resistance is determined according to the map.

The details of the defensive organization are determined after reconnaissance not only of the terrain that the division must occupy, but also of its surroundings, of the routes that the enemy may use for his approaches, of the obstacles that may hinder his march, and of the possible positions for his artillery.

The work involved in putting a strongpoint in a state of defense is carried out, in principle, by the infantry troop that is to occupy this strongpoint. The divisional commander may assign engineer detachments for this organization.

The support points are chosen in such a way as to flank each other and to escape, as far as possible, the distant views of the enemy artillery. It is sufficient that the field of fire in front be 800 to 1,000 meters, a distance that corresponds to the really effective range of the rifle. If the field of fire is more restricted, obstacles, accessory defenses and flankers are multiplied. The distances are

---

* A center of resistance can include one important support point, or several close support points.

marked, the field of fire is cleared. Searchlights are installed for the night.

The flanks not covered by the neighboring units are supported by impassable obstacles or, failing that, protected by overflowing echelons.

In the defense, the front lines, the advanced positions, are, in principle, to be avoided. They lead to the dissipation of forces and to partial failures likely to weaken the morale of troops maintained on the line of resistance.

The front to be defended is most often covered by surveillance elements simply charged with warning of the enemy's approach. These elements withdraw, when the time comes, through the wings and intervals of the line of resistance, avoiding being caught.

If the uncertainty about the enemy's plans makes it necessary, security detachments of all arms can be pushed forward from the front. Their role is to inform the command about the direction of the enemy's march and, if necessary, to delay the latter. These detachments then operate under the conditions indicated in Section VII.

Defense of support points.

Art. 114. When the attack takes shape, the infantry forces in charge of defending the strongpoints occupy the prepared locations and engage in the action.

Fire is opened as soon as it can be effective. It must be, from the beginning, violent enough to force the enemy to stop or, at least, to advance only very slowly.

In some cases, the artillery intervened usefully by slowing down the march of the enemy columns by firing from a great distance. It avoids being absorbed by the fight against the enemy artillery. It must, above all, reserve the possibility of firing on the attacking infantry, when the latter offers vulnerable objectives. If necessary, batteries or parts of batteries are concealed until the last moment to surprise the assaulting columns by flanking fire.

Counter-attacks can be executed by the available troops, who seize a favorable opportunity, for example a pause in the attack or the moment of the assault.

In the case where the enemy has seized a strong point, the garrison which has been dislodged has the duty to try, by offensive returns, to take back the lost ground and to drive out the adversary; it is. if necessary, supported by the available troops which are in the vicinity.

The counter-attacks and the offensive returns must be organized by the command in order to ensure, to the infantry which executes them, the effective support of the other arms.

GOING ON THE OFFENSIVE.

Art. 115. It may happen that, contrary to the forecasts of the superior command, a division placed on the defensive is not attacked or is attacked by obviously inferior forces. The commander of the division must then go on the offensive, if the instructions he has received do not formally forbid it.

Similarly, the commander of a division placed on the defensive has the duty to go on the offensive when an opportunity arises to inflict a serious defeat on the enemy, by taking advantage of a fault committed by the latter.

In both cases, the divisional commander makes arrangements for his forces to act on a more restricted front than that which they occupied in the defensive. He indicates, in a very precise manner, the objectives and the points to be attacked; he immediately proceeds to the attack.

Chapter V – Pursuit

Art. 116. The assault, the conquest of the terrain, is not sufficient to decide victory. Only a relentless pursuit, begun as soon as the adversary begins to bend, will finish off the enemy by breaking his last resistance and putting him in no condition to face the struggle again.

This pursuit, carried out with troops who have often already had to make considerable efforts during the battle, requires indomitable energy and extreme endurance on the part of the commanders and the executors.

While the most tested forces are designated to ensure the occupation of the conquered ground, all the rest of the division launches out on the tracks of the enemy.

The concern to maintain tactical links becomes a secondary consideration. Nor is there any consideration for the men who would remain behind. The main thing is to leave the enemy neither the time nor the means to recover, and success authorizes all boldness.

The pursuit is carried out on a wide front in order to outflank the enemy and to reach his lines of retreat.

When the infantry is out of breath, it is up to the cavalry, the cyclists and the artillery to continue the pursuit, pushing it to the extreme limit of the forces of men and horses.

Chapter VI – Retreat

Art. 117. By day, retreat under fire is always a difficult operation, because of the losses it entails and the disorganization that results.

When the enemy has made himself master of the ground defended by the division and all efforts to drive him out have failed, it is nevertheless necessary, at all costs, to stop him until nightfall.

The troops who were in contact with the enemy try to hold on by clinging to the ground and organizing summary shelters with their portable tools.

The division commander prepares the arrangements for the retreat. On the general direction indicated by the higher command, he chooses, to rally his division, an area of terrain presenting solid support points or covered by natural obstacles, cuts, woods, etc., and sufficiently distant so that contact with the enemy is broken. He established a withdrawal to an intermediate position using the first reconstituted units, which he reinforced with artillery and cavalry.

The division withdrew under the cover of night and reached

the rallying zone indicated. It then took up a marching position allowing it to move quickly.

The withdrawing troop must hold, until complete destruction if necessary, to ensure the flow of the division. In favorable circumstances, it can employ offensive procedures. It withdraws when the bulk of the division is safe from enemy attack.

Chapter VII – Particulars Relating to Combat in Various Terrain

Art. 118. Cut or covered terrain allows the approaches to be hidden from the distant action of the enemy artillery and from the enemy's view; it facilitates maneuver and surprises.

But, when the accidents of the ground have a very marked character, the overall direction of the combat is difficult to achieve for the command. The combat can even take the form of more or less separate and distinct actions.

It is then necessary that the commander of the division distribute his forces *a priori*, while keeping troops at his disposal to exploit partial successes or to deal with the unexpected. In many cases, the artillery cannot, for lack of sufficiently extensive views, support the progression of its infantry from afar; the terrain does not always allow it to be maintained under a single command. It is therefore sometimes necessary to divide it between the different attacks. The commander of an attack then has complete control of the artillery forces assigned to that attack.

In rugged terrain, it is essential to determine with the greatest care the directions, to ensure the connections and to prepare in advance the exit, beyond the various covers, of the units in combat formation.

In particular, in the woods, the maintenance of order and the respect of tactical links are of the utmost importance.

Chapter VIII – Particulars Relating to Night Combat[*]

Art. 119. Once the combat has begun, it shall be continued without interruption until a decision is obtained. If this decision is not reached before daylight, it is sought by means of night operations. Night combat thus prolongs the combat begun during the day.

Night actions can also be aimed at surprising an enemy who is poorly guarded or who is in a state of moral inferiority, at pushing back outposts, and at removing the support points necessary for subsequent operations.

The leader who prescribes a night attack determines the moment according to the situation, the state of his troops and the subsequent goal he proposes.

Sometimes, it will be in his interest to attack a strong point in the early hours of the night, so as not to give the enemy time to put it in a state of defense. But the immediate exploitation of success

---

[*] Some of the indications for night combat are applicable to combat in the woods.
Fighting in fog is very similar to night fighting, but it is always necessary to take into account the possibility that the fog may suddenly dissipate.

is then difficult, and an action of this kind can only have a limited objective, generally consisting of seizing a point of the terrain and ensuring its preservation.

In other cases, it is better to attack a little before daylight, in order to be able to exploit the success immediately. The night attack is then the prelude to an action that will take its fullest form in the early hours of the day.

A night attack is all the more delicate to lead and execute as the attacking troop is stronger. In the darkness, the number of troops loses its importance; the moral value of the troops makes up for their numerical inferiority and makes it possible to obtain important results with weak means. It is therefore in the interest of the company to limit the number of troops employed in a night operation.

On the other hand, this number of troops must be proportionate to the front to be attacked; if this front is large, the use of large forces, such as a brigade or a division, may become necessary. A general action being difficult to carry out at night, it is then advisable to organize distinct attacks, each aiming at the removal of a well determined objective and preserving a relative independence. The simultaneity of the different attacks is obtained by determining the time of departure of each of them.

In the middle of the night, only the infantry is capable of fighting. The attacking troops act straight ahead, with the bayonet. The units are kept together in the hand of their leaders, in deep or staggered formation.

If the operation is carried out towards the end of the night, the attack formation is more open. A first echelon, consisting solely of infantry, is responsible for removing the attack objectives before daylight. In the rear, temporarily reserved infantry units, artillery, and cavalry approached under cover of darkness and were ready to move in at dawn to complete and exploit the results of the night attack.

The success of a night attack depends, in large part, on the manner in which it is prepared. The preparation must, above all, seek to guarantee the secrecy of the attack and require only very simple preliminary movements.

The directions of attack are fixed, as much as possible,

according to natural landmarks visible on the ground.

It is essential to reconnoiter the terrain beforehand. This reconnaissance is, as far as possible, extended until nightfall, so that the terrain is seen under the different aspects that it presents in daylight and at night.

All measures are taken to ensure order and to avoid causes of error or confusion. Simple signals and easily distinguishable means of recognition are chosen. The watches are set. The conduct to be followed after the success of the attack, the rallying points in case of failure are indicated in a precise way.

In any night attack, surprise is sought. The approach of the troops in charge of the operation is concealed; the arrangements for the attack are made safe from any enemy intervention.

At the fixed signal or time, the attacking troops move forward, bayonet to the gun, in the greatest silence, preceded by a few patrols; the distances and intervals between the units are reduced. If the enemy uses searchlights, one lies down as soon as the light beam approaches and the march is resumed when this beam has moved away. All noise from weapons and equipment is avoided; horses are left behind.

When close to the enemy, the march is accelerated, without firing, in order to throw oneself on him with a bayonet. Each unit pushes forward until it has taken its objective.

The conquered position is quickly organized and occupied in order to stop any offensive return. Positions are pushed forward, ambushes established on the directions by which the enemy may present himself.

The different attacks are linked together by patrols.

Chapter IX – Action of the Command

Art. 120. The dispositions to be taken by the division commander in view of combat vary according to the mission assigned, the situation of the division, that of the enemy, the morale of the troops, etc.

Once the division commander has made his decision, he puts all his energy into carrying it out. He avoids going back on an order given during the battle.

His decisions must be transmitted quickly and reliably. It is essential not only that his staff be familiar with his way of seeing and doing things, but also that there be, as far as combat is concerned, unity of doctrine between him and his troops, as well as between the different arms. The efforts of the troops will be all the more concordant, all the more energetic, as the will of the leader and the goal he wants to reach will be better known by all.

From the beginning, the division commander directs the battle.

He establishes the general conditions of the engagement by an order in which he makes known the points of the terrain that the advance guard must conquer or of which it must ensure possession, the role of the division's artillery in the engagement, the zone where this artillery must establish itself, the mission of the cavalry and the engineers, the points on which the main body of the division must direct itself or eventually assemble, the location of its command post.

During the engagement, the division commander gives, if necessary, the necessary orders for the reinforcement of the vanguard by units taken from the main body of the division.

He regulates and coordinates the attacks of the main body. His order of attack determines the mission of the division, the goal he proposes, the attacks to be executed; the general direction, the zone of action and the successive objectives of each of them; the distribution of the infantry between the attacks; the mission of the artillery, possibly its positions and its distribution in view of the support it must lend to the infantry; the mission of the cavalry and the engineers; the time of the beginning of the attacks.

The orders concerning the engagement and the attacks must be given in writing.

During the battle, the division commander makes his directing action felt by the use of artillery and troops still available; he avoids, in principle, reinforcing secondary attacks in order to devote as many forces as possible to the main attack.

Once his orders have been given, he leaves the choice of means of execution to those in charge; it is his duty not to hinder the initiative of his subordinates.

In order to achieve victory, he does not hesitate to throw all his strength into the struggle.

In the event of a setback, he must hope and fight to the end; he strives, by all means, to raise the morale of his subordinates and to restore confidence.

A leader who capitulates in open country is dishonored.

The commanders of the brigades, the artillery, the cavalry and the engineers of the division, have the duty to constantly inform the division commander on the progress of the battle and the situation of the troops under their command.

The artillery commander, constantly oriented on the intentions of the division commander, gives the execution orders to all the artillery available to the division commander;[*] he determines the distribution and locations of the artillery groups on the ground and assigns them their mission. He keeps himself informed of the development of the battle and proposes, in due course, to the division commander, measures to coordinate the action of the artillery. He modifies, if necessary, the initial distribution of the batteries; he studies in advance the changes of position and prescribes them on his own initiative in case of emergency, when it is a question of a forward movement.

---

[*] Both the divisional artillery and the units of corps artillery or heavy artillery that the corps commander may have placed momentarily under the orders of the division commander, in order to give more power to the attack that is entrusted to this division.

Chapter X – Duties of the Leaders and Troops

Art. 121. The closest liaison between the different organs of command in combat is an essential guarantee of success and a necessity of the first order.

The leaders of important units, as well as of smaller forces, must keep abreast of what is happening around them, provoke orders if they do not receive them, and act at all times, not only with a view to their special mission, but in the best interest of the general public.

The leader of any troop in a waiting position has the obligation to consider in advance the various missions that may fall to him, to inform himself of the situation and to reconnoiter or have the terrain reconnoitered accordingly. In this way, he will be able, when the time comes, to get the troop he commands into action without any loss of time and under the best conditions.

In addition, the leader of any troop that marches into battle has the duty to anticipate it, as far as circumstances and the proximity of the enemy allow, in order to personally assess the situation and make arrangements with full knowledge of the facts.

In this order of ideas, the artillery reconnaissance will be, in the columns on the march, pushed forward under the protection of

Duties of the Leaders and Troops 223

the most advanced elements, in order to constantly foresee and prepare the possible entry into action of the batteries.

In the event of an unforeseen encounter with the enemy, every troop commander should strive to achieve the goal assigned to him; in general, he should attack in order to be able to continue the prescribed operation as soon as possible, or at least to try to see the situation clearly, to take prisoners and to be in a position to give useful information.

The most perfect union and an unfailing devotion to duty must characterize the relations between the different leaders. One must always march with the cannon or with the fusillade when the mission allows it. A complete solidarity must exist between the various arms.

The leaders of the infantry and cavalry units are obliged to ensure the protection of any artillery in their vicinity. When this protection is not achieved by the general disposition of the troops, the artillery receives special support.[*]

Whatever the number of troops engaged, whatever the skill of the leader's combinations, it is always necessary to march at any cost to the enemy and drive him out of his position, or, on certain points, to resist until the end and be killed on the spot.

It is the value of the troops which, in last resort, decides of the victory.

All their qualities, discipline, instruction, skill in the shooting, training in the march, maneuvering aptitude and, above all, moral qualities, are indispensable elements to ensure the success.

The morale of an untrained troop can be shaken in the first fights. It is therefore important, during peacetime, to raise the mind and heart of the soldier and to convince him that the salvation of the country will depend on his ability to virilely endure the fatigues

---

[*] The commander of an artillery support is not under the orders of the commander of this artillery. The latter gives the commander of the support all useful indications for the accomplishment of his mission, but he does not intervene in the choice of the means of execution.

The mission of a unit of infantry placed in support of artillery ceases if ordered by the authority which has constituted this support or when the artillery changes position.

and privations of war, as well as on his tenacity, his bravery and his spirit in the fire.

Before the battle, it will be necessary to remind him of all that can make us hope for victory; during the fight, we will not be afraid to point out to him in advance the perils to be run, because a foreseen danger impresses less than a surprise; we will also show him that once on the march for the assault, the best way to diminish the danger consists in approaching the enemy as soon as possible.

Officers and non-commissioned officers have the duty to work energetically to maintain discipline and to keep in their place,[*] by all means, the soldiers under their command; if necessary, they force their obedience. Finally, they must be well penetrated with the idea that their first and most beautiful mission consists in giving the example to their troops. Nowhere is the soldier more obedient and more devoted than in combat. His eyes are fixed on his leaders. Their bravery and coolness will pass into his soul and make him capable of all energies and all sacrifices.

Reports. Mention in the order and in dispatches.

Art. 122. The company, squadron and battery commanders and all the senior and general officers, up to the commander-in-chief, contribute, each in his own area, to the written report of the day. The officers report the men who have distinguished themselves; on the other hand, the soldiers who have failed in their duty are always the subject of special reports.

When a soldier appears to have deserved a special mention for his fine conduct, for having taken a flag, a gun, saved his general or his commander, or for any other act of bravery and devotion, he is the subject of a report which is transmitted to the commander in chief. The latter decides whether he should be cited in the army order, and, in addition, in the dispatches of operations; this latter mention cannot be obtained without the first having taken place.

---

[*] In particular, soldiers must never leave their places in combat to assist wounded comrades, and the recovery of the wounded is the exclusive responsibility of stretcher bearers and medical service personnel.

Duties of the Leaders and Troops 225

The report is written and signed by the superior officer or other officer under whose eyes the event took place, even when it concerns an officer without troops; it is carefully verified by the brigadier general and by the division general; these general officers record their reasoned opinion, so that it is well established that the mention in the order of the army and the mention in the bulletin, as well as the rewards which must result, were really deserved.

The dispatches contain individual praise only if all these formalities have been exactly fulfilled; the report of the day, which often has to be written and sent immediately, contains only general praise and the account of operations.

Section VI – Cavalry

Chapter I – General Role of the Cavalry

Art. 123. Apart from its tactical role in battle, the cavalry has the constant duty of informing the command.

Whether it is army cavalry in charge of exploration, or corps cavalry in charge of contributing to the safety and protection of the troops against surprises, its mission is most often summarized in providing, in a timely manner, the command to which it is subordinate with the information it requires.

In battle, the cavalry fights in combination with the other arms. It helps them and completes their action by putting at their service the speed, mobility and rapidity of attack that are its own.

It is above all, and par excellence, the weapon of surprise, and that is its main strength. By surprise, by the instantaneous violence of its attacks, it can obtain considerable and sometimes decisive results in the battle.

The increase in the power of fire gives to a daring cavalry opportunities to intervene that are more favorable and more frequent than before; but it is necessary that the cavalry desires these opportunities and that it seeks them.

Chapter II – Army Cavalry

Cavalry in exploration.

Art. 124. The army cavalry is usually formed into divisions.

During periods of marching and before battle, the cavalry divisions are charged with *exploration*.

The purpose of exploration is to provide the army commander with the information he deems necessary, both to guarantee his freedom of action, and consequently the safety of the army, and to develop his maneuver plan.

The instructions given by the command to the cavalry in view of the exploration must clearly determine the goal to be attained, and, in the form of simple and precise questions, the information to be sought: they indicate, if necessary, the region where the bulk of the exploration cavalry will have to go.

The chief of this cavalry has the widest initiative in the execution of the task which falls to him. He has the duty to keep himself in constant communication with the commander of the army.

His task is simplified if he manages to gain the upper hand over the enemy cavalry. He seeks, consequently, to put this cavalry out of action, whenever his mission does not oppose it. To this end, he must always be in a position to fight, that is to say, to keep the bulk of his forces together. When the opposing cavalry has been defeated, reconnaissance is facilitated, and information can be easily transmitted to the rear.

The task of searching for the information requested by the command is entrusted to light elements, which constitute the "discovery."

Discovery includes *discovery patrols* and *officer reconnaissance*. The composition, strength and number of discovery patrols depend on the strength of the cavalry, the purpose and the circumstances. As a rule, officer reconnaissances march as long as possible with the discovery patrols, which are then responsible for supporting them, collecting them if necessary, and providing their information.

The essential role of the discovery elements is to observe. Detachments of a certain size may have to fight, but mobility is, for them as for reconnaissance, the main condition for the success of their mission.

It is important to select with the greatest care the leader of any discovery element.

The instructions to the leader of a discovery element should specify the objective to be achieved, the nature of the information to be gathered, and contain directions for the transmission of the information.

Timely delivery of information is often more difficult than collecting it. The constant concern of the leader of a discovery element must be to ensure the delivery of information by any means available to him.

Discovery is often halted by the surveillance network the enemy surrounds himself with. The bulk of the cavalry then supports the discovery, seeking to dislocate the opponent's surveillance network.

In all cases, the cavalry must indicate with precision not only the points or regions that are occupied by the enemy, but also those that are not. This last information, sometimes called negative information, is often of great importance.

Cavalry in battle.

Art. 125. The army cavalry takes part in the battle in the same way as the troops of the other arms.

Its commander receives instructions from the command that establish its role and give it its mission. Within the framework of these instructions, it must constantly look for opportunities to participate in the battle: it is especially by intervening by surprise that it will be able to obtain important results.

The army cavalry is sometimes placed on one wing, sometimes on the front, sometimes in the rear; it can be kept grouped under the direct orders of either the army commander or a corps commander; finally, it can be distributed among the army corps and, in this case, it participates in their action.

Towards the end of the battle, the role of the army cavalry becomes capital with respect to an exhausted infantry and an artillery without ammunition.

In particular, the cavalry contributes to the exploitation of the success by a relentless pursuit, to which it devotes all its forces until the last limit.

In the pursuit, the cavalry endeavors to disorganize the enemy by reaching its flanks and rear, or by acting directly against its retreating columns.

In case of failure, the cavalry sacrifices itself if necessary to protect the retreat.

Chapter III – Corps Cavalry

Art. 126. In principle, a cavalry regiment is assigned to each army corps operating within an army.

When an army corps operates in isolation, it is generally assigned a larger number of cavalry.

The mission of the corps cavalry is:

a) To provide such intelligence as the corps commander deems necessary for its safety;

b) To participate in the protection of the troops against surprises.

According to the needs of the moment, the general commanding the corps will divide the cavalry at his disposal between these two missions: he will retain, for his own safety, the free disposal of part of this cavalry, and will allocate to the divisions, for protection, the forces that he considers necessary.

Cavalry under the direct orders of the commander of the corps.

Art. 127. The commander of the corps gives the unit of the corps cavalry responsible for guaranteeing its safety a precise indication of the directions to be reconnoitred and the information to be sought.

When the army cavalry is operating in front of the front of the corps, the corps cavalry will be able to gather the necessary information from it. Its role is to link the corps to the army cavalry.

If the army cavalry has outrun the corps' front of march, or if it is too far away, the corps cavalry assumes the entire burden of intelligence gathering in the area assigned to it. It may then be necessary to have it supported by detachments of infantry and artillery, especially when the commander of the corps deems it useful to assemble the entire corps to search for important information (see Section VII, Art. 141).

But, while employing procedures similar to those of exploration, corps cavalry could not replace army cavalry in terms of the scope of operations. Its radius of action, that is, the range of its reconnaissance, can hardly exceed practically one day's march ahead of the main body of the army. This distance is sufficient to guarantee the freedom of action of the corps commander.

When the battle begins, the corps cavalry covers the deployment of the corps. When there is no more room for it in front of the infantry, it is either grouped behind the front or on one wing, or distributed among the divisions of the corps. In all cases, it continues to enlighten and inform, and seeks, by all means, to intervene usefully in the action.

Cavalry attached to the infantry divisions.

Art. 128. The commander of the corps determines the portion of the corps cavalry responsible for participating in the protection of the troops against surprises and distributes it among the infantry divisions.

The number of cavalry attached to an infantry division depends on the mission of the division, its place in the corps, and the terrain; it must never be less than one platoon; in certain circumstances, it may be several squadrons, especially when the commander of the corps, during the course of the battle, has assigned to the infantry divisions all or part of the cavalry which he had previously retained at his disposal.

The cavalry thus temporarily attached to an infantry division is generally designated as *divisional cavalry*: it is not organically part of the division.

In principle, in the forward march, the divisional cavalry is in the vanguard and constitutes the vanguard point of the division: it detaches, if necessary, patrols to the rear guard and on the flanks of the column; it marches on the flank of the division if the latter is on one wing. In retreating marches, it forms the rear guard point of the division.

When a long halt is ordered, the divisional cavalry establishes posts or patrols at points favorable for observation.

At the end of the march, it covers the establishment of outposts and complies with the requirements of Article 94 of the section "Security."

Since the divisional cavalry service is very busy, it is important to give most of this cavalry the rest it needs: for this purpose, it is generally quartered in the shelter of the infantry outposts.

When intelligence indicates that an action is imminent, the divisional cavalry commander multiplies reconnaissance to inform the division commander of the enemy's movements and situation in the division's zone of action. During the battle, he makes sure that the divisional general is informed in time of what is happening, not only in the direction where the battle is engaged, but also on the flanks and in the rear; he constantly looks for the opportunity to intervene usefully in the action, in close liaison with the infantry, which he must at all times enlighten and support.

Cavalry of a detachment.

Art. 129. The safety of a detachment composed of troops of all arms requires the functioning of all the organs destined to ensure the freedom of action of the commander and the protection of the troops.

The division of the cavalry into two groups assigned respectively to each of these two missions is made by the commander of the detachment.

The group designated to contribute to the protection of the detachment operates like divisional cavalry; the group assigned to ensure the freedom of action of the leader operates, all things considered, like corps cavalry. The distance at which it illuminates depends on the instructions of the detachment commander.

When the number of cavalry does not allow it to be divided into two groups, the single group is assigned to the protection of the column: the mission of searching for distant information is then entrusted to reconnaissance units directed, if necessary, by officers mounted in other arms.

Chapter IV – Particulars Concerning the Safety of a Cavalry Troop Operating in Isolation on the March and on Station

Art 130. The principles concerning security set forth in Chapter IV are applicable to any cavalry troop operating in isolation, whatever the role, situation and strength of the troop. On station as well as on the march, the leader has the duty to assume:
 1. His freedom of action;
 2. The protection of his troop.

The leader's freedom of action is guaranteed by the information sought far enough away so that the leader has time to make his arrangements. On station the reconnaissance and patrols sent out for this purpose during the day are transformed, during the night, into posts intended to warn the commander of the approach of the enemy, sufficiently in advance so that the troop can, if necessary, mount its horse and leave its billet: these posts are generally placed at crossroads, road junctions, bridges, etc.

In marching, the protection of the troop is ensured by a vanguard, a rear guard and flankers.

The strength of these elements is proportionate to the number of troops they cover; it depends on the situation, the goal to be reached and the terrain.

The march of the vanguard is executed by successive jumps with a sufficient advance to carry out the reconnaissance without delaying the column.

In the same way, in a retreat, the rear guard marches by jumps, facing the enemy every time it is stopped1.

The flankers, or flank patrols, are provided either by the vanguard, or by the main body of the column: they march on the flanks, preceding the element which has detached them.

At the station, the protection of the troops is guaranteed by the arrangement of the cantonments staggered in depth, by the defensive measures taken in each cantonment, and by the surveillance1 exercised by means of posts.

These posts are placed, some near the barricades established at the exits of the cantonment, the others on the access routes through which the enemy may come. These provisions are completed by a very active patrol service.

No precise rules can be given concerning the strength to be attributed to the outposts. The column commander determines in each particular case the arrangements to be made according to the tactical situation and the terrain.

Even more than for the infantry, it is essential to assign only the minimum of necessary forces to cavalry outposts, in order to ensure that the greater part of the troop is rested, without which it would be promptly out of condition to render any service.

The cavalry is only likely to resist on the spot by making use of its fire. Consequently, when cavalry outposts have to hold against an attack, it is by fighting on foot that they fulfill their mission.

Particulars concerning the march of a cavalry column operating in isolation.

Art. 131. The march of a cavalry column is executed in a different manner, according to whether an encounter with the enemy is considered impossible, possible or probable.

When the march is executed at such a distance from the enemy that any encounter is considered impossible, one tries to facilitate the movement and to reduce fatigue. The column is set in motion at a walking pace: at 4 or 5 kilometers from the starting point, it makes a stop of a few minutes, during which the officers have the packs rectified and the horses re-groomed. Later on, the stops are subordinated to the extent of the route and can be staggered from two to two hours; there are no hourly stops.

The march is generally executed in columns of four or two: the walk and the trot are alternated, avoiding in principle the use of the trot on sloping ground; the platoons can take a distance of about ten meters between them, in order to maintain a regular pace and to avoid breaks.

At the walk, the cavalry columns make 6.5 kilometers per hour. When the walk and the trot are alternated, the speed of march varies with the nature of the road: a speed of 8 kilometers per hour is considered a normal pace for columns of any size (regiment, brigade, division). If one walks constantly at a trot, one covers 10 kilometers in about forty minutes: this speed is difficult to achieve for strong columns.

When an encounter with the enemy is possible, one marches by four, the platoons close together, the squadrons alone keep a short distance between them to avoid jolts. If the width of the road allows it, one can also march in column of platoons; but this formation, which decreases the depth of the column, is, in general, very tiring because of the tightening that occurs and the lengthening that results.

Near the enemy, the cavalry leaves the roads and marches across the fields in an approach formation; this disposition is only taken as late as possible, because of the fatigue it imposes and the decrease in speed it entails.

In forced marches, i.e. during very long routes, the average speed of cavalry columns must be reduced. The number and extent of trotting times are reduced and, if the length of the route requires a rest, it is extended for at least five hours.

The battle trains are kept behind the main body. In principle, the hand horses march with the battle trains; they can be intercalated as needed between the various elements of the column. The regimental trains always form a separate column.

Chapter V – The Cavalry Division

Marches far from the enemy.

Art. 132. As long as it is far from the enemy, the division marches on the road in one or several columns.

The march in one column ensures the rapid concentration of forces; the march in several columns facilitates the movement.

The cycling infantry marches, as much as possible, outside the cavalry columns; but it is always necessary to ensure its protection.

When the enemy is signaled, the division passes to the approach march.

Approach march.

Art. 133. The approach maneuver begins from afar; in practice, it is begun as soon as an encounter with the enemy cavalry is deemed likely to occur that very day.[*]

---

[*] Two cavalry divisions 30 kilometers apart can approach each other in less than two hours, and intelligence, even if transmitted under the best conditions, gains little time on the cavalry it announces.

The Cavalry Division

The division uses the roads as long as possible, provided that the situation requires it, and that it switches to the cross-country march, which often alternates with the road march, in the case of the passage of defiles.

The approach formation depends on the use that the commander intends to make of his division, the proximity of the enemy and the terrain; it can be modified during the approach maneuver and must be able to be transformed rapidly into a combat formation.

The division marches together, that is to say that all its elements must be able to participate in the same overall action; for this purpose, it is articulated in depth or in width, so as to be ready to pass instantaneously to the attack: during the stops, the articulated gatherings, covered by the vanguard or the security elements, are hidden from view; they must have wide and easy approaches.

The purpose of the approach march is to transport the division from one favorable terrain to another: it is executed by leaps from plateau to plateau and from ridge to ridge; it generally includes a succession of passes through defiles. The division does not enter a defile until its exit is assured: it crossed the defiles at a rapid pace.

The leader's skill consists in taking the initiative of the attack, in keeping the advantage of the terrain, or, at least, in never letting the division be surprised in an unfavorable situation.

Vanguard. The division is covered and illuminated by a vanguard.

The vanguard is more or less strongly constituted according to the role it has to fulfill: it is generally joined by the cycling group, possibly by machine guns and by artillery.

Its mission is to search the terrain, to make contact with the enemy, to push back his advanced parties and to mask, if necessary, the maneuver of the main body.

During certain periods of the approach, the role of the advance guard takes on a particular importance. In front of the successive defiles, it forms the bridgeheads under the shelter of which the division crosses and exits the defiles. The considerable offensive strength given to it by the addition of the rifles of the cycling group allows it, if it finds the strong points it must hold already occupied, to attack them resolutely and take them.

At the moment of the encounter, the vanguard returns to the division's combat system; the safety mission it was fulfilling is then entrusted to a few light elements, scout platoons or combat patrols. Sometimes the vanguard may be given a specific combat mission while the division extends its maneuver around it.

Combat Discovery. In addition to the long-range discovery, the divisional general sends officer reconnaissance to the enemy from the beginning of the approach to determine his situation and direction of march. This is the *combat discovery*. The leader, who is oriented the fastest on the enemy cavalry, can be the first to give his approach the speed and decision necessary to arrive on his adversary, before the latter has had time to make his own arrangements for attack.

But, to be informed quickly, one must go ahead of the information and not wait for it; to act quickly, one must make his decision without trying to know everything.

The purpose of the combat discovery is to enlighten and orient the divisional general until the moment when, the division being close to the probable battlefield, the general goes ahead of it with the commanders of the brigades, the artillery, and the cycling group, and gives his attack orders according to what he sees of the enemy and the terrain.

Combat against other cavalry.

Art. 134. Cavalry combat is decided in the melee with saber and lance point.

The charge is only the means of arriving at the melee, by imposing hand-to-hand combat on the adversary, and by throwing, by the brutality of the shock, disorder into his ranks. It is all the more powerful that the squadrons have, at the time of the boarding, more speed and more cohesion, which excludes any complicated movement.

The Cavalry Division

Cavalry combat generally includes a main attack that the other attacks are intended to facilitate or support.

The orders of the division general indicate the objective of the main attack, the troops who are to execute the attack, and the role of other units in the division, particularly the artillery and the cycling group. The best chance of success lies in surprise, which ensures the priority of the attack.

The best chance of success lies in surprise, which ensures the priority of the attack. Surprise is achieved by a maneuver based primarily on the speed of the approach and the judicious use of the terrain.

If the surprise succeeds, one has on the enemy not only the moral superiority of the offensive, but also the tactical advantage given by the priority of the combat dispositions: the main attack is then launched right on the mass of the enemy.

Against an informed opponent ready for combat, the maneuver requires in addition a combination of attacks aiming at either the envelopment of the enemy cavalry, or the envelopment or the crushing of a part of his formation.

When envelopment is sought, the battle array is wide open: the main attack is directed at the point in the enemy's array chosen by the commander; the battle groups in charge of the other attacks use the terrain to conceal their approach and converge on the enemy by narrowing their intervals.

If the enveloping maneuver on both wings of the enemy seems to lead to too great an extension of the front of attack, efforts can be concentrated on one wing only, or on a part of the enemy's position judged particularly vulnerable.

It is then necessary to fix the other enemy forces by secondary attacks, or to contain them momentarily by the fire of the cycling group, the machine guns and the artillery. The essential thing, in fact, if one cannot be the strongest everywhere, is to be the strongest for a given time on a given point.

Whatever the form of the maneuver, the main attack must be covered by echelons on its wings, and followed by supporting squadrons. The mission of the echelons is to attack the enemy forces that would threaten the wing they are guarding; if they have nothing in front of them, they fall back on the enemy's wings. The role of the support squadrons was to fill any gaps that might occur in the line of attack or to flank any enemy forces that crossed it: their presence alone constituted an important moral support for this line.

The divisional general could, depending on the circumstances, either lead the main attack himself, or keep at his disposal a certain number of squadrons, with which he would intervene personally. *But any conception which would not ensure the participation of the totality of the forces of the division in the attack must be absolutely rejected.*

All the swords and lances of the division must be at the melee, because it is there alone that the cavalry combat will be decided.

A cavalry that attacks another must always propose to destroy it: it has no other way of doing so than to penetrate the ranks of the latter and to cut down by the edge the cavalrymen who compose it, beginning with the officers; success is no longer in doubt from the moment when there is no longer any command on the opposing side.

No officer or rider should remain outside the melee. No officer or cavalryman should leave the melee as long as there is an enemy on horseback.

Use of the cavalry division against troops of all arms.

Art. 135. A cavalry division may have to attack troops of all arms, either in battle, or when it receives a mission to support reconnaissance, to force a passage, to slow down a column, etc.

When enemy cavalry is not to be feared, the division is largely organized into battle groups.

The division must be split into combat groups out of sight of the enemy. Each group moves against its assigned objective and makes its attack according to the enemy's situation, circumstances and terrain. The role of the division general is to coordinate the action of the combat groups in view of the objective to be achieved.

The attack on horseback is the most effective mode of combat against surprised or demoralized troops.

The Cavalry Division

An attack by fire involving the action on foot of numerous squadrons can only be considered if the opposing cavalry is in no condition to intervene in force.

If an enemy cavalry attack is to be feared, the division uses the fire of its artillery and cyclists: the commander keeps the bulk of his cavalry together.

When a cavalry division is given the mission of stopping or slowing down a marching column, it strives to give the enemy the illusion that he is not dealing with cavalry alone. The leader combines the action of the combat groups by attacking the column at the head and on the flanks, so as to slow down its speed of march and force it to multiply its security detachments. Most often, the cycling group is kept on the marching road and attacks the vanguard by blocking its path, while the cavalry and artillery units move to the flanks. The division renewed its ventures whenever it could exploit other favorable opportunities.

In all cases, cavalry action against intact infantry troops is likely to result in considerable losses for the cavalry: it must therefore be ordered by the command only with good reason.

Section VII – Detachments

Composition and mission of detachments.

Art. 136. The formation of a detachment must respond to a well-defined need.

The mission given to the detachment is either an action subordinate to that of a large unit (security detachments, cover groups, etc.), or an independent operation.

The composition and strength of a detachment is determined by the role it is to perform.

A detachment always includes cavalry. This last weapon, even if it is in small quantities, is indispensable to enable the detachment to light its way. (See Art. 129.)

Artillery is only assigned to a detachment if the number of infantry or cavalry reaches one regiment. In each case, it must be assessed whether the advantages of the presence of artillery outweigh the disadvantages of its protection.

Command of detachments.

Art. 137. The commander of a detachment is always designated by the authority ordering its formation.

A detachment composed of forces taken from different corps of troops must, as far as possible, be commanded by an officer superior in rank to the leaders of these forces.

Detachment commanders have the same authority as corps commanders for the policing, discipline and service of the troops under their command.

Conduct of a detachment.

Art 138. The conduct of a detachment depends, above all, on the mission received.

The leader of the detachment avoids dispersing his forces. He shall keep all his troops grouped together for the execution of his mission and shall use only the indispensable elements for his safety.

The artillery is kept at a sufficient distance behind the first elements of the column or formation. In the immediate vicinity of the enemy, it moves by leaps and bounds, if necessary, to avoid falling, in column of road, under the fire of the enemy batteries. In combat, it is, as much as possible, provided with support.

Security detachments.

Art. 139. The role and mode of action of the vanguards, rearguards and flank-guards in the march, the stationing and the combat of the division have been specified in sections IV and V.

The other security detachments, especially those operating on behalf of units superior to the division, always receive a well-defined mission.

When they have to fight, these detachments conform to the instructions given for the division's combat. In the event that they are ordered to delay the enemy, they operate as stated in article 140 below.

Detachments in charge of delaying the enemy.

Art. 140. A detachment may be given the mission of delaying a superior enemy, that is to say, of preventing him from crossing a certain line before a certain time.

In order to accomplish this mission, the offensive is justified, when circumstances require it. Boldness is then the best guarantee of success.

Generally, the detachment resorts to the defensive or to maneuver in retreat.

The defensive maneuver is the rule, when the area available to the detachment for its resistance is shallow or when the terrain presents favorable breaks.

The retreating maneuver is used when the detachment is operating in a relatively deep area.

It consists of holding, for a limited time, on successive positions and each time with only a fraction of the forces. The enemy is thus forced to initiate several deployments, or to march across fields, and, consequently, to lose time. The detachment maneuvering in retreat aims especially for long distance fire. Successive units withdraw before they are encircled by the enemy, because retreating under fire, in daylight and in open terrain, would lead to the rapid disorganization of the troop.

The maneuver in retreat is only possible for small detachments. It is in the interest of lightening the infantry troops who are charged with a mission of this nature.

This form of combat is particularly applicable to covering groups.

In the defense, as in the maneuver in retreat, the detachment must be particularly concerned with protecting its flanks.

Cavalry Support Detachment.

Art. 141. Detachments attached as support to a cavalry troop under the conditions of article 127 are placed under the authority of the cavalry commander, who gives them his instructions. He employs them either to support his attacks or to ensure his withdrawal.

When stationed, the infantry of the detachment may cooperate in the safety of the cavalry.

Generally speaking, it is necessary to abstain from asking the infantry, supporting the cavalry, for excessive efforts, which would have the result of ruining it and putting it out of state to fulfill its role.

Under certain circumstances, the higher command may have to form detachments charged, if necessary, with collecting the cavalry. If he does not place them under the orders of the cavalry commander, he himself determines their mission.

Detachments in charge of an independent operation.

Art. 142. The minor operations (removal of a post, surprise of a convoy, of a staging post, destruction, requisitions, etc.), require a complete preparation and the most absolute secrecy in the execution.

The authority that prescribes the operation gives the commander of the detachment very precise written instructions on the mission to be carried out.

The commander of the detachment studies in advance, according to the instructions he has received, the operation entrusted to him, and prepares its execution. He communicates, before departure, to the one who would have the command after him, the instructions, orders and information he has received.

During the march, the commander of the detachment takes all necessary precautions to hide his presence from the enemy. He shall turn away from towns, villages and main roads. If he is forced to cross inhabited places, he has them carefully searched; if he has to stay there, he takes, if necessary, the notables of the locality as hostages; he establishes small posts and lookouts to prevent the inhabitants from communicating outside.

When he has to fight, he entrusts each part of his troop with a precise mission, for example, to remove the small posts or sentries, to cut the lines of the carriages, to deliver the prisoners, etc. He designates a rallying point and a line of retreat that all the men must know.

For the attack, he acts suddenly and with the utmost energy.

The retreat is ordered as soon as the result is obtained.

On the return of the detachment, the commander reports to the authority who ordered the formation of the detachment.

To attack a troop on the march, if possible, a terrain where the enemy would have difficulty deploying, for example a defile, is chosen.

To attack a convoy, the detachment commander takes the enemy escort as his objective, in order to disperse it and then seize the convoy. He can also immediately seek to destroy the convoy, by simply protecting himself against the action of the escort.

In the force in charge of attacking automobiles, some men seek to cut the lines, others move on the first and last cars of the convoy to put them in the way.

The commander of a detachment whose mission is to execute, in enemy country, a requisition, a forage, a destruction, etc., generally divides his troop into two parts. One, the weaker one, stays in the immediate vicinity of the locality, occupies the exits and carries out the operation. The other, the stronger one, protects the operation.

Conduct and protection of convoys.

Art. 143. Any convoy whose security is not ensured by the presence of neighboring troops, shall receive an escort.

The convoy and its escort then constitute a single detachment, the leader of which is designated by the authority that orders the formation of this detachment (Art. 137).

The strength and composition of the escort are calculated according to the nature of the convoy, its size, the dangers it may face, the nature of the country to be crossed, the length of the journey, etc.

The officers, civil servants and employees of all kinds, who march with the convoy, exercise their functions under the superior authority of the commander of the detachment.

The latter has at his disposal, in the interest of the service, all the soldiers present who are equal to or inferior to him in rank.

When a convoy is large, it is essential to divide it into several subdivisions. A special guard is assigned to each of them, and, if there are requisition cars in the convoy, soldiers are distributed from distance to distance to watch the drivers.

The march of a convoy is regulated according to the proximity of the enemy, the nature of the place and the state of the roads.

The leader of the detachment is given, on these different points, very detailed information, whose accuracy he has to verify.

He generally divides the escort into two parts. One, the weaker one, is assigned to the guard of the cars, and to the immediate protection of the convoy. It is split accordingly. The bulk of the escort marches, concentrated under the direct orders of the detachment commander, on the side most exposed to enemy attacks.

The convoys rarely make a long stop, and only in places recognized in advance and favorable to their defense.

In case of an attack, if the convoy is unable to continue its route, the commander will park it. The park is formed outside the road, in a square, with the rear wheels facing outwards.

If it is not possible to leave the road, the cars double the rows; each car clamps on the previous ones, the tiller, placed inside the road and obliquely; the drivers put their feet on the ground and place themselves at the head of their horses.

The escorting of prisoners of war requires special vigilance and a lot of firmness.

The officer in charge of driving prisoners of war forms them into a column, having them go ahead, follows and accompanies this column, which marches in close order. He forbids any conversation between the men of the escort and the prisoners, and prevents the latter from communicating with the inhabitants.

At the start, the escort loads its weapons in the presence of the prisoners, who are warned that any attempt at resistance or refusal to obey would be suppressed by the weapons with the utmost severity.

To quarter the prisoners, one chooses localities containing large buildings where the prisoners can be easily guarded and which are always illuminated. Only one door remains open and a guard is established there.

In case of an attack on the march, the prisoners are made to lie down; part of the escort, in charge of their immediate guard, remains close to them and fires on anyone who gets up before being ordered to do so; the rest of the escort maneuvers to repel the enemy.

Section VIII – Fieldworks

Generalities.

Art. 144. The purpose of fieldworks is:
1. To facilitate the progression of troops;
2. To increase, in combat, the strength of resistance of a unit momentarily obliged to stop;
3. To allow a troop, placed on the defensive, to take full advantage of the terrain.

The creation and improvement of communications make possible, in all circumstances, the movement of troops, and favor maneuver.

In the offensive, conquered terrain must never be abandoned. Any unit that has advanced under fire, or that has seized a strong point, is obliged, if it cannot push further, to hold on to the ground by exploiting and increasing, by all means, the protection offered by the terrain.

In the defense, the organization of well-chosen strongpoints can allow the enemy to be contained with inferior forces. The choice of these support points must correspond to the tactical situation and the intentions of the command.

Fieldworks in the offensive.

Art. 145. In the offensive, the best guarantees against the effects of fire, for the skirmishers as well as for the reinforcements, are the rapidity of the forward movement, the use of sufficiently flexible formations and the use of defile routes.

But a troop marching forward is sometimes obliged to stop under fire. It then makes the most of the protection offered by the terrain. It uses the natural shelters and improves them, if necessary, to be able to make a more effective use of its weapons, and, eventually, to ensure a more complete protection.

In open terrain, a line of skirmishers, which can no longer advance, clings to the ground with the determination not to give up the ground. It shelters itself by creating, if necessary, a protective cover in the ground. These first works are perfected by the reinforcements and the available units that come successively to occupy them. When a troop is forced to remain in place during the night, it takes advantage of the darkness to reinforce the structures it has begun.

Sometimes, the attacking troop, having taken advantage of the night to get closer to the objective to be taken, ensures the possession of the ground gained by entrenching itself there.

Any support point conquered during the fight is immediately entrenched and occupied, so as to be able to offer serious resistance to counter-attacks. Generally, this work is carried out by the very troops who have taken the strongpoint.

During the attack, passages are opened through the obstacles that hinder the forward march. The infantry and the artillery carry out themselves all the minor works that concern their own movement. The engineers carry out the more important works. During the approach march, they build bridges over rivers, lay tracks, create crossing points for vehicles, destroy obstacles, etc. Before the assault, they open breaches in the defenses that cover the strong points to be removed.

For this purpose, engineering units are placed at the head of the attacking troops.

Fieldwork in the defense.

Art. 146. The positions to be defended, the centers of resistance and the strongpoints to be occupied are determined by the command according to the mission to be accomplished. The organization of a strongpoint is regulated by the officer designated as commander of the strongpoint.

All work must be continuous, so that at any time, if the enemy attacks, the strongpoint can be effectively defended.

An infantry fire line must have a good field of fire up to the medium combat distances (800 to 1,000 meters). It should also be very inconspicuous and, if possible, shielded from enemy artillery fire.

The aim is to make the most of existing shelters, by arranging them judiciously. Efforts are made to reduce the visibility of the trenches. The use of false trenches to deceive the enemy may be indicated in certain cases.

One should avoid occupying the edges of localities or woods that are exposed to enemy artillery fire. On the other hand, a point that the enemy artillery cannot reach constitutes a very strong support point.

The batteries are protected by more or less substantial works. If necessary, they are completely buried.

The reinforcements placed near the line of fire are also covered by shelters.

The troops themselves entrench the terrain they have to defend.

Engineering units are normally used to open communications, or to create important structures (methodical defense of villages and woods, construction of high profile works, installation of passive obstacles, etc.).

As a rule, engineer troops work in units that do not go below the section level.

Tools.

Art. 147. The portable tools of the infantry and engineers and the tools placed on the artillery carriages are used by the very troops to which they belong.

The tools of the combat train of the infantry regiments are placed, at the moment of need, and according to the orders of the commanders of the corps, at the disposal of the battalions or companies which have to execute important works.

In principle, the sapper-miners' cars of the combat train of the engineer company remain at the exclusive disposal of this company.

The tools carried by the tool extensions of the engineer depot company of the army corps, are placed at the disposal of the troops, according to the orders of the corps commander. In the absence of orders, the commander of the engineer depot company issues, when a division commander directly requests it, tool extensions, up to three per division. On the battlefield, in case of emergency, the extensions of the depot company will issue tools to any troop that requests them.

Requisitions in the villages provided tools, but in limited numbers. On the other hand, the troops will often be able to find in the localities precious resources of materials for certain works (plows, harrows, wood, iron, etc.).

Section IX – Operation of the Aeronautical service and the Telegraphic Service

Chapter I – Aeronautical Service

Aerial reconnaissance.

Art. 148. The aeronautical service is an army service.

In each army, the Chief of Staff defines and assigns missions.

These must be given in writing and in a precise form. Members of the unit retain all initiative regarding the choice of execution methods.

The transmission of reports from the landing grounds to the headquarters or command post is handled by the staff using the resources available to them. It generally includes a car service and a telegraphic or telephone link.

Movement of squadrons. Landing grounds.

Art. 149. The squadrons move by leaps and bounds of varying amplitude.

Landing fields are, as far as possible, established in the evening for the following day, so that aircraft leaving at dawn can, on their return, land on the new field.

When it is necessary to establish a new landing field, the Chief of Staff of the Army will indicate to the Director of the Aeronautical service the area where this field must be located. The Director of Aviation shall conduct reconnaissance and make all necessary arrangements. He shall exercise command over the landing field; he shall in particular have under his command the troops and gendarmerie detachments designated to ensure the police and general surveillance of this field.

When it is necessary to guarantee the protection of the landing ground, the head of the detachment designated for this purpose receives instructions concerning his mission from the Chief of the Army Staff. He will obtain information from the Director of Aviation on the conditions to be met in order to carry out the mission, but will remain responsible for the measures to be taken. He reports in a timely manner to the Director of the Aviation Department, events that may affect the safety of the squadrons.

It is strictly forbidden for any troop or detachment to cross a landing field.

Assistance to be given to aeronauts and airmen.

Art. 150. All troops must render assistance to airmen and airwomen who land or are in distress in their vicinity.

They must also ensure the transmission of the information they report.

Chapter II – Telegraphic Service

General rules concerning the establishment of telegraphic and telephone networks.

Art. 151. Each army, army corps, cavalry corps or division has at its disposal the lines existing in its zone of action, with the exception of those reserved by the superior unit and those of the specialized railway network.

In the organization of its network, a unit is required to:

1. Connect to the network of the superior unit, in a point fixed by the latter;

2. Push its lines as close as possible to the subordinate units and detachments, and to fix the points where these will come to connect;

3. Establish all useful internal communications.

Army telegraph and telephone network.

Art. 152. The army network is subdivided into: *the forward network*, organized and operated by the first line service, and *the* *network of the staging area*, organized and operated by the second line service. The second line technical section can, in case of insufficient means of action of the first line service, be called to participate in the latter service.

The connection of the front line network with the staging area network is made at the *junction station*, the location of which is determined by the army commander.

The army network connects with the army group network at the *connection point* set by the rear director.

The forward network connects the army *quartermaster general's station* with the junction station and the *army stations*. The latter are intended to ensure liaison with the army corps and the intelligence bodies directly dependent on the army.

The organization of the forward network is regulated by the army chief of staff, who determines the locations of the army posts and informs each corps commander of the army post by which he will be served, as well as the parts of the existing network to be reserved for the needs of the army.

The network of the staging area connects the *post of the staging and service directorate* to the junction post, to the various elements of the staging service and to the organs of the army's communication line.

Its organization is regulated by the chief of staff of the director of stages and services.

Army radio-telegraphic network.

Art. 153. In the army, radiotelegraphy is intended to supplement wire communications, whenever they are not assured, particularly during their installation, and, if necessary, to double these communications.

The Chief of Staff of the army indicates, each day, the communications to be ensured, the number of posts necessary for each link and the authorities to which the posts will be detached.

The radiotelegraph sets are at the disposal of the authority to which they are detached to the exclusion of any subordinate authority.

The assignment of the posts is temporary. The authority which has them at its disposal shall ensure their custody and, if necessary, give orders for their removal.

Army optical network.

Art. 154. The army chief of staff determines the optical communications to be established by means of the resources of the telegraph company and the telegraph detachments of subordinate units. He informs the corps chiefs of staff of the optical stations to be established and serviced by them.

Corps Telegraphic Service.

Art. 155. The essential purpose of this service is to ensure communications between the corps headquarters and the designated army post.

In addition, stations may be organized to establish communication between the headquarters and the command post and to connect the corps commander with certain elements (divisions, cavalry, outposts, depots, convoys, etc.). These elements are connected to the corps posts by couriers, cyclists or orderlies.

The wire connection with the neighboring corps is, in principle, done through the army network.

In addition, the telegraphic detachment of the army corps establishes the optical stations set by the army chief of staff, as well as those whose creation is ordered by the army corps chief of staff.

Telegraphic service of a cavalry division.

Art. 156. The purpose of this service is to connect the cavalry division to an army post, in order to ensure rapid communications with the army commander. In execution, it operates in accordance with the rules established for the light telegraphy service in the cavalry troops.

Radiotelegraph stations are, as far as possible, detached to the large cavalry units.

Prescriptions concerning the use of telegraphic communications.

Art. 157. The telegraphic network must include only essential communications.

In principle, communications are used only by the authorities designated by the army commanders for the army network, and by the army corps commanders for the army corps networks. However, the intelligence organs may use at any time the offices or posts of any kind within their reach. The same applies to troops in combat.

The use of telegraphy must be reserved only for cases where such use presents a real advantage.

Telegrams and radiograms must be as concise as possible.

As soon as a post is set up, its chief reports to the authority designated to use the post. The latter will provide the necessary messengers for the transport of dispatches. The same applies when an authority uses a civilian office.

All telegrams must be given to the postmaster, written and signed by the authority sending it. It is forbidden for the telegrapher to write a telegram under dictation. Only the technical personnel of the military telegraphy has the right to transmit communications.

Telephone transmissions are made either in the form of telephoned messages or in the form of conversation between officers.

Construction of lines.

Art. 158. Telegraphic detachments have the right to cut and double the lines when their service requires it.

The troops are required to take, in all circumstances, the

necessary precautions to avoid the deterioration of the lines.

It is forbidden, especially for the personnel of the telephone workshops of the troops, to try to disrupt the communications, exchanged on the lines, by establishing devices in parallel.

Section X – Trains, Depots and Convoys

Generalities concerning the organization and the use of trains, depots and convoys.

Art. 159. The ammunition, foodstuffs and material which the troops need to fight and to subsist are transported by the combat trains, the regimental trains, the depots and the convoys.

The ammunition and material useful on the battlefield are distributed between the corps combat train, the division and corps combat train, the artillery depot and the engineer depot.

Food is carried by the regimental trains of the corps and headquarters as well as by the convoys.

The combat trains and the regimental trains of the troops, the regimental trains of the headquarters, the depots and the convoys each have a commander designated by the specific regulations of the various arms and services.

In the division and the army corps, the combat train generally includes constituted elements (ambulances, artillery depot echelons, etc.) belonging to different services.

In the same way, artillery or engineer depot elements, convoy elements, medical formations, etc., may be called upon to follow each other on the same route, or to station themselves in the same area.

In order to ensure order, discipline and the transmission of the command's instructions, it is essential to group together, for the march and stationing, the various elements thus temporarily united. These groups are placed under the orders of leaders designated, in principle, by the commander of the army corps.

The operational orders determine, according to the situation and the urgency of the needs to be met, the composition of each group, its place in the general set-up, as well as the place of the group leader.

The authority of the leader of a group over the elements constituting this group ceases when these elements receive instructions to go into action. From that moment on, they resume their autonomy to move to the point where they are to be employed.

Command orders and technical instructions are addressed directly to the group leaders, who regulate the splitting, marching and stationing of their group accordingly. Group commanders are responsible for protection, order and discipline, both on the march and at the station, but have no influence on the service and internal administration of the units. Their powers are the same as those of the detachment commanders.

In principle, the decisions of the command concerning the use of the different organs of the trains, depots and convoys, are taken on the proposal of the heads of service concerned. They are supplemented by technical instructions.

The commander of an element not attached to a grouping shall receive directly, through the command, the orders and technical instructions that concern him.

Discipline of trains, depots and convoys.

Art. 160. The regularity of the operation of supplies and the orderly movement of trains, depots and convoys have a considerable influence on the morale of the troops. The command, at all levels, has the duty to take the most severe measures to ensure absolute discipline in all formations that follow the columns.

The number of cars entering into the composition of trains, depots and convoys, must be exactly maintained within the regulatory limits. The military authorities, at all levels of the hierarchy, frequently ensure this.

The cars cannot receive other objects than those included in their regular load, nor carry more weight than that for which they were built. It is forbidden to allow any man to ride in them without the authorization of the corps commander or the commander of the column.

Combat trains of the troops.

Art. 161. During marches to the enemy, each combat train immediately follows the corps to which it belongs.

In combat, the combat trains keep close to their corps, but at a sufficient distance so as not to be exposed to fire directed at the line of combat. They use the shelters offered by the terrain. According to the orders of the corps commander, they are gathered in a single group, or divided into several forces.

Regimental trains.

Art. 162. The regimental trains follow the movement of the columns, at a place as close to their corps as the situation allows.

Insofar as the distance from the enemy and the conditions of the march lend themselves to it, the regimental trains or a more or less important element of these trains immediately accompany the corps and march with their combat trains.

The cars that do not accompany the troops are formed, under the orders of a designated officer, into groups corresponding to the marching columns.

As long as an encounter is not likely, these groups march behind the rear-guards of the combat columns. At the end of the march, the cars join their corps and station with it.

When the encounter is imminent, and during the battle, the regimental trains are kept far enough back so as not to interfere with the movements of the troops, the battle trains and the depots.

As a rule, they are then split into two echelons, one of which, comprising the cars immediately needed by the troops, forms an advanced echelon that is pushed in the wake of the corps.

As the troops progress, the command gives orders for these two echelons of the regimental trains to be directed to closer locations.

For the night, part of the regimental trains, distribution sections, meat cars, rolling kitchens, etc. join the troops. Once the distributions have been made, these cars are billeted with their corps or are brought back to the rear.

The supply sections of the regimental trains are formed each day by groups which correspond respectively to a station or a supply center. They meet at fixed points, under the orders of a designated officer or, failing that, the most senior supply officer, and are directed to the station or supply center where they are to be loaded. According to the orders given, they then join special billets, their regimental trains or their corps.

In any column, regimental trains are staggered in the same order as the units to which they belong.

In principle, the regimental trains are guarded by the troops who belong to the regimental trains. An escort is given to them only if the situation and the distance of the troops make it absolutely necessary.

Groups constituted with the combat trains of the divisions and the corps, the depots and the convoys.

Art. 163. On the march, the combat trains of the divisions and of the corps are placed at the tail of the combat columns, but before the rear guards.

The groups formed with the depots and convoys follow at a variable distance according to the situation and the distance from the enemy, but always sufficient to ensure the regularity of their march.

When combat begins, the command sends instructions to the leaders of these groups, as well as to the leaders of the combat trains, for the use of the ammunition sections, the medical units and, if necessary, the engineer depot and the bridge crew. These instructions prescribe the dispatch of these elements to suitably chosen points; they may also fix points where each group will go to be dispersed. The service chiefs take charge of the groups placed at their disposal and ensure the technical functioning of the services, in accordance with the instructions of the command.

As long as their use is not foreseen, the convoys march far enough back so as not to hinder the movements of the columns.

When the necessity of using their supplies is anticipated, the administrative convoy sections are staggered so as to be able, in due course, to make contact with the supply sections of the regimental trains and to avoid any backward movement by the latter.

Mobile reassembly depot.

Art. 164. The mobile remount depot is intended to provide replacement saddle, draft and pack horses for dismounted troops.

In principle, it works with a part of the convoy.

Special provisions for retreating marches.

Art. 165. In retreating marches, trains, depots and convoys precede the troops.

The combat trains of the corps, divisions and army corps march at a short distance in front of their units, conforming to their movements.

The regimental trains are clearly ahead of the columns.

The depot and convoy groupings are, in due course, pushed well forward.

Section XI – Supply and Evacuation, Requisitions

Chapter I – Generalities

Art. 166. The objective of supplies is to bring to the troops all that is necessary to enable them to subsist and to fight.

The purpose of evacuations is to bring back to the rear the personnel and material whose retention with the troops would be a hindrance.

The supplies and evacuations provide either for normal and daily needs - such as food supplies - or for momentary and eventual needs - such as ammunition supplies and evacuations of wounded after a battle.

In war, the methodical exploitation of local resources can rarely be ensured by the troops themselves; it is more particularly the responsibility of the services. The supply of troops is ensured by their combat trains and their regimental trains. These trains are in turn replenished by convoys, depots or direct shipments from the rear.

The emptied supply units are replenished at points called:

Supply stations, if the supply is carried out by rail;

Supply centers, if the supply is carried out by land.

Daily evacuations are generally carried out at stations or

supply centers. In the case of very large evacuations, especially after a battle, the number of stations and evacuation centers is increased.

The measures to be taken to ensure supplies and evacuations cannot be the subject of precise rules; they are subordinate to the situation and may not be uniform for an entire army corps. *In any case, these measures must never have the consequence of impeding the freedom of operations.*

The command has the duty to orient the services on its projects, so as to allow them to foresee in time the technical measures of execution, without being surprised by events.

He must also stagger resources in order to get them to the desired points in a timely manner, while avoiding congestion.

Chapter II – Supply of Foodstuffs

Action of the command.

Art. 167. It is the duty of the command to ensure, in the best possible conditions, the feeding of men and horses. Defective feeding is a cause of indiscipline, as men are encouraged to seek their own sustenance. It can also be the cause of serious epidemics.

In marches towards the enemy, the constant preoccupation of the command must be to push forward the resources destined for the subsistence of the troops, in order to reduce to a minimum the journeys that the necessities of supply may impose on the crews of the troops and the convoys of the army corps.

In retreating marches, trains and convoys must clear the road network and leave it at the exclusive disposal of the troops. It may then be advantageous to unload the supplies and to set up depots where the troops will refuel as they pass.

The command determines the feeding and refueling procedures to be used.

In case of *force majeure*, every corps or detachment commander has the duty to prescribe, on his own initiative, the necessary measures to ensure, in due time, the feeding of his men and horses.

Role of the quartermasters.

Art. 168. Under the authority of the command, the quartermasters direct the food supply service.

They propose all measures to be taken in order to ensure food supplies.

The quartermasters or military deputy quartermasters have authority, as far as the execution of the quartermaster's service is concerned, over all the personnel permanently or temporarily attached to their service.

Personnel in charge of the execution of the service.

Art. 169. The execution of the service is ensured by the technical personnel under the orders of the stewardship officials.

In addition, in each corps or headquarters, a supply officer is in charge of the direct daily distribution to the units or parts of this corps or headquarters. This officer contributes, if necessary and on the order of the command, to the exploitation of local resources.

Foodstuffs of different categories. [*]

Art. 170. The supplies carried into the field include:
1. The reserve supplies;
2. The supplies of the regimental trains;
3. The supplies of the administrative convoys.

The reserve supplies are carried, in part on men or horses, in part on the cars marching immediately behind the troops. They are intended to be consumed by half-day and by type of food on the

---

[*] During strategic transport and upon arrival in the concentration zone, the troops are fed with food taken from the garrisons (*food from the railways*) or distributed at the rest stops, and with food from the *landing zone*.

order of the head of the corps or detachment, when any other method of feeding is impossible. They must then be replaced as soon as possible.

The regimental trains ensure, in principle, the distribution of food to the men and horses every day. The food carried by the administrative convoys is intended to supply the regimental trains.

Each army corps is equipped with a herd of cattle which provides the troops with fresh meat.

Rations tariff.

Art. 171. The composition of rations and the number of rations to be allocated to each rank are determined by tariffs set by the Minister.

These tariffs provide for three types of rations:
The reserve food ration;
The normal ration;
The heavy ration.

The latter is allocated in circumstances where the troops have to endure a great deal of fatigue, or when the weather is very cold.

In some cases, extraordinary supplements may be collected in addition to the daily ration. In principle, these supplements are not taken from the reserve food.

The commander of an army has the authority to modify the ration rates established by the Minister, to determine the transition from one ration to another, to grant supplements to rations, to prescribe substitutions and to allocate food allowances.

The commanders of army corps and cavalry divisions, as well as the generals commanding detachments operating in isolation, have the same rights with regard to the passage from one ration to another, supplements, substitutions and representative allowances, in charge of accounting for them.

Divisional commanders have the right to prescribe substitutions and to allocate the representative allowance.

When living on the land, every corps and detachment commander has the right to prescribe substitutions.

Distributions.

Art. 172. Food intended to be consumed daily is called *daily rations.*

In principle, the daily rations are distributed each day,[*] namely: bread, small foodstuffs, oats for the whole day of the following day; meat, fodder, fuel, for the evening of the day and the morning of the following day; sleeping straw, for the same day.

The distribution of bread, small foodstuffs, oats and brandy is done by the regimental trains; fresh meat is brought in by meat cars or mobile kitchens.

Fuel, fodder and liquids other than brandy are, in principle, purchased or requisitioned on the spot by the supply officers.

If the regimental trains cannot ensure timely distribution, local resources are first used to provide the troops with as much of the day's food as possible. If this is not possible, every corps or detachment commander has the absolute duty to ensure food supplies by having the strictly necessary amount taken from the reserve food. He will immediately report on the situation in order to ensure the replacement, as soon as possible, of the foodstuffs thus consumed.

The corps or service chiefs fix the locations and times of the distributions. The supply officer drives his cars or has them assembled at the designated place. He gives to each company, squadron or battery, as well as to any detachment attached to his corps for food, the number of rations that are due to him.

The officer of the day presides over the distributions.

As far as isolated parties are concerned, the supply officer has the same attributions as the company, squadron or battery commanders.

Supply of regimental trains.

Art. 173. The loading of regimental trains must be completed

---

[*] For the cavalry, see article 178.

Supply of Foodstuffs

the day after the day of distribution, as much as possible, in the morning.

It is necessary, however, to leave the men and horses the necessary time to eat and rest.

The regimental trains are replenished, either at the supply centers by the administrative convoys of the army corps or the automobile convoys, or at the supply stations by direct shipments from the rear. They can also be replenished by means of purchases or requisitions.

The daily order of the army corps determines the location of the supply centers (generally three per corps), or makes known the supply stations. These centers or stations are chosen in such a way as to accelerate supply operations as much as possible and to reduce to a minimum the distances to be covered by the regimental trains.[*]

Whatever the method of supply employed, all movements must be regulated by the command with the greatest care.

Each corps or headquarters is represented in the supply of its regimental train by its supply officer.

A staff officer and a quartermaster are present, as far as possible, at the supply of the regimental trains. Their mission is to ensure the quality of the foodstuffs, to hear the complaints of the corps, and to act on them, if necessary. The staff officer presides over the supply operations and ensures the execution of the command's orders.

Supply of fresh meat.

Art. 174. The supply of fresh meat is generally ensured, for the entire corps, by the herd of cattle of the corps. In principle, this herd does not move. Meat cars transport the slaughtered meat from the organized *abattoirs* near the location of the herd, to the *delivery centers*, where the corps meat cars come to load.

---

[*] Regimental trains should not be required to travel more than 35 kilometers in any twenty-four hour period, and backward marches should be kept to a minimum.

In some cases, the command may direct the corps to use local live stock resources; it has the herd of cattle deliveries reduced accordingly.

Food at the local resident's.

Art. 175. The command may have the men and horses fed at the local resident's.

The food is requested by half-day or by whole day, in the form of a friendly agreement or requisition.

The composition of meals for the troops and officers, as well as the price of reimbursement, if any, shall be fixed by the command.

In determining the composition of meals, account shall be taken both of the need to give the troops food equivalent to the regulation ration and of local resources.

The right to prescribe food in the home may be delegated to corps or detachment commanders operating in isolation.

This method of feeding can normally be applied only to isolated and small detachments (correspondence posts, telegraph operators, cyclists, etc.); these receive printed orders and receipts for requisitions, as well as half-day food vouchers filled out in advance.

Instead of having the men fed directly by the local inhabitants, the command can instruct the municipalities to ensure their meals.

Special provisions for the cavalry.

Art. 176. The cavalry, especially when it operates in front of the columns, must, more than any other troop, live in the country.

It does not carry daily rations; distributions are made upon arrival at the cantonment, for the evening of the day and the morning of the following day.

In a cavalry division, the food wagons of the regimental trains are generally combined into a single group forming the division's convoy.

Supply of Foodstuffs

When local resources are insufficient, cavalry divisions are supplied from the rear. For this purpose, sections of motorized convoys can be placed at their disposal.

Chapter III – Supply of Ammunition

General provisions.

Art. 177. In the armies, it is of the utmost importance to maintain a complete supply of ammunition. The command must take the greatest care to ensure the timely replacement of consumed munitions.

On the battlefield, supplies are always provided from the rear to the front. It is up to the echelons in the rear to contact those in front.

In an army, ammunition is divided into three main echelons:

a) *Ammunition of the battle line, comprising:*

    1. Ammunition carried by the men, machine gun sections and batteries;

    2. Ammunition carried by the combat train of the troops.

b) *The ammunition of the corps depot*, divided between the infantry ammunition sections and the artillery ammunition sections constituting this depot, and intended to supply the battle line.

c) *The ammunition of the large army artillery depot*, intended to supply the artillery depots of army corps.

The corps artillery commander informs the various elements of the artillery depot of the infantry or artillery units they are to supply. Nevertheless, the ammunition sections must, in combat, and if there is an emergency, deliver ammunition to any troops placed in their vicinity.

Similarly, the commander of the artillery depot of an army corps must, unless there are major reasons, satisfy any request for ammunition, even if it emanates from a troop not belonging to the army corps.

Replacement of infantry ammunition in the line of battle.

Art. 178. *In station and on the march*, individual supplies (cartridges carried by the men) are supplied, above all, by means of cartridges withdrawn from sick or absent men, etc.; ammunition wagons are used only in case of insufficiency of the preceding resources.

The ammunition cars whose loading would be incomplete are replenished, as soon as possible, by the artillery depot.

In combat, the individual supply is first of all *increased* by means of the cartridges of the corps ammunition cars. These cartridges are distributed as soon as an engagement is imminent.

General officers may have cartridges from the ammunition cars of one corps distributed to another corps of the unit under their command.

Corps ammunition cars are not replenished during action by the artillery pool.

During the battle, the individual supply is fed, either by means of the cartridges withdrawn from the killed or wounded men, or by the artillery depot, whose different elements (sections of infantry ammunition), are brought closer and distributed according to the needs, by the command, behind the troops under fire.

In order to supply the firing line with cartridges, one takes advantage of all favorable circumstances, such as a pause in the battle, slowing down of the enemy's fire, etc.

Any sending of men or cars from the front to the rear, in order to replace ammunition, is strictly forbidden on the battlefield.

In case of emergency and in the absence of orders from higher authority, regimental or battalion commanders may transfer ammunition to another troop.

Replacement of artillery ammunition on the battle line.

Art. 179. On the battlefield, the battery group is split into two portions:
1. *The group of firing batteries*, comprising the guns and part of the shells of each battery;
2. *The group of combat echelons*, including, in particular, the rest of the shells of the batteries.

The replacement of the ammunition is done, first of all, by exchange of cars between each gun battery and its combat echelon.

The ammunition sent to the firing batteries is then replaced at the combat echelons by ammunition from the artillery ammunition sections. This supply is done by transfer, not by exchange of cars.

Provisions relating to the cavalry divisions.

Art. 180. Cavalry divisions must be supplied by any army corps from which they request ammunition, in the same way as the troops of the army corps itself.

Supply after a day of combat.

Art. 181. At the end of a day's fighting, supply operations shall continue without interruption during the night.

They are always carried out according to the same principles, that is to say from the rear to the front, by first replenishing, and, as far as possible, before daylight, the most advanced elements.

Supply of the army corps by means of the large army artillery depot.

Art. 182. The large army artillery depot is an element belonging to the rear service.

The supplies of the large depot are divided into a certain number of echelons distributed in the area of the stages and along the lines of communication.

The first echelon, known as the "road echelon," is loaded onto cars in order to ensure supplies by land.

The supply of the corps depots by the large depot is carried out either by the echelon on the road, or by convoys with mechanical or animal traction, or by means of the railroads.

Chapter IV – Evacuations

Art. 183. Evacuations must always be carried out in the shortest possible time, so as to rid the troops of everything that is likely to diminish their capacity for movement.

On the march or in station, the sick and wounded are evacuated each day according to the orders of the command, which directs them to the stations or supply centers, the wrecking yards or the hospitals.

Their transport is ensured by the automobile medical sections and, failing that, by requisitioned cars.

After the battle, the evacuation of the wounded often takes on considerable importance.

When they have been dressed, the transportable wounded are evacuated to specific stations or localities in the stage area. Those who are able to walk are transported as soon as possible to these stations or localities by detachments; the others are transported there later by motorized or animal-drawn convoys, after having received the necessary care.

The command fixes the points of assembly of the wounded, the stations or localities to which they will be directed, the means placed at the disposal of the medical service for the transport of the wounded, and the routes of the evacuation convoys.

The medical officers shall have authority over all military and civilian personnel permanently or temporarily attached to their service, as far as the execution of the medical service is concerned.

Chapter V – Requisitions

Requisitions proper.

Art. 184. The generals commanding armies, corps, divisions or detachments operating in isolation, have the authority to impose upon the populations, by means of requisition, the obligation to provide foodstuffs, materials, lodging, means of transportation and, in general, all objects or services necessary for the needs of their troops. They may delegate the right to requisition to the quartermasters, to the commanders of troops and detachments, and to the authorities of the stage service.

No requisition can be executed except by virtue of a written and signed order, emanating from a military authority having the right to requisition. Any military authority ordering a requisition is obliged to give receipt of the services provided.

The command, at all levels of the hierarchy, has the duty to ensure the maintenance of order and discipline in the execution of requisitions. Any abuse of authority and any act of plunder must be punished with the utmost rigor.

The commander-in-chief, the army and corps commanders respectively assign to each of the units under their command, the zone in which it will have the right to exercise requisitions.

In an army, the marching and stationing zones of the corps form, in principle, the zone of requisition of these large units, and this zone extends, towards the rear, to the forward limit of the staging area. In the staging area, requisitions are made under the authority of the director of the stages and services of the army.

In general, in each army corps or division, the generals entrust the quartermasters with the task of requisitioning the general supplies necessary for all the troops and services. The troops will exercise the right of requisition directly only for the satisfaction of their urgent and daily needs.

When several troops are grouped together in the same cantonment, the requisition orders are transmitted through the intermediary of the commander of the cantonment.

In all circumstances, the military authorities who have the right to requisition must not lose sight of the fact that it is advantageous, in order to retain or attract resources, to have recourse to requisition only in the absence of all other means, such as direct purchases or friendly agreements.

Requisition orders are addressed by the military authority to the municipalities or, in their absence, to local notable residents.

Requisition orders and receipts must always mention the type, quality and, if applicable, the duration of the services provided.

The orders and receipts are detached from counterfoil books, which must be provided to the officials in charge of requisitioning.

Exceptionally, any troop commander or detachment commander operating alone may, even without carrying a requisition book, request under his personal responsibility the services necessary for the daily needs of his troop. The requisition orders are then drawn up in duplicate and signed; one of these duplicates is sent, through the hierarchical channel, to the commander of the army corps, the other is given to the municipality.

If the local authorities refuse to comply with the requisition orders, the military authority has recourse to force to seize the foodstuffs and materials it needs. The strictest orders are given so that the seizures are exactly limited to the necessary services, and the detachments in charge of their execution are, as far as possible, commanded by officers.

In general, the principles and rules set forth above are applicable in enemy country as well as in national territory.

Contributions in money.

Art. 185. In certain circumstances, it may be necessary, in enemy territory, to replace the requisition of benefits in kind by contributions in money.

These contributions shall always be the subject of a written order. They can only be prescribed by the commander-in-chief or by the army commanders.

For all contributions, a receipt must be issued to the taxpayers.

Section XII – Service of the Gendarmerie in the Field

Role of the gendarmerie.

Art. 186. In the field, the gendarmerie is responsible for the judicial police, the general police and the maintenance of order in the army zone. Except in the case of absolute necessity, it provides escorts, other than those provided for, or dispatchers only on the orders of the commander-in-chief.

The gendarmerie service is organized by the army.

Relations of the gendarmerie with the command.

Art. 187. The gendarmerie detachments assigned to the different headquarters take the name of provostship. From the point of view of their service, as well as from the disciplinary point of view, they are, in principle, only responsible to their direct chiefs, to the generals to whom they are assigned, and to the chiefs of staff of the latter.

In addition, gendarmes assigned to a detachment, cantonment, stage command, etc., or in charge of the service of order in a convoy, a station, etc., are, from the point of view of police and general discipline, respectively placed under the orders of the head of the detachment, of the commander of the cantonment or of the stage, of the commander of the convoy or of the military commissioner of the station, etc.

Judicial Police.

Art. 188. The gendarmerie has a double role in the armed forces from a judicial point of view.

It searches for the perpetrators of crimes and misdemeanors and delivers them to the authority in charge of pursuing the repression.

In addition, it constitutes, outside the national territory, exceptional courts, called "provost courts," called to assist the councils of war.

Provost Marshals exercise their jurisdiction in the area occupied by the unit to which they are attached.

Any soldier or employee in the army who has knowledge of a crime or misdemeanor must immediately notify a gendarmerie officer or any other soldier in the army; he is obliged to answer categorically any questions put to him by them.

As soon as they become aware of a crime or misdemeanor, the provost marshals or gendarmerie officers, having the status of judicial police officers, begin the necessary information, in accordance with the provisions of the Code of Military Justice.

The gendarmerie officers shall search for and arrest the accused and shall take the measures prescribed by the regulations.

General police.

Art. 189. The gendarmerie must exercise incessant surveillance in the army zone, particularly with a view to preventing or repressing espionage.

In general, it ensures the execution of the regulations and orders or instructions emanating from the command. It protects the

Service of the Gendarmerie in the Field

inhabitants of the country against looting or any other violence, and removes from the army dubious individuals, whose action or even simple contact would be harmful to the country.

It brings back to their corps the soldiers it arrests, if they have only committed minor faults. When the charge brought against them is within the competence of the councils of war, it takes them to the prison of the headquarters of their unit.

It searches for deserters. For this purpose, the reports of these men must be sent by the corps and detachments as soon as possible to the provost marshal of the unit.

The gendarmerie keeps a special watch on non-military individuals in the army zone; both those attached to the army, employees, food vendors and merchants, and those who are not attached to it.

Any head of a service where non-army personnel are employed is required to declare them to the provost marshal. The Provost Marshal shall enter them in a special register.

The provost marshals have the authority to grant, after investigation, permissions and issue patents to persons requesting to practice any profession following the army. The patents are stamped by the chief of staff to whom the provost marshal reports and who issues them. The gendarmerie must have them represented frequently and ensure the identity of the individuals who hold them.

Licensed merchants and vendors are required to wear a tag on their arm with their registration number and occupation. The same information must be displayed on their vehicles.

The servants of employees, vendors or authorized merchants are required to have a certificate from the person who employs them. This certificate is valid only after it has been approved by the provost marshals and by the chief marshals. Every servant shall, in addition, wear on his arm a plate or armband on which his name and that of the person employing him are inscribed.

Prisons.

Art. 190. Prisons destined to receive soldiers of all ranks, people without confession or suspects, etc., are established in the headquarters by the care of the provosts. They are under the authority of the latter. The chief of staff is in charge of their supervision.

Role of the gendarmerie during marches and stationing.

Art. 191. The gendarmerie shall exercise surveillance in and around the area occupied by the troops. It shall see to the sanitation and the maintenance of order and shall ensure the custody of the prisoners.

To facilitate the execution of their service, the gendarmes are authorized to enter at any time, day and night, the cantonments, the bivouacs and the camps. For this purpose, they are given the password.

During the marches, the main role of the gendarmerie is to provide police protection behind the columns, by arresting marauders and bringing in stragglers.

They are particularly active in the area near the front of the stage area. The gendarmerie of the stages interrogates and gathers all the isolated persons it finds behind the army corps. It directs them to the nearest stage command, and, depending on their situation, places them at the disposal of the stage commander, or takes them to a medical facility, or, finally, keeps them in prison as deserters.

In principle, gendarmerie detachments are sent to the stations and supply centers and marched with the regimental trains, especially when these form separate columns.

Hunting is forbidden in the army zone to military personnel of any rank, as well as to persons outside the army.

The gendarmerie reports violations of this rule.

In combat, the gendarmerie ensures the police and the maintenance of order behind the troops. It sends back to their corps men who stray without a valid reason, directs those who are wounded to medical facilities, clears the roads, protects the wounded and prisoners of war and prevents looting.

Duties of the troops towards the gendarmerie.

Art. 192. The officers and men of the troops are obliged to lend a hand to the gendarmerie and to comply with its requisitions when it needs support.

Paris, December 2, 1913.
The President of the French Republic,
R. POINCARÉ

For the President of the Republic:
The Minister of War,
Eug. ETIENNE.

Appendices

Appendix No. 1 – Right to Command of Foreign Officers
Appendix to Section I.

EXCERPT from the order of February 18, 1844, on the rights to command of foreign officers.

Foreign officers may not exercise, either incumbently or provisionally, the command-in-chief of an army, or of an army corps.

They may exercise the command of a stronghold or a war post only in the absence of a French officer; if, therefore, there is one in the stronghold or post, the most senior officer in the highest rank among them, whatever that rank may be, shall perform the duties of the commander of the stronghold. The foreign officer retains command of the troops if he is superior in rank.

Foreign officers may temporarily exercise command of detachments in which troops from French regiments and troops from foreign corps are combined, but only because of superiority of rank and never according to seniority, command, in the case of equal rank, always going to the most senior French officer of that rank who is part of the detachment. As for the interim command of the constituted parts of foreign corps and the provisional command of detachments composed solely of troops of these corps, all officers belonging to them compete to exercise them, at equal rank, according to their seniority ranking and without distinction of origin.

Only officers born or naturalized French, who are given their rank in accordance with the law on promotion, are considered as French officers; French officers or naturalized French serving in a foreign capacity are assimilated in all circumstances to foreign officers and have no other rights than those enjoyed by such officers.

The preceding provisions are applicable to the indigenous corps within the limits set by the constitutive orders of these corps.

Appendix No 2 – Executive Agencies of the Services
Appendix to section 1.

I. ARTILLERY SERVICE.

The artillery service has at its disposal in each army:
In the front, the resources of the *corps artillery depots*;
In the rear, the resources of the *large army artillery depot*.

Corps artillery depot.

The corps artillery depot is normally divided into two echelons.
These echelons are interchangeable. They include artillery ammunition sections and infantry ammunition sections, constituted with containers.
The artillery depot also includes spare guns, as well as the personnel and material necessary for routine repairs.

Large army artillery depot.

The supplies of the large depot are divided into *ammunition lots* and *material reserves*.
The ammunition lots are of identical composition. They

include ammunition for 75 mm guns, small arms and machine guns.

The material reserve includes equipment, small arms ammunition and explosives.

In addition, the large stockpile includes lots of heavy artillery ammunition.

All ammunition in the large stockpile is in white boxes.

The large stockpile is divided into four echelons:

The road echelon consists of a number of depot sections. Each depot section carries one batch of ammunition.

The regulating station echelon is made up of loaded trains, designated as "mobile supplies," and placed at the regulating station. It includes a number of ammunition lots varying with the strength of the army and its situation, as well as a reserve of material.

The store station echelon is stored in one of the store stations assigned to the army. It also includes a variable number of ammunition lots.

The arsenal echelon is stored in the arsenal assigned to the army.

Its initial supply includes all the batches assigned to the army and not included in the first three echelons.

The ammunition for the heavy artillery is divided into two batches, one placed at the regulating station echelon, the other at the arsenal echelon.

II. ENGINEERING SERVICE.

The engineer service has, in each army:

At the front, the *corps engineer depot companies* and the *corps bridge crew companies*.

In the rear, the *army engineer depot* (to which a *telegraphic detachment of the engineer depot* is attached) and a *bridge crew*.

Engineer depot company.

The corps engineer depot carries depot tools, spare portable tools and explosives.

Bridge Crew Company.

The bridge crew equipment available to the deck crew company forms two divisions and a reserve. Each division itself consists of two groups; the first group alone is capable of establishing a short span bridge.

Army engineer depot.

The army engineer depot carries tools, explosives and bridge material. The *telegraph detachment* of the army engineer depot carries line equipment and devices for the supply of the army sapper-telegraph company.

There are *two army depot reserves*, the first one at the store station, the second one in a place in the interior.

III. AERONAUTICAL SERVICE.

The aeronautical service includes the *aerostation* service and the aeronautical service.

Aerostation service.

The aerostation service includes: *airships* with their crews, *home ports* or *resting stations, aerostation companies, reserves of material.*

Aeronautical service.

The aeronautical service includes
    In the front, *squadrons* and *air parks*, repair and supply organs;
    In the rear, various echelons of supply in personnel and equipment.

IV. TELEGRAPH SERVICE.

The telegraph service has at its disposal the personnel and material resources relating to:

Electric and optical networks of all kinds existing in the army zone, with the exception of the special electric network of the railroads;

Telegraph and radiotelegraphic field formations.

TELEGRAPHY.

a) Army Group.

The Army Group telegraph and telephone network is established using existing lines and equipment. It is operated by the personnel of the post and telegraph administration.

The staff of the army group has, in addition, a *telegraphic detachment* (military personnel of the post and telegraph administration).

b) Army.

In an army, the service includes:

A first-line service (forward network), having as its operational organ a *company of sappers-telegraphers*;

A second-line service (stage area network), having as its operational organ a *technical section* (military personnel of the post and telegraph administration).

c) Corps.

In an army corps, the service is provided by a *corps telegraph detachment.*

d) Cavalry division.

In a cavalry division, the service is provided by the *light telegraph* workshops and a *telegraph detachment.*

RADIOTELEGRAPHY.

a) Army group network.

This network has: fixed radiotelegraph stations, located in the army zone, and a *radiotelegraph detachment*, equipped with a number of field radiotelegraph stations.

b) Network of an army.

Each army has a *radiotelegraph detachment*, comprising a variable number of field radiotelegraph sets.

V. QUARTERMASTER SERVICE.

The quartermaster service has the following organs:

a) In the front, in each army corps.

1. The *administrative convoy* of the army corps, comprising two sections, each of which transports one day's worth of food for the strength of the army corps.

2. The *livestock herd* of the army corps, comprising a number of days of meat on the ground fixed by the command and to which is attached an automobile section of supply of fresh meat, serving for the transport of the slaughtered meat.

3. The *reserve of clerks and administrative workers* of the corps.

b) At the rear in each army.

1. The *administrative convoy* of the army, comprising two sections per army corps, which transport the same quantities of food as those of the administrative convoy of the army corps.

2. The *army livestock herd*, comprising, per army corps, a

number of days of meat on the ground fixed by the command.

3. The *army bakery*, comprising as many *field bakeries* as there are army corps.

4. The *reserve of clerks and workers of army administration*.

5. The *regulating station* supplies maintained at a number of rations fixed by the director of the stages and services of the army.

6. The supplies of the *store-stations*, whose stock is also maintained at a fixed number.

VI - HEALTH SERVICE.

The health service includes:

At the front, in each army corps:

1. The *regimental service* which gives first aid to the sick and wounded.

It is provided by the physicians of the troops who have the regimental personnel and equipment.

2. The following medical units:

    a) *Groups of stretcher-bearers*, intended to relieve the wounded and to transport them to the ambulances;

    b) *Ambulances*, whose mission consists of: completing the action of the regimental service, preparing the evacuation of the sick and wounded, and assuring their temporary hospitalization;

    c) *Hospitalization sections*, which transport complementary material for the ambulances and provide them with the necessary hospitalization objects to enable them to be immobilized;

    d) A *motorized sanitary section* intended to assure the normal daily evacuations.

In principle, the corps has, per division in its composition, four ambulances and three hospitalization sections. At the rear, in each army:

1. *Evacuation hospitals* (in principle, one per army corps), intended to sort out, hospitalize temporarily and evacuate the sick and wounded.

Each evacuation hospital can be divided into two sections that can function separately.

From the evacuation hospitals, "evacuation trains" (improvised or permanent medical trains) and "evacuation convoys" by road or water travel.

To the evacuation hospital are attached the personnel and equipment corresponding to four improvised medical trains.

2. *Ambulances* and *army hospitalization sections* comprising, in principle, eight ambulances and six hospitalization sections per army corps.

3. The *infirmaries of stations, overnight lodges, ports*, established on the route of the trains or evacuation convoys. They provide food, care and medicine to the sick and wounded passing through, collect those who cannot continue their journey and direct them to a hospital.

4. *Ambulances immobilized* in the area of the lodges to treat on the spot the sick and wounded whose evacuation has not yet been possible, or men suffering from epidemic or contagious diseases.

5. *Temporary or permanent hospitals and hospices*, existing in the occupied territory.

6. *Auxiliary hospitals*, organized by assistance societies or private individuals.

7. *Convalescent warehouses.*

8. The *reserves of army medical personnel and equipment.*

9. The *reserves of station-storage.*

MILITARY CHAPLAINCY IN THE ARMIES.

In armies in the field, chaplains of the various faiths are attached to stretcher-bearer groups and to the ambulances of cavalry divisions.

VII. RAILROAD SERVICE.

The service of the railroads of the network of the armies is assured, under the authority of the director of the railroads:

a) In national territory, whenever circumstances permit, by the ordinary personnel of the companies, under the direction of the *network commissions;*

b) In national territory, when the companies cannot assure the operation, and in enemy territory, by the railroad troops *(railroad sappers and sections of field railroad).*

Each army is assigned, in principle, a *line of communication*, which ensures all supplies or evacuations to or from the army. The line of communication includes a set of railroad tracks coming from the national territory, passing through the storage stations where the supplies placed at the disposal of the army are stored, and ending at a specially chosen station, located behind the army and named *regulating station.*

At the regulating station, supplies are loaded on wagons (mobile supplies) or deposited in stores.

Trains destined for the army are directed from the regulating station to stations as close as possible to the troops, which are called *supply stations.* It is at these stations that the contact between the railroad service and the crews of the armies or army corps takes place.

VIII. STAGING SERVICE.

The direction of the staging and services of an army has under its authority:

1. *Staging personnel and troops*, with the aid of which are organized the staging commands, which assure the administration, the police and the security of the territories of the staging zone;

2. *Elements on rail*, maintained, until the moment of their use, at the regulating station or in neighboring stations. These elements have been enumerated above;

3. *Elements on the road*, which move in the staging zone, following the general movement of the army. These elements have also been listed above among the organs belonging to the different services. Stage troops may also march with the road elements to provide communications protection in the stage area.

The director of staging and services disposes of supplies of all kinds stored in the stage area, in store stations, and in other establishments assigned to the army.

In the event that the railroads cannot serve the army directly, part of the army's line of communication is constituted by *staging roads*. The line of communication of the army may possibly use waterways.

Transport on the staging roads is ensured by *motor convoys*, by *army depot and administrative convoy sections*, by *auxiliary convoy sections*, assigned to the army and transported, in due time, to the staging area; finally, by *possible convoys*, organized by requisition in the staging area.

Appendix No 3 – Prescriptions Concerning Orders and Reports
Appendix to Section II.

Drafting of orders.

I. An order must be clear, precise and complete. It must not contain anything vague. Imprecise expressions, such as "at daybreak, at night, etc.," are never used.

Abbreviations are avoided. Important times and numbers are spelled out after they have been expressed in figures. Hours are counted from 0 to 24.

Names of places are spelled correctly and given in full, if necessary, in both languages of the border countries.

Mention is made of the map used to draw up the order.

If one wishes to designate a point that is not very distinct and not named on the map, or a hill, its position is indicated in relation to another point that is clearly defined and easy to find.

The orientation terms "North, South, East, West" should be used in preference to "forward, backward, right, left." When the latter terms are used, it should be made clear what they are used for.

Writing of minutes and reports.

II. An account or report must contain the precise indication of the place, date and time where the facts related took place.

The person who draws it up must, moreover, expressly distinguish in it what he has seen for himself from accounts whose accuracy he has not been able to verify personally. In the latter case, he must mention the source of his information.

An account established during an encounter with the enemy must specify:

1. The forces recognized (strength, arms to which they belong, possibly regimental numbers);
2. The precise moment (day and hour) when the presence of these forces was noted;
3. The locations they occupied at that moment;
4. Their situation and what could be appreciated of their movements;
5. The forces engaged and the locations occupied by the unit from which the report originates, the strength of its elements still available and the intentions of its leader.

A report does not include any assumptions about unrecognized forces and presumed enemy intentions.

Reports should be written very legibly, in ink or black pencil. Every precaution must be taken to ensure that the writing is not erased during transportation. Any unit, detachment, or reconnaissance commander, who has conquered valuable intelligence, sometimes at the cost of the greatest efforts and serious losses, must not forget that if the leader, for whom it is intended, cannot read it in full, the energy expended and the sacrifices made are in vain.

Transmission of orders and reports.

III. The authority who, *exceptionally*, gives a verbal order, always has it repeated by the one who is charged with transmitting it. The latter shall endeavor to grasp the spirit as well as the letter of the order and to be aware of the circumstances to which it relates.

During his mission, an officer in charge of carrying an order tries to be aware of the events he may witness, so as to be able to inform both his chief and the authority to which he is carrying the order.

If the situation to which the order relates has changed during the journey, the officer shall nevertheless transmit the order as he received it; he shall then add the necessary explanations as to the purpose of the leader at the time he left him.

If the order requires immediate execution, he shall be present at the beginning of the execution in order to give an account of it.

Every non-commissioned officer, dispatch rider, planton or cyclist, carrying an order or a written report, is given, at the start, the indication of the speed at which he must march and the route to be followed first.

A rider walking at the ordinary speed makes, on average, 2 kilometers of trot for 1 kilometer of step and travels at this pace about 10 kilometers per hour.

At the fast speed, he trots and covers about 15 kilometers per hour.

At fast speed, he travels at a gallop and thus walks at an average speed of 5 kilometers per quarter hour.

Upon arrival, an order or report carrier hands the letter to the addressee or to the person who replaces him; he waits for the acknowledgement of receipt and, if necessary, the reply.

Any subordinate who receives an order or a report, instead of his superior, sends it to him according to the instructions he has received. He shall take cognizance of the contents of this letter, if it is not marked "personal"; he shall prescribe on his own initiative the measures required by the circumstances and shall report to his superior.

In the outposts and in the vanguard, the leaders of the various forces are entitled to take note, as they pass by and with the least possible delay in transmission, of all the information coming from the front.

Appendix No. 4 – Supply of Food to the Troops
Appendix to Section XI.

The total supply of food includes, for all the arms, except for the cavalry divisions:

The reserve supplies, two days; oats, one day;

The supplies of the regimental trains, about two days;[*] oats, two days;

The supplies of the administrative convoys of the army corps, about two days; oats, two days;

The supplies of the administrative convoy of the army, about two days; oats, two days;

That is to say, in total, eight days[†] of supplies; 7 days of oats.

In the cavalry divisions:

The reserve food supplies include about one day's worth of food (except for sugar and coffee, which are supplied for three days) and two kilograms of oats.

---

[*] Except for canned meat, which is constituted at 1 day only.

[†] Except for canned meat, which is made up to 7 days only.

The regimental trains carry only one day's supply of food and oats.

Appendix No. 5 – Logs of Marches and Operations of the Staffs and Corps of Troops

Instruction for the drafting of the histories of the corps of troops.
(General Staff; 3rd Bureau, Military Operations, etc.)

Versailles, December 5, 1874.

In the future, the histories of the troops will be established in accordance with the attached model.
They will bear the title of:

Diary of the marches and operations of the (regiment, battalion, etc.) during the campaign undertaken in
      of   *on*   *19* .

One will observe, for the drafting of this diary the following rules:

Number of personnel on the day of departure.

Indicate the composition of the corps on the day of departure.
List the names of the officers classified by battalion, company,

squadron or battery.
Number of non-commissioned officers and men.
Number of horses.

Setting out.

Indicate the date of departure and the point of concentration to which the corps is directed.
The corps travels by rail or by stages.
Date of arrival at the point of concentration and indication of the army corps, division and brigade to which the corps belongs.

Writing of the history.

In writing the history, no comments or judgments should be made on the origin and causes of the campaign undertaken.
The history of a corps is only the faithful account, day by day, of the facts, from the beginning to the end of the operations; it should never be established after the fact.

Bivouacs or billets.

Location of the bivouac or billets. Indicate the corps that are bivouacked on the right or left. State if one is in first or second line. Location of the grand guards.

Reconnaissance.

Their strength and composition. Purpose of the reconnaissance. Results obtained.

Fighting.

Position of the corps before the action. Indicate the hour of the beginning of the action, and in general *always give* the hour of the day when an important fact occurs during the engagement, such as: change of position, march forward or in retreat, occupation of a remarkable point of the line of battle, retreat of a neighboring corps fighting on the right or on the left.

Mention if the corps covers itself by temporary works:

Trench shelters, farms or villages put in a state of defense and being used as point of support.

After the action, indicate the position kept by the corps at the moment when the combat stopped. Mention the time.

Losses.

We will try to indicate *very exactly* the losses suffered by the corps in each affair, in killed, wounded, prisoners and missing. The officers, non-commissioned officers and soldiers will all be designated by name. For the statement of losses after each encounter, no matter how small, model A will be used. This statement will be inserted in the body of the story, following the action that motivated it. If, during the day, men are killed or wounded at the outposts or in reconnaissance, the statement will be made according to the same model.

As a general rule, indicate all losses as they occur.

As for the soldiers of all ranks who died as a result of their injuries or illnesses, they will be mentioned at the end of the history, in conformity with the model B statement.

Finally, all the losses will be totaled on a model C statement which will end the work.

Awards.

Promotions, decorations and commendations in the order of the army should be mentioned as they come to the attention of the head of the command. As far as citations are concerned, only those in the army order should be mentioned. These are the only ones that are awards and appear on the statement of services. Changes that occurred during the campaign, among the officers, as a result of promotion, replacement, etc., will be noted on a model D statement.

Outstanding Actions.

Outstanding actions will be mentioned in all their details, in order to be able to be cited later as examples to follow.

Situations.

After a serious affair where the corps has suffered significant losses, a new table of the composition of the corps in officers will be established. This table will also mention the remaining strength (non-commissioned officers and troops).

General observations.

Personal assessments must be scrupulously avoided. The orders received will not be the object of any comment.

Each day of the campaign, from the day of departure, will have its date written in the margin of the journal.

Do not lose sight of the fact that the corps' diary must be used to establish an overall history.

This history will only be possible on the condition that the facts related by the corps having participated in the same affair can be easily compared between them, and this comparison, in order to be made, imperatively requires the exact indication of dates and times.

If the corps takes prisoners from the enemy, the number of prisoners will be indicated. The names and ranks of enemy officers taken prisoner should be given as far as possible.

The dimensions of the paper on which these histories will have to be established will be those of the format having twenty-six by eighteen centimeters.

MM. general officers in command, either in the field, or during major maneuvers, will see to it that a register-journal is kept at their headquarters in a form similar to that which is prescribed for the keeping of the histories of the troops. This log shall record all events as they occur. None of the important incidents which occur, either on the march, or on station, or during maneuvers and combat, must be passed over in silence.

On this register, day by day, without gaps or scrapes, will be recorded the summary of the orders received and given, the information gathered, and all the details relating to the marches, billets or bivouacs, the security service, the reconnaissance, the maneuvers and the fighting.

It will be attached a file of supporting documents, such as summary situations, copies of general and particular orders, additional reports, tables of marching, encampments, orders of movements, etc.

JOURNAL

DES MARCHES ET OPERATIONS

du (1)

pendant (2)

du   *au*   19

(1) Numéro du régiment ou bataillon.
(2) La campagne d   , ou les grandes manœuvres.

DATES.	HISTORIQUE DES FAITS.

Modèle A.

⁕ REGIMENT.

Etat nominatif des officiers, sous-officiers et soldats tués, blessés, faits prisonniers ou disparus au combat de   le   19.

NOMS	GRADES	TUÉS	BLESSÉS	PRISONNIERS	DISPARUS	CHEVAUX TUÉS ou perdus	OBSERVATIONS
	Totaux...						
	Total général...						

Modèle B.

ᵉ REGIMENT.

État nominatif des officiers, sous-officiers et soldats morts des suites de leurs blessures, ou morts dé maladie dans les hôpitaux.

NOMS	GRADES	DATES	LIEUX	MORTS DES SUITES de blessures	MORTS de MALADIE	OBSERVATIONS
			Totaux			

Modèle C.

⚫ RÉGIMENT.

État-général des pertes éprouvées par le corps pendant la durée de la campagne.

NOMS DES BATAILLES combats et rencontres de toute nature	DATES	SOUS-OFFICIERS ET SOLDATS							OFFICIERS							CHEVAUX tués ou perdus
		TUÉS	BLESSÉS	MORTS des suites de blessures	MORTS de maladie	PRISONNIERS	DISPARUS	TUÉS	BLESSÉS	MORTS des suites de blessures	MORTS de maladie	PRISONNIERS	DISPARUS	

Totaux..........

Totaux..........

Total général des pertes..........

Modèle D.   • RÉGIMENT.

Relevé des mutations survenues pendant la campagne parmi les officiers.

NOMS ET PRÉNOMS	GRADES	MUTATIONS

Circular concerning the transmission of the logs of marches and operations.
(Staff of the Army; Office of Military Operations and General Instruction of the Army.)

Paris, October 20, 1908.

The instruction of December 5, 1874 determined the conditions under which the logs of the marches and operations of the staffs and corps of troops should be established.

The following rules will be applied for the communication of these documents to the Minister:

1. *War operations.* The staffs and corps of troops, as soon as they return to their garrisons, after the end of the campaign, will send to the Minister (Army Staff; 3rd Bureau) their log of marches and operations, enclosing the file of supporting documents (situation, general and particular orders, reports, etc.) which must be appended to the log in execution of the prescriptions of the last paragraph of the instruction of December 5, 1874.

For long campaigns, these documents will be sent periodically every six months, as often as possible on the dates of June 30 and December 31.

2. *Maneuvers.* The diaries of marches and operations established for the periods of maneuvers will be communicated to the Minister only if he prescribes it. The directors of maneuvers are authorized to have the original logs of the staffs and corps of troops having operated under their direction sent to them.

Appendix No. 6 – Campaign Diaries of Quartermasters

Circular concerning the keeping of a campaign logbook by the quartermasters.
(Directorate of military intendance.)

Paris, September 20, 1907.

In the field and during the duration of maneuvers, the quartermaster's officers will keep a field notebook, the sheets of which will be marked and initialed before being given to the interested parties, by the military quartermaster of the mobilized army corps, in the first case, and by the director of the quartermaster's office of the region of the army corps, in the second case.

Each official will insert, day by day, in his handwriting, on the field notebook, a brief summary of the orders and notices received and given, concerning his service, as well as the measures taken to ensure it and the incidents that may be of interest. The exact time at which each of the reported failures occurred must be scrupulously indicated.

The provision of the campaign books will be the responsibility of the central administration.

These books will be in conformity with the model appended to the present regulations.

Format :
14 centimètres sur 19.

CARNET DE CAMPAGNE

DES FONCTIONNAIRES DE L'INTENDANCE

° CORPS.   ° DIVISION.

M

Le présent carnet, contenant   feuillets, a été côté et paragraphé par nous (3)

A   , le   19

(1) ° armée, *ou* Corps expéditionnaire de   , *ou* Grandes Manœuvres de 19   .
(2) Intendant militaire de corps d'armée, *ou* Directeur de l'intendance de la   ° région de corps d'armée.

NUMÉROS des ORDRES et avis reçus ou donnés.	DATES et HEURES.	ANALYSE SOMMAIRE DES ORDRES ET AVIS	
		REÇUS (indiquer de qui ils émanent).	DONNÉS (indiquer à qui ils ont été adressés).

EXECUTION DU SERVICE RÉSULTANT DES ORDRES et avis ci-contre.	OBSERVATIONS. Relater dans cette colonne les incidents pouvant présenter quelque intérêt.

Part II – International Law

1. International Convention of Geneva.

An Act approving the convention signed in Geneva on 6 July 1906 for the amelioration of the condition of the wounded and sick in armies in the field.

The Senate and the Chamber of Deputies have adopted,
The President of the Republic promulgates the following law:

Sole article. The President of the French Republic is authorized to ratify and to execute, if necessary, the convention signed in Geneva, on July 6, 1906, for the improvement of the condition of the wounded and sick in armies in the field.

An authentic copy of this act shall be attached to the present law.

The present law, deliberated and adopted by the Senate and the Chamber of Deputies, will be executed as a law of the State.

Done at Paris, June 12, 1913.

R. POINCARÉ.

For the President of the Republic:
The Minister of Foreign Affairs,
S. PICHON.

The Minister of War,
Eug. ETIENNE.

The Minister of the Navy,
Pierre BAJUDIN.

International Convention of Geneva of July 6, 1906, for the improvement of the lot of the wounded and sick in the field.[*]

(List of sovereigns and heads of state.)

Equally animated by the desire to diminish, as far as it depends on them, the evils inseparable from war, and wishing, for this purpose, to perfect and complete the provisions agreed upon in Geneva, August 22, 1864, for the improvement of the lot of wounded or sick soldiers in armies in the field,

Have resolved to conclude a new convention for this purpose, and have appointed as their plenipotentiaries, namely:

(Follows the designation of the plenipotentiaries.)

Who, after having communicated their full powers to each other, found in good and due form, have agreed as follows:

---

[*] The convention has been signed by Argentina, Austria-Hungary, Belgium, Bulgaria, Chile, China, Denmark, Germany, the Independent State of Congo, Korea, Spain, the United States of America, and the United States of America. Austria-Hungary, Belgium, Bulgaria, Chile, China, Denmark, France, Germany, Greece, Guatemala, Honduras, Italy, Japan, Luxembourg, Montenegro, the Netherlands, Norway, Peru, Spain, the United States of America, the Independent State of Congo, the United States of America, the United States of America, the United States of America, Guatemala, Honduras, Italy, Japan, Luxembourg, Montenegro, the Netherlands, Norway, Peru, Persia, Portugal, Romania, Russia, Serbia, Siam, Spain, Sweden, Switzerland, the United Kingdom, the United States of America, Uruguay, the states of Cuba, Paraguay, Costa Rica, and El Salvador. Colombia, Nicaragua, Turkey and Venezuela have joined.

Chapter I – Of the Wounded and Sick

Art. 1. Military personnel and other persons officially attached to the armies, who are wounded or sick, shall be respected and cared for, without distinction of nationality, by the belligerent who has them in his power.

However, a belligerent who is obliged to abandon the sick or wounded to his adversary shall leave with them, as far as military circumstances permit, part of his medical personnel and equipment to help care for them.

Art. 2. Subject to the care to be given to them in accordance with the preceding Article, the sick or wounded of an army who have fallen in the field of battle shall be treated in the same way as the wounded.

The belligerent states, which are not members of the other belligerent's power, are prisoners of war and the general rules of the law of nations concerning prisoners are applicable to them.

However, the belligerents remain free to stipulate between themselves, with regard to wounded or sick prisoners, such clauses of acceptance or favour as they may deem useful; they shall in particular have the right to agree :

To mutually recover, after a battle, the wounded left on the battlefield;

To return to their country, after having put them in a condition to be transported, or after recovery, the wounded or sick whom they do not wish to keep as prisoners;

To hand over to a neutral State, with the consent of the latter, the wounded or sick of the adverse party, on condition that the neutral State intern them until the end of hostilities.

Art 3. After each battle, the occupant of the battlefield shall take measures to search for the wounded and to protect them, as well as the dead, against pillage and ill-treatment.

He shall see that the burial or cremation of the dead is preceded by a careful examination of their corpses.

Art. 4. Each belligerent shall send, as soon as possible, to the authorities of their country or army, the marks or military identity papers found on the dead and the names of the wounded or sick collected by him.

The belligerents shall keep each other informed of internments and transfers, as well as of entries into hospitals and of deaths among the wounded and sick in their power. They shall collect all objects of personal use, valuables, letters, etc., which are found on the battlefields or left behind by the wounded or sick who have died in medical establishments and units, in order to have them transmitted to the persons concerned by the authorities of their country.

Art. 5. The military authority may appeal to the charitable zeal of the inhabitants to collect and care for, under its control, the wounded or sick of the armies, granting special protection and certain immunities to the persons having responded to this appeal.

Chapter II – Medical Units and Establishments

Art. 6. Mobile medical units (i.e. those intended to accompany armies in the field) and fixed establishments of the medical service shall be protected and respected by the belligerents.

Art. 7. The protection due to medical units and establishments ceases if they are used to commit acts harmful to the enemy.

Art. 8. The following are not considered as being of such a nature as to deprive a medical formation or establishment of the protection provided by Article 6:
1. The fact that the personnel of the formation or establishment are armed and that they use their weapons in their own defense or that of their sick or wounded;
2. The fact that, in the absence of armed nurses, the formation or establishment is guarded by a picket or sentries with regular warrants;
3. The fact that weapons and cartridges withdrawn from the wounded and not yet turned over to the competent service are found in the formation or establishment.

Chapter III – Personnel

Art. 9. Personnel assigned exclusively to the removal, transport and treatment of the wounded and sick, as well as to the administration of medical units and establishments, and chaplains attached to the armies, shall be respected and protected in all circumstances; if they fall into enemy hands, they shall not be treated as prisoners of war.

These provisions shall apply to the personnel on guard duty in training and medical establishments, in the case provided for in Article 8, paragraph 2.

Art. 10. The personnel of voluntary relief societies, duly recognized and authorized by their governments, who are to be employed in the medical formations and establishments of the armies, shall be assimilated to the personnel referred to in the preceding Article, provided that the said personnel shall be subject to military laws and regulations.

Each State must notify to the other, either in time of peace, or at the outbreak or during hostilities, and in any case before any actual employment, the names of the societies which it has authorized to lend their assistance, under its responsibility, to the official medical service of its armies.

Art. 11. A recognized society of a neutral country may only lend the assistance of its medical personnel and formations to a belligerent with the prior consent of its own government and the authorization of the belligerent itself.

The belligerent who has accepted the assistance is obliged, before any use, to notify his enemy.

Art. 12. The persons designated in Articles 9, 10 and 11 shall continue, after they have fallen into the power of the enemy, to perform their duties under his direction.

When their assistance is no longer indispensable, they shall be sent back to their army or to their country within the time limits and by the route compatible with military necessities.

They will then take with them the effects, instruments, weapons and horses which are their particular property.

Art. 13. The enemy shall assure to the personnel referred to in Article 9, as long as they are in his power, the same allowances and the same pay as to the personnel of the same rank in his army.

Chapter IV – Equipment

Art. 14. The mobile medical units will keep, if they fall into the power of the enemy, their equipment, including the carriages, whatever the means of transport and the driving personnel. However, the competent military authority shall have the right to use them for the care of the wounded and sick; the return of the equipment shall take place under the conditions laid down for the medical personnel, and, as far as possible, at the same time.

Art. 15. The buildings and equipment of fixed establishments shall remain subject to the laws of war, but may not be diverted from their use as long as they are necessary for the sick and wounded.
However, the commanders of the operating troops may dispose of them, in case of important military necessity, by assuring in advance the fate of the wounded and sick who are in them.

Art. 16. The equipment of the societies admitted to the benefits of the convention in accordance with the conditions determined by the latter is considered as private property and, as such, is respected in all circumstances, except for the right of requisition recognized to the belligerents according to the laws and customs of war.

Chapter V – Evacuation Convoys

Art. 17. Evacuation convoys shall be treated as mobile medical units, except for the following special provisions:

1. The belligerent intercepting a convoy may, if military necessity so requires, dislocate it by loading it with the sick and wounded which it is carrying;

2. In this case, the obligation to return the medical personnel, provided for in Article 1, shall be imposed on any military personnel in charge of the transport or guarding of the convoy and having a regular warrant for this purpose.

The obligation to return medical equipment provided for in Article 14 shall apply to the railways and ships of the inland waterways, specially organized for evacuations, as well as to the equipment of the ordinary cars, trains and trucks belonging to the medical service.

The military cars and the health service cars may be taken with their own vehicles.

Civilian personnel and the various means of transport resulting from the requisition, including the iron and steel equipment and the vehicles used for the convoys, shall be subject to the general rules of the law of nations.

Chapter VI – The Distinctive Sign

Art. 18. As a tribute to Switzerland, the heraldic sign of the Blue Cross on a white background, formed by the interweaving of the federal colors, shall be maintained as the distinctive sign of the sanitary service of the armies.

Art. 19. This emblem shall appear on the flags, armbands, as well as on all the material related to the sanitary service, with the permission of the competent military authority.

Art. 20. The personnel protected by virtue of articles 9 (paragraph 10), 10 and 11 shall wear, attached to the left arm, an armband with a red cross on a white background, issued and stamped by the competent military authority, accompanied by a certificate of identity for persons attached to the health service of the armed forces and who do not have a military uniform.

Art. 21. The distinctive flag of the Convention may be flown only on the medical units and establishments which it orders to be respected and with the consent of the military authority. It must be accompanied by the national flag of the belligerent to which the formation or establishment belongs.

However, medical formations which have fallen into the hands of the enemy shall not display any other flag than that of the Red Cross, as long as they are in that situation.

Art. 22. Medical units of neutral countries which, under the conditions provided for in Article 11, have been authorized to provide their services, must fly, together with the flag of the Convention, the national flag of the belligerent to which they belong.

The provisions of the second paragraph of the preceding Article shall apply to them.

Art. 23. The emblem of the red cross on a white ground and the words "Red Cross" or "Geneva Cross" may be used, either in time of war or in time of peace, only to protect or designate medical units and establishments, personnel and material protected by the Convention.

Chapter VII – Application and Execution of the Convention

Art. 24. The provisions of the present Convention shall be binding only upon the Contracting Powers, in case of war, between two or more of them. These provisions shall cease to be binding from the moment when one of the belligerent Powers is not a signatory of the Convention.

Art. 25. The Commanders-in-Chief of the belligerent armies shall provide for the details of the execution of the preceding Articles, as well as for cases not provided for, according to the instructions of their respective Governments and in conformity with the general principles of the present Convention.

Art. 26. The signatory Governments shall take the necessary measures to instruct their troops and, especially, the protected personnel, in the provisions of the present Convention, and to bring them to the notice of the population.

Chapter VIII – On the Repression of Abuses and Infractions

Art. 27. The signatory Governments whose legislation is not at present adequate undertake to take or to propose to their legislatures the measures necessary to prevent at any time the use, by private persons or by societies other than those entitled thereto under the present Convention, of the emblem or name of the "Red Cross" or "Geneva Cross," particularly for commercial purposes, by means of trade marks.

The prohibition of the use of the emblem or name in question shall take effect from the time determined by each legislation and, at the latest, five years after the entry into force of the present Convention. As from such entry into force, it shall no longer be lawful to use a trademark contrary to the prohibition.

Art. 28. The signatory Governments also undertake to take or to propose to their legislatures, in case of inadequacy of their military penal laws, the measures necessary to repress, in time of war, individual acts of pillage or ill-treatment of the wounded and sick of the armies, as well as to punish, as usurpation of military insignia, the improper use of the flag and armband of the Red Cross by military personnel or private persons not protected by the present Convention. They shall communicate to each other, through the intermediary of the Swiss Federal Council, the provisions relating to this repression, at the latest within five years of the ratification of the present Convention.

They shall communicate to each other, through the Swiss Federal Council, the provisions relating to such repression, at the latest within five years of the ratification of this Convention.

General Provisions

Art. 29. The present Convention shall be ratified as soon as possible.

The ratifications shall be deposited at Berne.

A record shall be drawn up of the deposit of each ratification, a certified copy of which shall be transmitted through diplomatic channels to all the contracting powers.

Art. 30. The present Convention shall come into force for each Power six months after the date of deposit of its ratification.

Art. 31. The present Convention, duly ratified, shall replace the Convention of August 22, 1864, in the relations between the contracting States.

The Convention of 1864 shall remain in force as between the parties which have signed it and which have not also ratified the present Convention.

Art. 32. The present Convention may, until the 31st day of December next, be signed by the Powers represented at the

Conference which opened at Geneva on the 11th day of June, 1909, as well as by the Powers not represented at that Conference, which have signed the Convention of 1864.

Those powers which, on 31 December 1906, have not signed the present Convention shall remain free to accede to it thereafter. They shall make known their accession by means of a written notification addressed to the Swiss Federal Council and communicated by the latter to all the Contracting Powers.

The other Powers may request accession in the same form, but their request shall not be effective unless, within a period of one year from the date of notification to the Federal Council, the latter has not received any objection from any of the Contracting Powers.

Art. 33. Each of the contracting parties may denounce the present Convention. Such denunciation shall not take effect until one year after written notification has been made to the Swiss Federal Council, which shall immediately communicate the notification to all the other contracting parties.

Such denunciation shall be valid only in respect of the Power which has notified it.

In *witness thereof*, the plenipotentiaries have signed the present Convention and have affixed their seals.

Done at Geneva, this sixth day of July, one thousand nine hundred and six, in a single copy, which shall remain deposited in the archives of the Swiss Confederation, and copies of which, certified true copies, shall be transmitted through diplomatic channels to the Contracting Powers.

(Signatures follow.)

2. Declaration of Saint-Petersburg

Imperial decree which approves the declaration signed in Saint Petersburg, on December 11, 1868, to the effect of prohibiting the use of certain projectiles in time of war.[*]

Paris, December 30, 1868.

NAPOLEON, by the grace of God and the national will, EMPEROR OF THE FRENCH, to all present and to come, WELCOME;

On the report of our Minister Secretary of State in the Department of Foreign Affairs,

We have decreed and decree the following:

Art. 1. A declaration having been signed in St. Petersburg on the third of December 1868, between the powers designated above, to the effect of prohibiting the use of certain projectiles in time of war between the contracting States and the States which will accede to this undertaking, the said declaration, the content of which follows, is approved and will be inserted in the *Bulletin of Laws*.

DECLARATION.

On the proposal of the Imperial Cabinet of Russia, an

---

[*] Powers having adhered to the declaration: Austria, Belgium, Brazil, Bulgaria, China, Denmark, France, Germany, Great Britain, Greece, Italy, Japan, Luxembourg, Montenegro, Netherlands, Persia, Portugal, Rumania, Russia, Serbia, Siam, Spain, Sweden and Norway, Switzerland and Turkey.

Declaration of Saint-Petersburg

international military commission having met in St. Petersburg to examine the propriety of prohibiting the use of certain projectiles in time of war between civilized nations, and this commission having fixed, by common agreement, the technical limits where the necessities of war must stop before the requirements of humanity, the undersigned are authorized, by the orders of their Governments, to declare as follows:

Considering that the progress of civilization must have the effect of mitigating as much as possible the calamities of war;

That the only legitimate aim which States must propose to themselves, during war, is the weakening of the military forces of the enemy;

That for this purpose it is sufficient to put out of action as many men as possible;

That this aim would be exceeded by the use of weapons which would unnecessarily aggravate the sufferings of the men put out of action or would make their death inevitable;

That the use of such weapons would therefore be contrary to the laws of humanity,

The contracting parties undertake to renounce mutually, in case of war between them, the use, by their land or sea forces, of any projectile of a weight of less than four hundred grams which is either explosive or charged with fulminating or inflammable matter.

They will invite all States which have not participated, by sending delegates, in the deliberations of the International Military Commission meeting in St. Petersburg, to accede to the present undertaking.

This undertaking shall be binding only upon the contracting or acceding parties, in case of war between two or more of them; it shall not be applicable to non-contracting or non-acceding parties.

It shall also cease to be binding from the moment when, in a war between contracting or acceding parties, a non-contracting or non-acceding party joins one of the belligerents.

The contracting or acceding parties reserve the right to come to an agreement at a later date, whenever a specific proposal is formulated with a view to future improvements which science may bring to the armament of troops, in order to maintain the principles which they have laid down and to reconcile the necessities of war with the laws of humanity.

Done in St. Petersburg, the   <u>twenty-ninth November</u>
                                                  eleventh December
one thousand eight hundred and sixty-eight.

(Signatures follow.)

Art. 2. Our Minister Secretary of State in the Department of Foreign Affairs is charged with the execution of the present decree.

Done at the Tuileries Palace, December 30, 1868.
Signed: NAPOLEON.

Seen and sealed with the seal of the State:
The Keeper of the Seals, Minister of Justice and Worship,
Signed: J. BAROCHE.

For the Emperor:
The Minister of Foreign Affairs,
Signed : LA VALETTE.

3. Acts of The Hague

Decree carrying promulgation of the international acts signed in The Hague on July 29, 1899, following the international conference of peace met in this city.

Paris, November 28, 1900.

The President of the French Republic,
  On the proposal of the Minister of Foreign Affairs,
    Decrees:

Art. 1. Following the international conference of peace meeting in The Hague, various international acts having been signed in this city on July 29, 1899, namely:

5. A declaration concerning the prohibition of the use of projectiles which have the sole purpose of spreading asphyxiating or lethal gases;
6. A declaration concerning the prohibition of the use of bullets which expand or flatten easily in the human body, etc.;

And the ratifications of these acts having been deposited at the Royal Ministry of Foreign Affairs at The Hague, the said conventions, declarations and final act, the content of which follows, will receive their full and complete execution between France and the contracting powers.

Done in Paris, on the 28th of November 1900.
Signed: EMILE LOUBET.

For the President of the Republic:

The Minister of Foreign Affairs,
  Signed: DELCASSÉ

Declaration concerning the prohibition of the use of projectiles whose sole purpose is to spread asphyxiating or noxious gases.[*]

DECLARATION

The undersigned, plenipotentiaries of the Powers represented at the International Peace Conference at The Hague, duly authorized for that purpose by their Governments;
Inspired by the sentiments which found expression in the St. Petersburg Declaration of 29 November - 11 December 1868,

Declare:

The Contracting Powers forbid each other the use of projectiles whose sole purpose is to spread asphyxiating or noxious gases.

The present declaration is binding only on the contracting powers, in case of war between two or more of them.

It shall cease to be binding from the moment when, in a war between contracting powers, a non-contracting power joins one of the belligerents.

The present declaration shall be ratified as soon as possible.

The ratifications shall be deposited at The Hague.

A record shall be made of the deposit of each ratification, a certified copy of which shall be transmitted through diplomatic channels to all the contracting powers.

The non-signatory Powers may accede to the present declaration. For this purpose, they shall make known their adherence to the contracting powers, by means of a written notification addressed to the Government of the Netherlands, and communicated by the latter to all the other contracting powers.

---

[*] Contracting Powers as of November 30, 1912: Austria-Hungary, Belgium, Bulgaria, China, Denmark, France, Germany, Greece, Italy, Japan, Luxembourg, Mexico, Montenegro, Netherlands, Norway, Persia, Portugal, Rumania, Russia, Serbia, Siam, Spain, Sweden and Norway, Switzerland, Turkey. Accepted by: Great Britain and Nicaragua. The United States of America has neither signed nor ratified.

If one of the High Contracting Parties should denounce the present declaration, such denunciation shall not take effect until one year after the notification has been made in writing to the Government of the Netherlands, and communicated by the latter immediately to all the other Contracting Powers. Such denunciation shall take effect only with regard to the Power which has notified it.

In witness whereof, the plenipotentiaries have signed the present declaration and have affixed their seals.

Done at The Hague, this 29th day of July 1899.

(Signatures follow.)

*Declaration concerning the prohibition of the use of bullets which expand or flatten easily in the human body, etc.**

DECLARATION.

The undersigned, plenipotentiaries of the Powers represented at the International Peace Conference at The Hague, duly authorized for that purpose by their Governments;
Inspired by the sentiments which found expression in the St. Petersburg Declaration of 29 November - 11 December 1868,

Declare:

The Contracting Powers forbid each other the use of bullets which expand or flatten easily in the human body, such as hard-cased bullets, the casing of which does not entirely cover the core or is provided with incisions.

The present declaration is binding only upon the Contracting Powers in case of war between two or more of them.

It shall cease to be binding from the moment when, in a war between contracting powers, a non-contracting power joins one of the belligerents.

The present declaration shall be ratified as soon as possible.

The ratifications shall be deposited at The Hague.

A record shall be made of the deposit of each ratification, a certified copy of which shall be transmitted through diplomatic channels to all the contracting powers.

The non-signatory powers may accede to the present declaration. For this purpose, they shall make known their accession to the contracting powers by means of a written

---

* Contracting Powers as of November 30, 1912: Austria-Hungary, Belgium, Bulgaria, China, Denmark, France, Germany, Greece, Italy, Japan, Luxembourg, Mexico, Montenegro, Netherlands, Norway, Persia, Rumania, Russia, Serbia, Siam, Spain, Sweden, Switzerland, Turkey. It has been accepted by Great Britain, Nicaragua and Portugal. The United States of America has neither signed nor ratified.

notification addressed to the Government of the Netherlands, which shall be communicated by the latter to all the other contracting powers.

If one of the High Contracting Parties should denounce the present declaration, such denunciation shall not take effect until one year after the notification has been made in writing to the Government of the Netherlands, and communicated immediately by the latter to all the other Contracting Powers.

This denunciation shall produce its effects only with regard to the Power which has notified it.

In witness whereof, the plenipotentiaries have signed the present declaration and have affixed their seals.

Done at The Hague, this 29th day of July 1899.

(Signatures follow.)

Decree promulgating the international convention signed at The Hague on 18 October 1907, for the peaceful settlement of international disputes.

Paris, 2 December 1910.

The President of the French Republic,
On the proposal of the Minister of Foreign Affairs and the Keeper of the Seals, Minister of Justice,

Decrees :

Art. 1. The Senate and the Chamber of Deputies having adopted the international convention for the peaceful settlement of international disputes, signed at The Hague, on October 18, 1907, by France, Germany, the United States of America, the Argentine Republic, Austria-Hungary, Belgium, Bolivia, Brazil, Bulgaria, Chile, China, Colombia, the Republic of Cuba, Denmark, the Dominican Republic, Ecuador, Spain, Great Britain, Greece, Guatemala, Haiti, Italy, Japan, Luxembourg, El Salvador, Mexico, Montenegro, Netherlands, Norway, Panama, Paraguay, Peru, Persia, Portugal, Romania, Russia, Serbia, Spain, Siam, Sweden, Switzerland, Turkey, Uruguay and Venezuela, and the ratifications of this act having been deposited at The Hague by France, Germany, the United States of America, Austria-Hungary, Belgium, Bolivia, China," Denmark, Haiti, Mexico, the Netherlands, Norway, Russia, El Salvador, Siam, Sweden and Switzerland; Nicaragua having acceded to the said Convention on the 16th day of December 1909, the said Convention, the content of which is as follows, shall be given its full and complete execution.

Convention I on the peaceful settlement of international disputes

(List of sovereigns and Heads of State.)

Animated by the firm will to contribute to the maintenance of general peace;

Resolved to promote with all their efforts the amicable settlement of international disputes;

Recognizing the solidarity which unites the members of the civilized nations;

Wishing to extend the empire of law and to strengthen the feeling of international justice;

Convinced that the permanent institution of an arbitral jurisdiction accessible to all, within the independent powers, can contribute effectively to this result;

Considering the advantages of a general and regular organization of the arbitral procedure;

Believing with the initiator of the international peace conference that it is important to enshrine in an international agreement the principles of equity and law on which rest the security of States and the well-being of peoples;

Desiring, to this end, to better ensure the practical operation of commissions of inquiry and arbitration tribunals and to facilitate recourse to arbitral justice in disputes of a summary nature;

Have deemed it necessary to revise in certain respects and to complete the work of the first peace conference for the peaceful settlement of international disputes.

The high contracting parties have resolved to conclude a new convention for this purpose and have appointed: their plenipotentiaries, namely:

(Designation of the plenipotentiaries follows.)

Who, having deposited their full powers, found in due form, have agreed as follows:

Section I – Of the Maintenance of the General Peace

Art. 1. In order to prevent as much as possible the recourse to force in the relations between States, the contracting powers agree to use all their efforts to assure the peaceful settlement of international disputes.

Section II – Good Offices and Mediation

Art. 2. In case of serious dissension or conflict, before resorting to arms, the contracting powers agree to have recourse, so far as circumstances permit, to the good offices or mediation of one or more friendly powers.

Art. 3. Independently of this recourse, the contracting powers deem it useful and desirable that one or more powers foreign to the conflict should, on their own initiative, so far as circumstances permit, offer their good offices or mediation to the States in conflict.

The right to offer good offices or mediation belongs to the powers foreign to the conflict, even during the course of hostilities.

The exercise of this right may never be considered by either of the parties to the conflict as an unfriendly act.

Art. 4. The role of the mediator consists in reconciling the opposing claims and in appeasing the resentments which may have arisen between the conflicting States.

Art. 5. The functions of the mediator shall cease from the moment when it is ascertained, either by one of the parties in dispute or by the mediator himself, that the means of conciliation proposed by him are not accepted.

Art. 6. Good offices and mediation, either at the request of the parties to the conflict or on the initiative of powers outside the conflict, have exclusively the character of advice and are never binding.

Art. 7. The acceptance of mediation may not have the effect, unless otherwise agreed, of interrupting, delaying or hindering mobilization and other preparatory measures for war.

If it takes place after the outbreak of hostilities, it does not, unless otherwise agreed, interrupt the military operations in progress.

Art. 8. The contracting Powers agree to recommend the application, in such circumstances as permit, of special mediation in the following form.

In the event of a serious dispute endangering the peace, the States in conflict shall respectively choose a power to which they entrust the mission of entering into direct contact with the power chosen on the other side, with a view to preventing the rupture of peaceful relations.

During the term of this mandate, which, unless otherwise agreed, shall not exceed thirty days, the States in dispute shall refrain from any direct contact with the subject of the conflict, which shall be considered as referred exclusively to the mediating Powers. The latter must make every effort to settle the dispute.

In the event of an actual breach of peaceful relations, these powers remain charged with the common mission of taking advantage of every opportunity to restore peace.

Section III – International Commissions of Inquiry

Art. 9. In disputes of an international character involving neither honour nor essential interests and arising from a difference of opinion on points of fact, the parties who have not been able to reach agreement by diplomatic means, shall consider it useful and desirable that they should be able to do so.

Art. 10. The parties shall establish a national commission of inquiry to facilitate the settlement of such disputes by clarifying the issues of fact through a conscientious and impartial examination.

The international fact-finding missions shall be subject to a special agreement between the parties to the dispute. It shall also determine, if necessary, the seat of the commission and the power to travel, the language to be used by the commission and the languages which may be used before it, the date on which each party shall file its statement of facts and generally all the conditions agreed upon by the parties.

If the parties deem it necessary to appoint assessors, the inquiry agreement shall determine the manner of their appointment and the extent of their powers.

Art. 11. If the inquiry agreement has not designated the seat of the commission, it shall sit at The Hague.

The seat, once fixed, can only be changed by the commission with the consent of the parties.

If the inquiry agreement has not determined the languages to be used, this shall be decided by the commission.

Art. 12. Unless otherwise provided, Boards of Inquiry shall be formed in the manner determined by Articles 45 and 57 of this Agreement.

Art. 13. In the event of the death, resignation or impediment, for whatever reason, of one of the commissioners, or possibly of one of the assessors, he shall be replaced in the manner laid down for his appointment.

Art. 14. The parties shall have the right to appoint special agents to the commission of inquiry with the task of representing them and serving as intermediaries between them and the commission.

They are, moreover, authorized to charge counsel or lawyers appointed by the judge, to expose and support their interests before the commission.

Art. 15. The International Bureau of the Permanent Court of Arbitration shall serve as a registry for the commissions sitting in The Hague, and shall place its premises and organization at the disposal of the Contracting Powers for the operation of the Commission of Inquiry.

Art. 16. If the commission sits elsewhere than in The Hague, it appoints a secretary general whose office serves as its clerk.

The clerk's office is responsible, under the authority of the president, for the material organization of the commission's meetings, the drafting of the minutes and, during the investigation, the custody of the archives, which will then be deposited at the International Bureau in The Hague.

Art. 17. With a view to facilitating the establishment and operation of commissions of inquiry, the Contracting Powers recommend the following rules, which shall be applicable to the inquiry procedure so long as the parties do not adopt other rules.

Art. 18. The commission shall regulate the details of the procedure not provided for in the special convention of inquiry or in the present convention, and shall carry out all the formalities involved in the taking of evidence.

Art. 19. The investigation shall take place in the presence of both parties.
On the scheduled dates, each party shall communicate to the Commission and to the other party the statements of facts, if any, and, in any case, the acts, documents and papers that it deems useful for the discovery of the truth, as well as the list of witnesses and experts that it wishes to be heard.

Art. 20. The commission has the right, with the consent of the parties, to go temporarily to the place where it deems it useful to have recourse to this means of information, or to delegate one or more of its members. The authorization of the State on whose territory the information is to be provided must be obtained.

Art. 21. All material findings and all visits to the premises must be made in the presence of the agents and counsels of the parties, or they must be duly called.

Art. 22. The commission has the right to request from the other party any explanations or information it deems useful.

Art. 23. The parties undertake to provide the Commission of Inquiry, to the fullest extent possible, with all the means and facilities necessary for the complete knowledge and accurate assessment of the facts in question.
They undertake to use the means at their disposal under their domestic law to ensure the attendance of witnesses or experts in their territory who are summoned before the commission.

If the latter cannot appear before the commission, they shall arrange for their hearing before their competent authorities.

Art. 24. For all notifications which the Commission may have to make in the territory of a third Contracting Power, the Commission shall apply directly to the government of that Power. The same shall apply if it is a question of proceeding on the spot to the establishment of any means of proof.

Requests addressed to this effect shall be executed according to the means available to the requested power under its domestic legislation. They can only be refused if the power considers them to be of such a nature as to prejudice its sovereignty or its security. The Commission shall also always have the right to have recourse to the intermediary of the power in whose territory it has its seat.

Art. 25. Witnesses and experts shall be called at the request of the parties or *ex officio* by the Commission, and in any case through the intermediary of the government of the State in whose territory they are located.

The witnesses shall be heard, successively and separately, in the presence of the agents and counsel and in an order to be determined by the commission.

Art. 26. The examination of witnesses shall be conducted by the chairman.

The members of the commission may, however, ask each witness the questions they deem appropriate to clarify or complete his or her testimony or to inquire into any matter concerning the witness within the limits necessary for the determination of the truth.

The agents and counsel for the parties may not interrupt the witness in his testimony, nor may they question him directly, but may request the president to ask the witness such additional questions as they deem useful.

Art. 27. The witness may testify without being allowed to read any written draft. However, he may be authorized by the president to use notes or documents if the nature of the facts reported requires it.

Art. 28. The minutes of the witness' testimony are drawn up from the outset and read to the witness. The witness may make such changes and additions as he or she sees fit, which shall be recorded following his or her deposition.

The witness's entire deposition is read to him and he is required to sign it.

Art. 29. The agents are authorized, during or at the end of the investigation, to present in writing to the commission and to the other party such statements, submissions or summaries of facts as they deem useful for the discovery of the truth.

Art. 30. The deliberations of the commission shall be held in camera and shall remain secret.

All decisions are taken by a majority of the members of the commission.

The refusal of a member to take part in the vote must be recorded in the minutes.

Art. 31. The meetings of the commission shall be public and the minutes and documents of the investigation shall be made public only by virtue of a decision of the commission taken with the consent of the parties.

Art. 32. When the parties have presented all the clarifications and evidence and all the witnesses have been heard, the president shall declare the investigation closed and the commission shall adjourn to deliberate and draft its report.

Art. 33. The report shall be signed by all the members of the commission.

If one of the members refuses to sign, this shall be noted; the report shall nevertheless remain valid.

Art. 34. The report of the commission shall be read in open session, with the agents and counsel of the parties present or duly called.

A copy of the report shall be given to each party.

Art. 35. The report of the commission, which is limited to a statement of the facts, shall in no way have the character of an arbitral award. It leaves the parties free to decide what to do with the findings.

Art. 36. Each party shall bear its own costs and an equal share of the costs of the commission.

Section IV – International Arbitration

Chapter I – Arbitral Justice.

Art. 37. The purpose of international arbitration is the settlement of disputes between States by judges of their choice and on the basis of respect for the law.

The recourse to arbitration implies the commitment to submit in good faith to the award.

Art. 38. In questions of law and, in the first place, in questions of interpretation or application of international conventions, arbitration is recognized by the contracting powers as the most effective and, at the same time, the most equitable means of settling disputes which have not been resolved by diplomatic means.

Accordingly, it is desirable that, in disputes on the above-mentioned matters, the contracting Powers should have recourse to arbitration, if necessary, in so far as circumstances permit.

Art. 39. The arbitration agreement shall be concluded for disputes which have already arisen or for possible disputes.

It can concern all disputes or only disputes of a certain category.

Art. 40. Independently of the general or particular treaties which at present stipulate the obligation of recourse to arbitration for the contracting powers, these powers reserve the right to conclude new agreements, either general or particular, with a view to extending compulsory arbitration to all cases which they may consider possible.

Chapter II – The Permanent Court of Arbitration.

Art. 41. In order to facilitate the immediate recourse to arbitration for international disputes which cannot be settled by diplomatic means, the contracting powers undertake to maintain, as established by the first peace conference, the permanent court of arbitration, accessible at all times and functioning, unless the parties stipulate otherwise, in accordance with the rules of procedure inserted in the present convention.

Art. 42. The permanent court shall have jurisdiction in all cases of arbitration, unless the parties agree to the establishment of a special jurisdiction.

Art. 43. The Permanent Court shall have its seat at The Hague.
An international office serves as the registry of the court; it is the intermediary of communications relating to the meetings of the court; it has custody of the archives and the management of all administrative matters.
The contracting powers undertake to communicate to the office, as soon as possible, a certified copy of any arbitration stipulation entered into between them and of any arbitral award concerning them and rendered by special courts.
They shall likewise communicate to the office the laws, regulations and documents which may establish the execution of the awards rendered by the court.

Art. 44. Each contracting power shall appoint not more than four persons of recognized competence in matters of international law, of high moral character and willing to accept the duties of arbitrator.

The persons so nominated shall be entered as members of the court on a list which shall be notified to all the contracting powers by the Bureau.

Any change in the list of arbitrators shall be brought to the notice of the Contracting Powers by the Bureau.

Two or more powers may agree on the joint appointment of one or more members.

The same person may be appointed by different powers.

The members of the court are appointed for a term of six years. They may be reappointed.

In the event of the death or retirement of a member of the court, he shall be replaced in the same way as for his appointment, and for a further period of six years.

Art. 45. When the contracting powers wish to apply to the permanent court for the settlement of a dispute which has arisen between them, the choice of the arbitrators who are to form the tribunal competent to decide the dispute must be made from the general list of the members of the court.

In the absence of the constitution of the arbitral tribunal by the agreement of the parties, the procedure shall be as follows:

Each party shall appoint two arbitrators, only one of whom may be its national or chosen from among those appointed by it as members of the permanent court. These arbitrators shall together select a referee.

In the event of a tie, the choice of the arbitrator shall be entrusted to a third party, designated by mutual agreement of the parties.

If there is no agreement on this matter, each party shall designate a different power and the choice of the umpire shall be made in agreement by the powers thus designated.

If, within two months, these two powers have not been able to agree, each of them shall present two candidates from the list of members of the permanent court, who are not nationals of either of the parties. The lot shall determine which of the candidates thus presented shall be the umpire.

Art. 46. As soon as the tribunal is composed, the parties shall notify the office of their decision to apply to the court, the text of their compromise and the names of the arbitrators.

The board shall promptly notify each arbitrator of the agreement and the names of the other members of the tribunal.

The court shall meet on the date fixed by the parties. The bureau shall provide for its installation.

The members of the tribunal, in the exercise of their functions and outside their country, shall enjoy diplomatic privileges and immunities.

Art. 47. The office is authorized to place its premises and its organization at the disposal of the contracting powers for the functioning of any special arbitration court.

The jurisdiction of the permanent court may be extended, under the conditions prescribed by the regulations, to disputes existing between non-contracting powers or between contracting powers and non-contracting powers, if the parties have agreed to have recourse to such jurisdiction.

Art. 48. The contracting Powers consider it their duty, in the event of a sharp conflict threatening to break out between two or more of them, to remind them that the permanent court is open to them.

Accordingly, they declare that reminding the parties to the conflict of the provisions of the present Convention, and advising them, in the best interests of peace, to apply to the permanent court, can only be considered as acts of good offices.

In the event of a dispute between two Powers, either of them may always address to the international office a note containing its declaration that it is prepared to submit the dispute to arbitration.

The office shall immediately bring the declaration to the knowledge of the other power.

Art. 49. The permanent Administrative Council, composed of the diplomatic representatives of the Contracting Powers accredited to The Hague and of the Minister for Foreign Affairs of the Netherlands, who shall act as President, shall have the direction and control of the International Bureau.

The Council shall adopt its own rules of procedure and all other necessary regulations. 1 It shall decide all administrative matters that may arise in connection with the operation of the court.

It shall have full power to appoint, suspend or dismiss the officers and employees of the office.

It fixes the salaries and wages, and controls the general expenditure.

The presence of nine members at duly convened meetings is sufficient for the council to deliberate validly. Decisions are taken by a majority vote.

The Council shall promptly communicate to the Contracting Powers the regulations adopted by it. It shall submit to them annually a report on the work of the court, on the operation of the administrative services and on the expenditures. The report shall also contain a summary of the essential contents of the documents communicated to the board by the powers under Article 43, paragraphs 3 and 4.

Art. 50. The expenses of the Bureau shall be borne by the contracting Powers in the proportion established for the International Bureau of the Universal Postal Union.

The costs to be borne by the adhering Powers shall be counted from the day on which their adherence takes effect.

Chapter III – Arbitration Procedure.

Art. 51. In order to promote the development of arbitration, the contracting Powers have laid down the following rules, which shall be applicable to arbitral proceedings, in so far as the parties have not agreed on other rules.

Art. 52. The powers which resort to arbitration shall sign a special agreement in which the subject-matter of the dispute, the time-limit for the appointment of the arbitrators, the form, order and time-limits within which the communication referred to in Article 63 shall be made, and the amount of the sum to be deposited by each party for costs shall be determined.

The agreement shall also determine, if necessary, the method of appointment of the arbitrators, any special powers of the tribunal, its seat, the language it shall use, and those which may be used before it, and generally all the conditions agreed upon by the parties.

Art. 53. The permanent court is competent to establish the compromise, if the parties agree to defer to it.

It is also competent, even if the request is made only by one of the parties, after an agreement through diplomatic channels has been tried in vain, when it is a question of:

1. A dispute falling within a treaty, of general arbitration concluded or renewed after the coming into force of this agreement and which provides for a compromise for each dispute, and does not exclude for the establishment of the latter either explicitly or implicitly the jurisdiction of the court. However, recourse to the court shall not be had if the other party declares that, in his opinion, the dispute does not fall within the category of disputes to be submitted to binding arbitration, unless the arbitration treaty confers on the arbitral tribunal the power to decide this question.

2. A dispute arising out of contractual debts claimed from one power by another as due to its nationals, and for the settlement of which the offer of arbitration has been accepted. This provision does not apply if the acceptance was made subject to the condition that the arbitration agreement be drawn up in some other way.

Art. 54. In the cases provided for in the preceding article, the arbitration agreement shall be drawn up by a commission consisting of five members appointed in the manner provided for in article 45, paragraphs 3 to 6.

Art. 55. The arbitration functions may be conferred on a sole arbitrator or on several arbitrators appointed by the parties at their own discretion, or chosen by them from among the members of the permanent court of arbitration established by this convention.

In the absence of the constitution of the tribunal by agreement of the parties, the procedure shall be as indicated in Article 45, paragraphs 3 to 6.

Art. 56. When a sovereign or a head of state is chosen as arbitrator, the arbitration procedure shall be regulated by him.

Art. 57. The referee is *ex officio* chairman of the tribunal.

When the tribunal does not include a referee, it appoints its own president.

Art. 58. In the event that the arbitration agreement is drawn up by a commission, as referred to in Article 54, and unless otherwise agreed, the commission itself shall form the arbitration tribunal.

Art. 59. In the event of the death, resignation or impediment, for whatever reason, of one of the arbitrators, "he shall be replaced in the manner fixed for his appointment.

Art. 60. In the absence of a designation by the parties, the tribunal shall sit at The Hague.

The tribunal may sit in the territory of a third power only with the consent of that power.

The seat, once fixed, may be changed by the tribunal only with the consent of the parties.

Art. 61. If the agreement has not determined the languages to be used, this is to be decided by the court.

Art. 62. The parties shall have the right to appoint special agents to the court to act as intermediaries between them and the court.

They are also entitled to appoint counsel or advocates to defend their rights and interests before the court.

The members of the permanent court may only exercise the functions of agents, counsel or advocates in favor of the power which has appointed them members of the court.

Art. 63. The arbitral proceedings consist, as a general rule, of two distinct phases: the written hearing and the debates.

The written hearing shall consist of the communication by the respective agents to the members of the tribunal and to the opposing party of the memorials, counter-memorials and, if necessary, replies; the parties shall attach thereto all the documents and exhibits invoked in the case. This communication shall take place, directly or through the intermediary of the international bureau, in the order and within the time limits determined by the agreement.

The time limits established in the arbitration agreement may be extended by mutual agreement of the parties or by the court when it deems it necessary to reach a fair decision.

The debates shall consist of the oral development of the parties' arguments before the court.

Art. 64. Any document produced by one of the parties must be communicated, in a certified copy, to the other party.

Art. 65. Unless there are special circumstances, the court shall not meet until the investigation is closed.

Art. 66. The debates are directed by the president.

They shall be public only by virtue of a decision of the court taken with the consent of the parties.

They are recorded in minutes drawn up by secretaries appointed by the president. These minutes shall be signed by the president and by one of the secretaries and shall be authentic.

Art. 67. Once the investigation is closed, the court has the right to exclude from the debate any new acts or documents that one of the parties may wish to submit to it without the consent of the other.

Art. 68. The court remains free to take into consideration new acts or documents to which the agents or counsel of the parties draw its attention.

In this case, the court has the right to require the production of these acts or documents, without the obligation to give notice of them to the opposing party.

Art. 69. The court can also require the agents of the parties to produce any documents and request any necessary explanations. In case of refusal, the court shall take note of it.

Art. 70. The agents and counsels of the parties are authorized to present orally to the court all the arguments which they consider useful for the defense of their case.

Art. 71. They have the right to raise exceptions and incidents. The decisions of the court on these points shall be final and shall not give rise to any further discussion.

Art. 72. The members of the tribunal shall have the right to ask questions of the agents and counsel of the parties and to request clarification of doubtful points.

Neither the questions asked nor the observations made by the members of the tribunal during the course of the proceedings may be regarded as an expression of the opinions of the tribunal in general or of its members in particular.

Art. 73. The court is authorized to determine its jurisdiction by interpreting the compromise and other acts and documents that may be invoked in the matter, and by invoking the principles of law.

Art. 74. The court has the right to issue procedural orders for the conduct of the trial, to determine the form, order and time limits within which each party must make its final submissions, and to carry out all the formalities involved in the taking of evidence.

Art. 75. The parties undertake to provide the court, to the greatest extent they consider possible, with all the means necessary for the decision of the dispute.

Art. 76. For all notifications which the tribunal may have to make in the territory of a third contracting power, the tribunal shall apply directly to the government of that power. The same shall apply if it is a question of taking evidence on the spot.

Requests addressed to this effect shall be executed in accordance with the means available to the requested power under its internal legislation. They may be refused only if that power considers them to be of such a nature as to prejudice its sovereignty or security.

The tribunal shall also always have the right to have recourse to the intermediary of the power in whose territory it has its seat.

Art. 77. When the agents and counsel of the parties have presented all the explanations and evidence in support of their case, the president shall declare the proceedings closed.

The president shall declare the proceedings closed.

Art. 78. The deliberations of the tribunal shall take place *in camera* and shall remain secret.

All decisions are taken by a majority of its members.

Art. 79. The arbitral award shall state the reasons on which it is based. It shall mention the names of the arbitrators; it shall be signed by the president and by the clerk or the secretary acting as clerk.

Art. 80. The award shall be read in open court, with the agents and counsel of the parties present or duly called.

Art. 81. The sentence, duly pronounced and notified to the agents of the parties, decides the dispute definitively and without appeal.

Art. 82. Any dispute that may arise between the parties, concerning the interpretation and execution of the award, shall, unless otherwise stipulated, be submitted to the judgment of the court that rendered it.

Art. 83. The parties may reserve in the compromise the right to request a review of the arbitral award.

In this case, and unless otherwise stipulated, the request must be addressed to the court that made the award. It can only be motivated by the discovery of a new fact, which would have been of a nature to exert a decisive influence on the award and which, at the time of the closure of the debates, was unknown to the tribunal itself and to the party who requested the revision.

The revision procedure can only be initiated by a decision of the tribunal expressly noting the existence of the new fact, recognizing it as provided for in the preceding paragraph and declaring the request admissible.

The compromise determines the time limit within which the application for review must be made.

Art. 84. The arbitral award is binding only on the parties to the dispute.

Where the interpretation of a convention in which powers other than the parties in dispute have participated is involved, the latter shall give due notice to all the signatory powers. Each of these powers has the right to intervene in the proceedings. If one or more of them have availed themselves of this right, the interpretation contained in the award is also binding on them.

Art. 85. Each party shall bear its own costs and an equal share of the costs of the court.

Chapter IV – Summary Procedure: Arbitration.

Art. 86. With a view to facilitating the functioning of arbitral justice, when disputes of a nature to require a summary procedure are involved, the contracting powers lay down the following rules, which shall be followed in the absence of different stipulations, and subject, if necessary, to the application of the provisions of Chapter III which are not contrary to them.

Art. 87. Each of the parties in dispute shall appoint an arbitrator. The two arbitrators thus appointed shall choose a referee. If they do not agree on this, they shall each present two candidates from the general list of the members of the permanent court, apart from the members indicated by each of the parties themselves and who are not nationals of any of them; the lot shall determine which of the candidates thus presented shall be the umpire.

The referee shall preside over the court, which shall render its decisions by a majority vote.

Art. 88. In the absence of prior agreement, the tribunal shall, as soon as it is constituted, set the time limit within which the two parties must submit their respective briefs to it.

Art. 89. Each party shall be represented before the court by an agent who shall act as intermediary between the court and the government which appointed him.

Art. 90. The proceedings shall be conducted exclusively in writing. However, each party has the right to request the appearance of witnesses and experts. The court, for its part, has the right to request oral explanations from the agents of both parties, as well as from experts and witnesses whose appearance it deems useful.

Section V – Final Provisions

Art. 91. The present Convention, duly ratified, shall replace the Convention for the peaceful settlement of international disputes of 29 July 1899 in the relations between the contracting Powers.

Art. 92. The present Convention shall be ratified as soon as possible.

The ratifications shall be deposited at The Hague.

The first deposit of ratifications will be recorded by a transcript signed by the representatives of the powers taking part and by the Minister of Foreign Affairs of the Netherlands.

Subsequent deposits of ratifications shall be made by means of a written notification, addressed to the Government of the Netherlands, accompanied by the instrument of ratification.

A certified copy of the transcript relating to the first deposit of ratifications, of the notifications mentioned in the preceding paragraph, and of the instruments of ratification, shall be immediately delivered by the Government of the Netherlands through diplomatic channels to the Powers invited to the Second Peace Conference, and to the other Powers which have acceded to the Convention. In the cases referred to in the preceding paragraph, the said Government shall at the same time inform them of the date on which it received the notification.

Art. 93. The non-signatory Powers, which have been invited to the Second Peace Conference, may accede to the present Convention.

The power which desires to accede shall notify its intention in writing to the Government of the Netherlands, transmitting to it the act of accession which shall be deposited in the archives of the said Government.

This Government shall immediately transmit to all the other Powers invited to the Second Peace Conference certified copies of the notification and of the act of accession, indicating the date on which it received the notification.

Art. 94. The conditions under which powers which have not been invited to the second peace conference may accede to the present Convention shall be the subject of a subsequent agreement between the powers concerned.

Art. 95. The present Convention shall have effect, for the powers which have participated in the first deposit of ratifications, sixty days after the date of the transcript; and, for the powers which shall subsequently ratify or accede, sixty days after the notification of their ratification or accession has been received by the Government of the Netherlands.

Art. 96. If one of the contracting powers should wish to denounce the present Convention, the denunciation shall be notified in writing to the Government of the Netherlands, which shall immediately communicate certified copies of the notification to all the other powers, informing them of the date on which it was received.

The denunciation shall have effect only with regard to the power which has notified it and one year after the notification has reached the Government of the Netherlands.

Art. 97. A register, kept by the Ministry of Foreign Affairs of the Netherlands, shall indicate the date of the deposit of ratifications made in accordance with Article 92 (paragraphs 3 and 4), as well as the date on which notifications of accession (Article 93, paragraph 2) or of denunciation (Article 96, paragraph 1) have been received.

Each Contracting Power is entitled to inspect this register and to request certified extracts from it.

In witness whereof the plenipotentiaries have signed the present Convention.

Done at The Hague, this 18th day of October 1907, in a single copy which shall remain deposited in the archives of the Government of the Netherlands, and of which certified copies shall be delivered through diplomatic channels to the Contracting Powers:

(Signatures follow.)

Art. 2. The Minister of Foreign Affairs and the Minister of Justice, are charged, each in what concerns him, with the execution of the present decree.

Done in Paris, on 2 December 1910.

A. FALLIÈRES.

For the President of the Republic:

The Minister of Foreign Affairs,
S. PICHON.

The Keeper of the Seals, Minister of Justice,
Théodore GIRARD.

Decree promulgating the international convention, signed at The Hague on 18 October 1907, concerning the limitation of the use of force for the recovery of contractual debts.

Paris, 2 December 1910.

The President of the French Republic,
On the proposal of the Minister of Foreign Affairs,
Decrees :

Art. 1. The Senate and the Chamber of Deputies having adopted the international convention concerning the limitation of the use of force for the recovery of contractual debts, signed at The Hague on 18 October 1907 by France, Germany, the United States of America, the Argentine Republic, Austria-Hungary, Bolivia, Bulgaria, Chile, Colombia, the Republic of Cuba, Denmark Republic of Cuba, Denmark, Dominican Republic, Ecuador, Great Britain, Greece, Guatemala, Haiti, Italy, Japan, Mexico, Montenegro, Norway, Panama, Paraguay, Netherlands, Peru, Portugal, Russia, Spain, Sweden, Switzerland, United Kingdom, United States of America: Persia, Portugal, Russia, El Salvador, Serbia, Turkey and Uruguay, and the ratifications of this act having been deposited at The Hague by France, Germany, the United States of America, Austria-Hungary, Denmark, Great Britain, Haiti, Mexico, Norway, the Netherlands, El Salvador and the Netherlands; China having acceded to the said Convention on January 15, 1910 and Nicaragua on December 16, 1909, with the following reservations *a)* With regard to debts arising from ordinary contracts between the national of a nation and a foreign government, recourse shall be had to arbitration only in the specific case of denial of justice by the courts of the country of the contract, which must first be exhausted; *b)* Public loans, with the issue of bonds, constituting the national debt, shall not give rise, under any circumstances, to military aggression or to the material occupation of the soil of the American nations; - the said convention, the content of which follows, shall receive its full and complete execution.

Convention II Concerning the Limitation of the Use of Force for the Recovery of Debts

(List of sovereigns and heads of state.)

Desiring to avoid between nations armed conflicts of pecuniary origin, arising from contractual debts, claimed from the government of one country by the government of another country as due to its citizens.

Have resolved to conclude a convention for this purpose, and have appointed as their plenipotentiaries, namely:

(Designation of plenipotentiaries follows.)

Who, having deposited their full powers found in due form, have agreed upon the following provisions:

Art. 1. The contracting powers have agreed not to have recourse to armed force for the recovery of contractual debts claimed from the government of one country by the government of another country as due to its citizens.

However, this stipulation shall not be applied when the debtor State refuses or leaves unanswered an offer of arbitration, or, in case of acceptance, makes it impossible to establish a compromise, or, after arbitration, fails to comply with the award made.

Art. 2. It is further agreed that the arbitration mentioned in paragraph 2 of the preceding article shall be subject to the procedure provided for in Section IV, Chapter III, of the Hague Convention for the Peaceful Settlement of International Disputes. The arbitral judgment shall determine, except for the particular arrangements of the parties, the validity of the claim, the amount of the debt, the time and the method of payment.

Art. 3. The present Convention shall be ratified as soon as possible.

The ratifications shall be deposited at The Hague.

The first deposit of ratification shall be recorded in a transcript signed by the representatives of the Powers which take part in it and by the Minister of Foreign Affairs of the Netherlands.

Subsequent deposits of ratifications shall be made by means of a written notification addressed to the Government of the Netherlands and accompanied by the instrument of ratification. A certified copy of the transcript relating to the first deposit of ratifications, of the notifications mentioned in the preceding paragraph, and of the instruments of ratification, shall be immediately transmitted, by the Government of the Netherlands, through diplomatic channels, to the Powers invited to the Second Peace Conference, and to the other Powers which have acceded to the Convention. In the cases referred to in the preceding paragraph, the said Government shall at the same time inform them of the date on which it received the notification.

Art. 4. Powers not signatory to the present Convention shall be admitted to accede thereto.

The Power desiring to accede shall notify its intention in writing to the Government of the Netherlands, transmitting to it the act of accession, which shall be deposited in the archives of the said Government.

This Government shall immediately transmit to all the other Powers invited to the Second Peace Conference, certified copies of the notification and of the act of accession, indicating the date on which it received the notification.

Art. 5. The present Convention shall take effect for the powers which have participated in the first deposit of ratifications, sixty days after the date of the transcript of this deposit, for the powers which ratify subsequently or which accede, sixty days after the notification of their ratification or accession has been received by the Government of the Netherlands.

Art. 6. If one of the contracting powers should wish to denounce the present Convention, the denunciation shall be notified in writing to the Government of the Netherlands, which shall immediately communicate a certified copy of the notification to all the other powers, informing them of the date on which it was received.

The denunciation shall have effect only with regard to the power which has notified it, and one year after the notification has reached the Government of the Netherlands.

Art. 7. A register kept by the Minister of Foreign Affairs of the Netherlands shall indicate the date of the deposit of ratifications made in pursuance of Article 3 (paragraphs 3 and 4), as well as the date on which notifications of accession (Article 4, paragraph 2) or of denunciation (Article 6, paragraph 1) have been received.

Each Contracting Power is entitled to inspect this register and to request certified extracts from it.

In witness whereof the plenipotentiaries have signed the present Convention.

Done at The Hague, on the 18th day of October 1907, in a single copy which shall remain deposited in the archives of the Government of the Netherlands, and of which certified copies shall be delivered through diplomatic channels to the Contracting Powers.

(Signatures follow.)

Art. 2. The Minister of Foreign Affairs is charged with the execution of the present decree.

Done in Paris, December 2, 1910.

A. FALLIÈRES.

For the President of the Republic:
The Minister of Foreign Affairs,
S. PICHON.

Decree promulgating the international convention, signed at The Hague on 18 October 1907, relating to the opening of hostilities.

Paris, December 2, 1910.

The President of the French Republic,
On the proposal of the Minister of Foreign Affairs, the Minister of the Navy and the Minister of War,

Decrees:

Art. 1. The Senate and the Chamber of Deputies having adopted the international convention relating to the opening of hostilities, signed at The Hague, on October 18, 1907, by France, Germany, the United States of America, the Argentine Republic, Austria-Hungary, Belgium, Bolivia, Brazil, Bulgaria, Chile, Colombia, the Republic of Cuba, Denmark, the Dominican Republic Ecuador, Great Britain, Greece, Guatemala, Haiti, Italy, Japan, Luxembourg, Mexico, Montenegro, Spain, the. Montenegro, Norway, Panama,. Norway, Panama, Paraguay, the. Peru, Persia, Portugal, Rumania, Russia, Salvndor, Serbia, Siam, Sweden, Switzerland, Turkey, Uruguay and Venezuela, and the ratifications of this act having been deposited at The Hague by France, Germany, the United States of America, Austria-Hungary, Belgium, Bolivia, Denmark, Great Britain, Haiti, Mexico, Norway, the Netherlands, Hussia, El Salvador, Siam, Sweden and Switzerland; - China having acceded to the said convention on the 15th day of January, 1910, and Nicaragua on the 1st day of November, 1909; the said convention, the content of which follows, will be given its full and complete execution.

Convention III Relating to the Opening of Hostilities

(List of sovereigns and heads of state).

Considering that, for the security of peaceful relations, it is important that hostilities should not begin without prior warning;

That it is important, likewise, that the state of war be notified without delay to the neutral powers;

Desiring to conclude a convention to this effect, have appointed as their plenipotentiaries, namely:

(The designation of the plenipotentiaries follows.)

Who, having deposited their full powers, found in due form, have agreed upon the following provisions:

Art. 1. The contracting powers recognize that hostilities between them must not commence without a previous and unequivocal warning, which shall take the form either of a declaration of war with reasons, or of an ultimatum with a conditional declaration of war.

Art. 2. The state of war must be notified without delay to the neutral powers, and will only take effect in their regard after receipt of a notification which may be made even by telegraphic means. However, the neutral Powers may invoke the absence of notification, if it is established in an unquestionable manner that they were in fact aware of the state of war.

Art. 3. Article 1 of the present Convention shall have effect in case of war between two or more of the contracting powers.

Article 2 shall be binding in the relations between a contracting belligerent and the neutral powers which are also contracting parties.

Art. 4. The present Convention shall be ratified as soon as possible.

The ratifications shall be deposited at The Hague.

The first deposit of ratifications shall be recorded by a transcript signed by the representatives of the Powers taking part in it and by the Minister of Foreign Affairs of the Netherlands.

Subsequent deposits of ratifications shall be made by means of a written notification addressed to the Government of the Netherlands and accompanied by the instrument of ratification.

A certified copy of the transcript relating to the first deposit of ratifications, of the notifications mentioned in the preceding paragraph, and of the instruments of ratification, shall be immediately delivered by the Government of the Netherlands through diplomatic channels to the Powers invited to the Second Peace Conference, and to the other Powers which have acceded to the Convention. In the cases referred to in the preceding paragraph, the said Government shall at the same time inform them of the date on which it received the notification.

Art. 5. Non-signatory Powers are admitted to accede to the present Convention.

The power which desires to accede shall notify its intention in writing to the Government of the Netherlands, transmitting to it the act of accession, which shall be deposited in the archives of the said Government.

This Government shall immediately transmit to all the other Powers certified copies of the notification and of the instrument of accession, indicating the date on which it received the notification.

Art. 6. The present Convention shall take effect for the Powers which have participated in the first deposit of ratification, sixty days after the date of the transcript of such deposit, and for the

Powers which ratify or accede subsequently, sixty days after the notification of their ratification or accession has been received by the Government of the Netherlands.

Art. 7. If one of the High Contracting Parties should wish to denounce the present Convention, the denunciation shall be notified in writing to the Government of the Netherlands, which shall immediately communicate a certified copy of the notification to all the other Powers, informing them of the date on which it was received.

The denunciation shall have effect only with regard to the Power which has notified it, and one year after the notification has reached the Government of the Netherlands.

Art. 8. A register kept by the Minister of Foreign Affairs of the Netherlands shall indicate the date of the deposit of ratifications made in accordance with Article 4, paragraphs 3 and 4, as well as the date on which notifications of accession (Article 5, paragraph 2) or of denunciation (Article 7, paragraph 1) have been received.

Each contracting power is entitled to take cognizance of this register and to request certified extracts from it.

In witness thereof the plenipotentiaries have signed the present Convention.

Done at The Hague, on the 18th day of October 1907, in a single copy which shall remain deposited in the archives of the Government of the Netherlands, and of which certified copies shall be delivered through diplomatic channels to the Powers which have been invited to the Second Peace Conference.

(Signatures follow.)

Art. 2. The Minister of Foreign Affairs, the Minister of the Navy and the Minister of War are charged, each in what concerns him, with the execution of the present decree.

Done in Paris, December 2, 1910.

A. FALLIÈRES.

For the President of the Republic:
The Minister of Foreign Affairs,
S. PICHON.

The Minister of the Navy,   *The Minister of War,*
DE LAPEYRÈRE.   BRUN.

Decree promulgating the international convention signed at The Hague on 18 October 1907, concerning the laws and customs of war on land.

Paris. December 2, 1910.

The President of the French Republic,
On the proposal of the Minister of Foreign Affairs and the Minister of War,

Decrees:

Art. 1. The Senate and the Chamber of Deputies having adopted the international convention concerning the laws and customs of war on land signed at The Hague, on October 18, 1907, by France, Germany, the United States of America, the Argentine Republic, Austria-Hungary, Belgium, Bolivia, Brazil, Bulgaria, Chile, Colombia, the Republic of Cuba, Denmark, the Dominican Republic, Ecuador, El Salvador, Greece, Guatemala, Haiti, Italy, Japan, Luxembourg, Mexico, Montenegro, Netherlands, Norway, Panama, Paraguay, Peru, Persia, Portugal, Romania, Russia, Serbia, Siam, Sweden, Switzerland, Turkey, United Kingdom, Uruguay, and Venezuela, and the ratifications of this Act having been deposited at The Hague by France, Germany, the United States of America. Austria-Hungary, Belgium, Bolivia, Denmark, Great Britain, El Salvador, Haiti, Mexico, the Netherlands, Norway, Russia, Siam, Sweden and Switzerland; – Nicaragua having acceded to the said Convention on the 16th day of December, 1909; the said Convention, the contents of which follow, shall be given full and complete effect.

Convention IV Concerning the Laws and Customs of War on Land

(List of sovereigns and Heads of State.)

Considering that, while seeking the means of safeguarding peace and preventing armed conflicts between nations, it is important to be concerned also with the case in which the call to arms would be brought about by events which their solicitude could not divert;

Animated by the desire to serve again, in this extreme scenario, the interests of humanity and the ever-progressive demands of civilization;

Believing that it is important, to this end, to review the general laws and customs of war, either with a view to defining them more precisely, or in order to draw certain limits intended to restrict their rigors as far as possible;

Have found it necessary to complete and clarify on certain points the work of the first peace conference, which, inspired by the Brussels conference of 1874, by those ideas recommended by a wise and generous foresight, adopted provisions having for its objective to define and regulate the usages of war on earth.

According to the views of the principal contracting parties, these provisions, the drafting of which was inspired by the desire to diminish the evils of war, as far as military necessities permit, are intended to serve as a general rule of conduct for the belligerents, in their relations with each other and with the populations. It was not possible, however, to agree on stipulations which would cover all practical circumstances.

On the other hand, it could not enter into the intentions of the principal contracting parties that the cases not foreseen were, for lack of written stipulation, left to the arbitrary appreciation of those who lead the armies.

Until a more complete code of the laws of war can be enacted, the High Contracting Parties deem it expedient to declare that, in cases not included in the regulations adopted by them, the populations and the belligerents remain under the protection and the rule of the principles and the laws of nations, as they result from the usages established between civilized nations, from the laws of humanity, and from the dictates of public conscience.

They declare that Articles 1 and 2 of the adopted regulations are to be understood in this sense.

The principal contracting parties, desiring to conclude a new convention for this purpose, have appointed as their plenipotentiaries, namely:

(Designation of plenipotentiaries.)

Who, having deposited their full powers, found in due form, have agreed as follows:

Art. 1. The Contracting Powers shall give to their land forces instructions which shall be in conformity with the regulations concerning the laws and customs of war on land, annexed to the present Convention.

Art. 2. The provisions contained in the Regulations referred to in Article 1, as well as in the present Convention, are applicable only between the Contracting Powers, and only if the belligerents are all parties to the Convention.

Art. 3. The belligerent party which violates the provisions of the said Regulations shall be liable for compensation, if any. It shall be responsible for all acts committed by persons forming part of its armed force.

Art. 4. The present Convention, duly ratified, shall replace, in the relations between the contracting Powers, the Convention of July 29, 1899, concerning the laws and customs of war on land.

The convention of 1899 shall remain in force as between the powers which have signed it and which have not also ratified the present convention. -1

Art. 5. The present Convention shall be ratified as soon as possible.

The ratifications shall be deposited at The Hague.

The first deposit of ratifications shall be recorded in a transcript signed by the representatives of the Powers taking part in it and by the Minister of Foreign Affairs of the Netherlands.

Subsequent deposits of ratifications shall be made by means of a written notification addressed to the Government of the Netherlands and accompanied by the instrument of ratification.

A certified copy of the transcript relating to the first deposit of ratifications, of the notifications mentioned in the preceding paragraph, and of the instruments of ratification, shall be immediately delivered by the Government of the Netherlands through diplomatic channels to the Powers invited to the Second Peace Convention, and to the other Powers which have acceded to the Convention. In the cases referred to in the preceding paragraph, the said Government shall at the same time inform them of the date on which it received the notification.

Art. 6. The non-signatory Powers are admitted to accede to the present Convention.

The power which desires to accede shall notify its intention in writing to the Government of the Netherlands, transmitting to it the act of accession, which shall be deposited in the archives of the said Government.

This Government shall immediately transmit to all the other Powers certified copies of the notification and of the instrument of accession, indicating the date on which it received the notification.

Art. 7. The present Convention shall take effect, for the Powers which have participated in the first deposit of ratifications, sixty days after the date of the transcript of such deposit, and, for the Powers which subsequently ratify or accede, sixty days after the notification of their ratification or accession has been received by the Government of the Netherlands.

Art. 8. If one of the Contracting Powers should wish to denounce the present Convention, the denunciation shall be notified in writing to the Government of the Netherlands, which shall immediately communicate a certified copy of the notification to all the other Powers, informing them of the date on which it was received.

The denunciation shall have effect only with regard to the Power which has notified it, and one year after the notification has reached the Government of the Netherlands.

Art. 9. A register kept by the Ministry of Foreign Affairs of the Netherlands shall indicate the date of the deposit of ratifications made in accordance with Article 5, paragraphs 3 and 4, as well as the date on which notifications of accession (Article 6, paragraph 2) or of denunciation (Article 8, paragraph 1) have been received.

Each Contracting Power is entitled to inspect this register and to request certified extracts from it.

In witness whereof the plenipotentiaries have signed the present Convention.

Done at The Hague, on the 18th day of October 1907, in a single copy, which shall remain deposited in the archives of the Government of the Netherlands, and of which certified copies shall be delivered through diplomatic channels to the Powers which were invited to the Second Peace Conference.

(Signatures follow.)

Appendix to the Convention – Regulations concerning the laws and customs of war on land

Section I – Belligerents

Chapter I – The Status of Belligerents.

Art. 1. The laws, rights and duties of war apply not only to the army, but also to militias and volunteer corps meeting the following conditions:
 1. To have at their head a person responsible for his subordinates;
 2. To have a fixed distinctive sign recognizable at a distance;
 3. To bear arms openly;
 4. To conform in their operations to the laws and customs of war.
In countries where militias or volunteer corps constitute the army or are part of it, they are included under the name of *army*.

Art. 2. The population of an unoccupied territory which, on the approach of the enemy, spontaneously takes up arms to fight the invading troops without having had time to organize itself in accordance with Article 1, shall be considered as belligerents if they openly bear arms and if they respect the laws and customs of war.

Art. 3. The armed forces of the belligerent parties may consist of combatants and non-combatants. In case of capture by the enemy, both are entitled to the treatment of prisoners of war.

Chapter II – Prisoners of War.

Art. 4. Prisoners of war are in the power of the enemy government, but not of the individuals or bodies which have captured them.
They must be treated with humanity.
All that belongs to them personally, except arms, horses and military papers, remains their property.

Art. 5. Prisoners of war may be subjected to internment in a city, fortress, camp or locality of any kind, with the obligation not to go beyond certain determined limits; but they may only be confined as a measure of indispensable security, and only for the duration of the circumstances which necessitate this measure.

Art. 6. The State may employ prisoners of war as workers, according to their rank and abilities, with the exception of officers. Such work shall not be excessive and shall have no connection with the operations of the war.
Prisoners may be authorized to work for public administrations or private individuals, or for their own account.
Work done for the State shall be paid according to the rates in force for soldiers of the national army performing the same work, or, if there are none, according to a rate in relation to the work performed.
When the work is done for other public administrations or for private individuals, the conditions are regulated in agreement with the military authority.
The wages of the prisoners shall contribute to the alleviation of their position, and the surplus shall be counted to them at the time of their release, except for the deduction of maintenance costs.

Art. 7. The government in whose power the prisoners of war are, shall be responsible for their maintenance.

In the absence of a special agreement between the belligerents, prisoners of war shall be treated, as regards food, bedding and clothing, on the same footing as the troops of the government which has captured them.

Art. 8. The prisoners of war shall be subject to the laws, regulations and orders in force in the army of the State in whose power they are. Any act of insubordination shall authorize the necessary measures of rigor in their regard.

Escaped prisoners who are recaptured before they have been able to rejoin their army or before they have left the territory occupied by the army which has captured them, shall be liable to disciplinary punishment.

Prisoners who, after having succeeded in escaping, are again taken prisoner, are not liable to any punishment for the previous escape.

Art. 9. Each prisoner of war is obliged to declare, if questioned on the subject, his true name and rank, and in the event of his violating this rule, he shall be liable to a restriction of the benefits granted to prisoners of war of his category.

Art. 10. Prisoners of war may be released on parole, if the laws of their country so authorize, and, in such a case, they are obliged, under the guarantee of their personal honor, to fulfill scrupulously, both towards their own government and towards the government which has made them prisoners, the engagements which they have contracted.

In the same case, their own government is obliged not to demand or accept from them any service contrary to the parole given.

Art. 11. A prisoner of war cannot be compelled to accept his freedom on parole; likewise, the enemy government is not obliged to accede to the prisoner's request for release on parole.

Art. 12. Any prisoner of war, released on parole and taken up again bearing arms against the government to which he was honour-bound, or against the allies of the latter, loses the right to the treatment of prisoners of war and may be brought before the courts.

Art. 13. Individuals who follow an army without being directly part of it, such as correspondents and reporters of newspapers, caterers, suppliers, who fall into the power of the enemy and whom the latter deems it useful to detain, shall have the right to the treatment of prisoners of war, on condition that they are in possession of a legitimation from the military authority of the army they were accompanying.

Art 14. From the outbreak of hostilities, an information bureau on prisoners of war shall be set up in each of the belligerent States and, if necessary, in neutral countries which have taken in belligerents on their territory. This office, in charge of answering all requests concerning them, shall receive from the various competent services all information relating to internments and transfers, releases on parole, exchanges, escapes, entries into hospitals, deaths, as well as other information necessary to establish and keep up to date an individual card for each prisoner of war. The office shall record on this card the service number, the name and surname, the age, the place of origin, the rank, the troop corps, the wounds, the date and place of capture, internment, wounds and death, as well as any particular observations. The individual card will be given to the government of the other belligerent after the conclusion of peace.

The intelligence office is also responsible for collecting and centralizing all objects of personal use, valuables, letters, etc., which will be found on the battlefields or left behind by prisoners released on parole, exchanged, escaped or deceased in hospitals and ambulances, and to transmit them to the interested parties.

Art. 15. Relief societies for prisoners of war, regularly constituted according to the law of their country and having for object to be the intermediaries of charitable action, shall receive from the belligerents, for themselves and for their duly accredited agents, all facilities, within the limits set by military necessities and administrative rules, to accomplish effectively their humanitarian task. The delegates of these societies may be admitted to distribute relief in internment depots, as well as in the staging areas of repatriated prisoners, in return for personal permission issued by the military authorities, and by undertaking in writing to submit to all measures of order and police that the latter may prescribe.

Art. 16. Post offices are free of postage. Letters, money orders and articles of money, as well as postal parcels intended for prisoners of war or dispatched by them, shall be free of all postal taxes, both in the countries of origin and destination and in intermediate countries.

Gifts and assistance in kind intended for prisoners of war shall be admitted free of all import and other duties, as well as of transport taxes on the railroads operated by the State.

Art. 17. Prisoner officers shall receive the pay to which officers of the same rank in the country where they are held are entitled, subject to reimbursement by their government.

Art. 18. All latitude is left to prisoners of war for the exercise of their religion, including attendance at the services of their religion, on the sole condition that they conform to the measures of order and police prescribed by the military authority.

Art. 19. The wills of prisoners of war are received or drawn up under the same conditions as for the soldiers of the national army.

The same rules shall also be followed with regard to the documents relating to the recording of deaths, as well as for the burial of prisoners of war, taking into account their rank and position. ,

Art. 20. After the conclusion of peace, the repatriation of prisoners of war shall take place as soon as possible.

Chapter III – The Sick and Wounded.

Art. 21. The obligations of the belligerents with regard to the service of the sick and wounded are governed by the Geneva Convention.

Section II – Hostilities

Chapter I – Means of Injuring the Enemy. Sieges and Bombardments.

Art. 22. Belligerents do not have an unlimited right to choose the means of harming the enemy.

Art. 23. In addition to the prohibitions established by special conventions, it is prohibited *in particular*:
 a) To use poison or poisonous weapons;
 b) To kill or wound by treason individuals belonging to the enemy nation or army;
 c) To kill or wound an enemy who, having no longer the means of defence, is at liberty to do so;
 d) To declare that no quarter will be given;
 e) To use weapons, projectiles or materials capable of causing superfluous injury;
 f) To make improper use of the parliamentary flag, the national flag or the military insignia and uniform of the enemy, as well as the distinctive signs of the Geneva Convention;
 g) To destroy or seize enemy property, in cases where such destruction or seizure is imperatively required by the needs of the enemy.
 h) To declare extinguished, suspended or inadmissible in court, the rights and actions of the citizens of the opposing side.
 It is also forbidden for a belligerent to force the citizens of the opposing side to take part in war operations directed against their country, even if they had been in his service before the beginning of the war.

Art. 24. The ruses of war and the use of the necessary means to obtain information on the enemy and on the ground are considered as lawful.

Art. 25. It is forbidden to attack or bombard by any means whatsoever towns, villages, dwellings or buildings which are not defended.

Art. 26. The commander of the attacking troops, before undertaking the bombardment, and except in the case of an attack by force, shall do everything in his power to warn the authorities.

Art. 27. In the case of bombardments, all necessary measures must be taken to spare, as far as possible, buildings dedicated to worship, the arts, science and charity, historical monuments, hospitals and places where the sick and wounded are gathered, provided that they are not used for military purposes.
The duty of the besieged is to designate its buildings or places of assembly by special visible signs which will be notified in advance to the besieger.

Art. 28. It is forbidden to deliver to pillage a city or even a town taken by assault.

Chapter II – Spies.

Art. 29. The only person who can be considered a spy is the individual who, acting clandestinely or under false pretences, gathers or seeks to gather information in the area of operations of a belligerent, with the intention of communicating it to the opposing party.
Thus, undisguised military personnel who have entered the area of operations of the enemy army in order to gather information are not considered spies. Likewise, the following are not considered spies: soldiers and non-military personnel who openly carry out their mission, and who are responsible for transmitting

messages intended either for their own army or for the enemy army. To this category also belong individuals sent in balloons to transmit dispatches and, in general, to maintain communications between the various parts of an army or a territory.

Art. 30. A spy caught in the act may not be punished without prior judgment.

Art. 31. A spy who, having joined the army to which he belongs, is later captured by the enemy, shall be treated as a prisoner of war and shall not incur any liability for his previous acts of espionage.

Chapter III – Parliamentarians.

Art. 32. The individual authorized by one of the belligerents to enter into negotiations with the other and presenting himself with the white flag is considered a parliamentarian. He has the right to inviolability as well as the trumpeter, bugler or drummer, the flag bearer and the interpreter who accompany him.

Art. 33. The commander to whom a parliamentarian is sent is not obliged to receive him under all circumstances.
He can take all necessary measures to prevent the parliamentarian from taking advantage of his mission to obtain information.
He has the right, in case of abuse, to temporarily detain the parliamentarian.

Art. 34. The parliamentarian loses his rights of immunity if it is proven, in a positive and irrefutable manner, that he has taken advantage of his privileged position to provoke or commit an act of treason.

Chapter IV – Capitulations.

Art. 35. Capitulations agreed upon between the contracting parties must take into account the rules of military honor.

Once fixed, they must be scrupulously observed by both parties.

Chapter V – The Armistice.

Art. 36. The armistice suspends war operations by mutual agreement of the belligerent parties. If the duration of the armistice is not determined, the belligerent parties may resume operations at any time, provided, however, that the enemy is warned in due time, in accordance with the terms of the armistice.

Art. 37. The armistice may be general or local. The former suspends the war operations of the belligerent States everywhere; the latter suspends them only between certain forces of the belligerent armies and within a specified radius.

Art. 38. The armistice must be officially notified in good time to the competent authorities and to the troops. Hostilities are suspended immediately after notification or at the fixed time.

Art. 39. It is for the contracting parties to determine in the clauses of the armistice the relations which may take place, in the theater of war, with the populations and between them.

Art. 40. Any serious violation of the armistice by one of the parties gives the other the right to denounce it and even, in case of emergency, to resume hostilities immediately.

Art. 41. The violation of the armistice by private individuals acting on their own initiative gives the right to claim only the punishment of the guilty parties and, if necessary, compensation for the losses suffered.

Section III – Military authority in the territory of the enemy State

Art. 42. A territory is considered to be occupied when it is in fact placed under the authority of the enemy army.

Occupation extends only to territories where such authority is established and capable of being exercised.

Art. 43. The authority of the legal power having passed de facto into the hands of the occupant, the latter shall take all the measures which depend on him with a view to re-establishing and ensuring, as far as possible, public order and life, respecting, unless absolutely prevented, the laws in force in the country.

Art. 44. A belligerent is forbidden to force the population of an occupied territory to give information on the army of the other belligerent or on its means of defence.

Art. 45. It is forbidden to compel the population of an occupied territory to swear an oath to the enemy power.

Art. 46. The honor and rights of the family, the life of individuals and private property, as well as religious convictions and the practice of worship, must be respected.

Private property may not be confiscated.

Art. 47. Pillage is strictly forbidden.

Art. 48. If the occupant levies in the occupied territory the taxes, duties and tolls established for the benefit of the State, he shall do so, as far as possible, according to the rules of assessment and distribution in force, and it shall be his obligation to provide for the expenses of the administration of the occupied territory to the extent that the legal government was obliged to do so.

Art. 49. If, in addition to the taxes referred to in the preceding article, the occupant levies other contributions in money in the occupied territory, it may only be for the needs of the army or the administration of this territory.

Art. 50. No collective punishment, pecuniary or otherwise, may be enacted against the populations for individual acts for which they cannot be considered jointly responsible.

Art. 51. No contribution shall be collected except by virtue of a written order and under the responsibility of a general in chief.

This collection shall be carried out, as far as possible, only in accordance with the rules of assessment and distribution of taxes in force.

For all contributions, a receipt shall be issued to the taxpayers.

Art. 52. Requisitions in kind and services can only be claimed from the communes or the inhabitants for the needs of the army of occupation. They will be in relation to the resources of the country and of such a nature that they do not imply for the populations the obligation to take part in the operations of the war against their fatherland.

These requisitions and services will only be claimed with the authorization of the commander in the occupied locality.

Benefits in kind shall, as far as possible, be paid in cash; if not, they shall be evidenced by receipts, and the payment of the sums due shall be made as soon as possible.

Art. 53. The army occupying a territory may only seize cash, funds and securities belonging to the State, arms depots, means of transport, warehouses and supplies and, in general, any movable property of the State which is likely to be used for war operations.

All means of transport assigned by land, sea or air to the transmission of news, to the transport of persons or things, except in cases governed by maritime law, arms depots and, in general, all kinds of munitions of war, may be seized, even if they belong to private persons, but must be returned and compensation shall be paid at peace.

Art. 54. Submarine cables linking an occupied territory to a neutral territory shall not be seized or destroyed except in case of absolute necessity. They must also be returned and the compensation paid at peace;

Art. 55. The occupying State shall consider itself only as administrator and usufructuary of the public buildings, immovables, forests and agricultural holdings belonging to the enemy State and situated in the occupied country. It shall safeguard the substance of these properties and administer them in accordance with the rules of ownership.

Art. 56. The property of the communes, of the institutions dedicated to worship, charity and education, education, the arts and sciences, even those belonging to the State, will be treated as private property.

Any seizure, destruction or intentional degradation of such establishments, historical monuments, works of art and science, is forbidden and must be prosecuted.

Art. 2. The Minister of Foreign Affairs and the Minister of War are charged, each in what concerns him, with the execution of the present decree.

Done in Paris, December 2, 1910.

A. FALLIÈRES.

For the President of the Republic:

The Minister of Foreign Affairs,
 S. PICHON.

The Minister of War,
 BRUN.

Decree promulgating the international convention signed at The Hague on October 18, 1907, concerning the rights and duties of neutral powers and persons in case of war on land.

Paris, December 2, 1910.

The President of the French Republic,
On the proposal of the Minister of Foreign Affairs, the Minister of War and the Minister of Public Works, Posts and Telegraphs,

Decrees:

Art. 1. The Senate and the Chamber of Deputies having adopted the international convention concerning the rights and duties of neutral powers and persons in case of war, signed at The Hague, October 18, 1907, by France, Germany, the United States of America, the Argentine Republic, Austria-Hungary, Belgium, Bolivia, Brazil, Bulgaria, Chile, Colombia, the Republic of Cuba, Denmark, the Dominican Republic, Ecuador, Spain, Great Britain, Greece, Guatemala, Haiti, Italy, Japan, Luxembourg, Mexico, the United States of America, the United Kingdom, the United States of America, and the United Kingdom, Japan, Luxembourg, Mexico, Montenegro, Netherlands, Norway, Panama, Paraguay, Peru, Persia, Portugal, Romania, Russia, El Salvador, Serbia, Siam, Spain, Sweden, Switzerland, Turkey, Uruguay and Venezuela, and the ratifications of this act having been deposited at The Hague by France, Germany, Austria-Hungary, Belgium, Bolivia, Denmark, Haiti, Mexico, the Netherlands, Norway, Russia, El Salvador, Siam, Sweden and Switzerland; – China having acceded to the said Convention on the 15th day of January, 1910, and Nicaragua on the 16th day of December, 1909; the said Convention, the content of which follows, shall be fully executed.

Convention V Concerning the Rights and Duties of Neutral Powers and Persons in Case of War on Land

(List of sovereigns and heads of state.)

With a view to specifying more precisely the rights and duties of neutral powers in case of war on land, and to regulating the situation of belligerents who are refugees in neutral territory;

Desiring also to define the status of neutrals until it is possible to regulate in its entirety the situation of individual neutrals in their relations with the belligerents;

Have resolved to conclude a convention for this purpose, and have accordingly nominated as their plenipotentiaries, namely:

(Designation of plenipotentiaries.)

Who, having deposited their full powers found in good and due form, have agreed upon the following provisions:

Chapter I – The Rights and Duties of Neutral Powers

Art. 1. The territory of neutral powers is inviolable.

Art. 2. It is forbidden for belligerents to pass through the territory of a neutral Power troops or convoys of munitions or supplies.

Art. 3. It is also forbidden for belligerents:
a) To install in the territory of a neutral Power a radio-telegraphic station or any apparatus intended to serve as a means of communication with belligerent forces on land or sea;
b) To use any such installation established by them before the war in the territory of the neutral Power for exclusively military purposes, and which has not been opened to the service of public correspondence.

Art. 4. Combatant corps may not be formed, nor enlistment offices opened, in the territory of a neutral Power for the benefit of the belligerents.

Art. 5. A neutral Power shall not tolerate on its territory any of the acts referred to in Articles 2 to 4.

It is obliged to punish acts contrary to neutrality only if such acts have been committed in its own territory.

Art. 6. The responsibility of a neutral power is not engaged by the fact that individuals cross the frontier in isolation to place themselves in the service of one of the belligerents.

Art. 7. A neutral power is not bound to prevent the export or transit, on behalf of either of the belligerents, of arms, ammunition, and, in general, of anything which may be useful to an army or a fleet.

Art. 8. A neutral power is not bound to prohibit or restrict the use by belligerents of telegraph or telephone cables, or of wireless telegraphy apparatus, which are either its own property or that of companies or individuals.

Art. 9. Any restrictive or prohibitive measures taken by a neutral Power with regard to the matters referred to in Articles 7 and 8 shall be uniformly applied by it to the belligerents.

The neutral power shall ensure that the same obligation is observed by companies or individuals owning telegraph or telephone cables or wireless telegraphy apparatus.

Art. 10. The fact that a neutral Power repels, even by force, attacks on its neutrality shall not be considered as a hostile act.

Chapter II – Belligerents Interned and Wounded Treated by Neutrals

Art. 11. A neutral power which receives on its territory troops belonging to the belligerent armies shall, as far as possible, intern them far from the theater of war.

It may keep them in camps and even confine them in fortresses or in places suitable for that purpose.

It will decide whether the officers can be left free by taking a parole to not leave neutral territory without authorization.

Art. 12. In the absence of a special agreement, the neutral Power shall provide the internees with the food, clothing and assistance required by humanity.

In the event of peace, the costs incurred by the internment shall be credited.

Art. 13. The neutral power which receives escaped prisoners of war shall let them go free. If it tolerates their stay in its territory, it may assign them a residence.

The same provision shall apply to prisoners of war brought by troops taking refuge in the territory of the neutral Power.

Art. 14. A neutral Power may authorize the passage through its territory of wounded or sick belonging to the belligerent armies, provided that the trains carrying them do not carry either personnel or war material. In such cases, the neutral Power is bound to take the necessary safety and control measures to this effect.

The wounded or sick brought into neutral territory under these conditions by one of the belligerents, and who belong to the adverse party, must be guarded by the neutral Power, in such a way that they cannot again take part in the operations of war. The said Power shall have the same duties with regard to the wounded or sick of the other army who are entrusted to its care.

Art. 15. The Geneva Convention shall apply to sick and wounded interned on neutral territory.

Chapter III – Neutral Persons

Art. 16. The nationals of a State which does not take part in the war shall be considered as neutrals.

Art. 17. A neutral may not avail himself of his neutrality:
a) If he commits hostile acts against a belligerent;
b) If he commits acts in favour of a belligerent, in particular if he voluntarily takes service in the ranks of the armed forces of one of the parties.

In such a case, the neutral shall not be treated more severely by the belligerent against whom he has withdrawn from neutrality than a national of the other belligerent State would be treated for the same act.

Art. 18. The following shall not be considered as acts committed in favor of one of the belligerents, within the meaning of Article 17, letter b:
a) Supplies made or loans granted to one of the belligerents, provided that the supplier or lender does not live in the territory of the other party or in the territory occupied by it, and that the

supplies do not come from such territories.

b) Services rendered in matters of police or civil administration.

Chapter IV – Railroad Equipment

Art. 19. Railroad material originating in the territory of neutral powers, whether belonging to such powers or to private companies or persons, and recognizable as such, may be requisitioned and used by a belligerent only in the case and to the extent that imperative necessity so requires. It shall be returned as soon as possible to the country of origin.

The neutral power may likewise, in case of necessity, retain and use, to the extent necessary, material coming from the territory of the belligerent power.

The neutral power may also, in case of necessity, retain and use, up to a certain amount, material coming from the territory of the belligerent Power. An indemnity shall be paid on both sides, in proportion to the material used and to the duration of its use.

Chapter V – Final Provisions

Art. 20. The provisions of the present Convention shall be applicable only as between the Contracting Powers, and only if the belligerents are all parties to the Convention.

Art. 21. The present Convention shall be ratified as soon as possible.

The ratifications shall be deposited at The Hague.

The first deposit of ratifications shall be recorded in a transcript signed by the representatives of the powers taking part and by the Minister of Foreign Affairs of the Netherlands.

Subsequent deposits of ratifications shall be made by means of a written notification, addressed to the Government of the Netherlands, accompanied by the instrument of ratification.

A certified copy of the transcript relating to the first deposit of ratifications, of the notifications mentioned in the preceding paragraph, and of the instruments of ratification, shall be immediately delivered by the Government of the Netherlands through diplomatic channels to the Powers invited to the Second Peace Conference, and to the other Powers which have acceded to the Convention. In the cases referred to in the preceding paragraph, the said Government shall at the same time inform them of the date on which it received the notification.

Art. 22. Powers which are not signatories shall be admitted to accede to the present Convention.

The power which desires to accede shall notify its intention in writing to the Government of the Netherlands, transmitting to it the act of accession, which shall be deposited in the archives of the said Government.

This Government shall immediately transmit to all the other Powers certified copies of the notification and of the instrument of accession, indicating the date on which it received the notification.

Art. 23. The present Convention shall take effect, in the case of the Powers which have participated in the first deposit of ratifications, sixty days after the date of the transcript of such deposit, and, in the case of the Powers which subsequently ratify or accede, sixty days after the notification of their ratification or accession has been received by the Netherlands Government.

Art. 24. If one of the contracting powers should wish to denounce the present Convention, the denunciation shall be notified in writing to the Government of the Netherlands, which shall immediately communicate a certified copy of the notification to all the other powers, informing them of the date on which it was received.

The denunciation shall have effect only with regard to the power which has notified it, and one year after the notification has reached the Government of the Netherlands.

Art. 25. A register kept by the Minister of Foreign Affairs of the Netherlands shall indicate the date of the deposit of ratifications made in accordance with Article 21, paragraphs 3 and 4, as well as the date on which notifications of accession (Article 22, paragraph 2) or of denunciation (Article 24, paragraph 1) have been received.

Each contracting power is entitled to take cognizance of these rules and to request certified extracts from them.

In witness thereof the plenipotentiaries have signed the present Convention.

Done at The Hague, on the 18th day of October 1907, in a single copy which shall remain deposited in the archives of the Government of the Netherlands, and of which certified copies shall be delivered through diplomatic channels to the Powers which were invited to the Second Peace Conference.

(Signatures follow.)

Art. 2. The Minister of Foreign Affairs, the Minister of War and the Minister of Public Works, Posts and Telegraphs are charged, each in what concerns him, with the execution of the present decree.

Done in Paris, December 2, 1910.

A. FALLIÈRES.

For the President of the Republic:

The Minister of Foreign Affairs,
S. PICHON.

The Minister of War,
BRUN.

The Minister of Public Works of Posts and Telegraphs,
L. PUECH.